THE WISDOM COMPASS

A 31-DAY JOURNEY TO WISDOM-FILLED LIVING

THEODORE HENDERSON

Soar
with
Eagles

A Publisher Driven
by Vision and Purpose
www.soarhigher.com

The Wisdom Compass: A 31-Day Journey to Wisdom-Filled Living

ISBN-13: 978-0-9814756-7-7
Library of Congress Control Number 2010932634

First Edition

Published by
Soar with Eagles
1200 North Mallard Lane, Rogers, AR 72756 USA
www.soarhigher.com

Design and editing by Carrie Perrien Smith

Printed in the United States of America

Contents

INTRODUCTION

Welcome to our journey together. Allow me to introduce myself as your tour guide. I have an MBA and over twenty years of sales and sales management experience in the business and technology field. More importantly, for your purposes, I am an avid and enthusiastic reader of the Bible. I love the Bible's how-to method of teaching life's lessons. I enjoy finding ways to apply the Bible to my everyday practical life as well as my spiritual life. In short, the principles in this book have allowed me to marry to spiritual and the practical for an overall enhanced life and better everyday living.

While reading the book of Proverbs, you'll find that there are no promises that if you do A plus B it will equal C. However, I would like to suggest that if you do A plus B, C is very likely to follow. In other words, learn the lessons, apply them, and things will often work out.

I am using the book of Proverbs, the twentieth book of the Bible, as the basis for the teachings in this book. The quotes are from the New International Version (NIV) because I have found it easier to read than the King James version — particularly for those who are not avid Bible readers. Personally, I like to read several versions. I learn something from each in the nuances of the language and find all of them very helpful. For our purposes, I decided to standardize on the NIV.

Here is what you'll need for our thirty-one-day journey of transformation:

- A Bible. The NIV is preferable as that is what we are using. A modern English version is okay also, but any version you are comfortable with will suffice.

- Thirty to forty minutes per day. Whether that is in the morning, afternoon, or evening is totally up to you. This study is designed with thirty-one chapters so that you may experience transformation in just one month. As you go through the book, you achieve the best results if you read the entire passage referenced in the book of Proverbs.

As you read through each chapter, make note of the sections or verses that strike you or relate to your current situation. Mark them off or underline them in the text or maybe write a couple of notes. I find there is something special about physically writing commentary about what you are reading or thinking — something that doesn't happen when you read without writing anything down. You more easily remember concepts and ideas when your hand moves to paper. You have probably experienced that if you've written goals — having them in your head just isn't enough. Writing them down reinforces and imprints them in your psyche more effectively.

I encourage you to make the time even if you feel you don't have it. Write out those passages, and then refer to them throughout the day and in the days to come. If time permits, begin your study time the next day by re-reading the work that you did the previous day. It will be time well-invested in your transformation. It's time to begin our journey.

Theodore Henderson
www.thewisdomcompass.com

PROVERBS *1*

Embracing Wisdom's Call

"Wisdom calls aloud in the street, she raises
her voice in the public squares."

Proverbs 1:20

If you have never read the book of Proverbs in its entirety or as a lesson in living, then this is the first day of the rest of a better life. As you read further, it is made plain the book was written to give us wisdom, instruction, perception, prudence, knowledge, judgment, learning, and advice. However, everything hinges on wisdom and all of these approaches are synonymous.

Wisdom is something available to all. No amount of money can buy it or make your mind open to it. You have to want it and listen for it whether it occurs in the written or verbal form. God's wisdom is responsible for all of the beauty and splendor around us. Take advantage of it as you begin your daily lesson.

The first chapter of Proverbs clearly identifies King Solomon and his lineage to King David. Notice also that it identifies these purposes for Proverbs beginning with Proverbs 1:2.

- For attaining wisdom and discipline
- For understanding words of insight
- For acquiring a disciplined and prudent life
- For the ability to make intelligent decisions especially in life's everyday matters
- For doing what is right and just and fair

Proverbs is a guide for doing what's right and making sound judgments in sometimes difficult circumstances. It is a fantastic guidebook for educating children and young people and providing practical application for the young. If you are already wise, spending time in the book of Proverbs only adds to your learning and discernment. Next, of course, you'll want to unravel the other proverbial teachings and parables to gain greater understanding through re-reading.

Those of the Christian faith want to attain fear of the Lord because that is the beginning of the transformation process. These five purposes noted in Proverbs 1:2 allow you to use your faith to get the benefit of living your life fully. Employing biblical principals opens the door for something supernatural to happen in your life. Once you begin the process, you'll grasp that it isn't just "positive thinking" or happening by your own initiative. If it were that easy, we could simply manifest our way out of trouble or avoid it. Fortunately, life has a different classroom in store for us.

So you may be thinking, "The five purposes sound great; but how do I actually do that in my daily life?" Well, let's look at some examples. First, let's pretend you are an athlete and you're training either for a team of some type (basketball, baseball, soccer, etc.) or maybe you're training for an event such as a triathlon. The first thing you do to be successful is practice. The coach sets up practice and encourages you to also practice outside of the bounds of the normally scheduled session.

If you've followed successful athletes, you probably noticed that most of their success is not always about athletic gifts. A lot of it is about discipline. They practice well before or beyond the regularly scheduled practice time because they want to hone their skills. You adopt the same discipline because you don't want to just remain on the team — you want to be the best on the team and you want to help the team win.

It's all about striving to reach the next level. If you're a high school player, you're trying to get a college scholarship. If you're a college player and think you have the talent, you're trying to make it to the pros. Even if you don't make it to a pro team, that same attitude of discipline will actually transform you into a person who can succeed in business and other avenues of life.

Whatever the area may be, the same principles work whether it is in the business arena or playing for a team. When you look into the life of most successful people (all areas of their life; not just the financial portion), you will see this pattern of disciplined sacrifice is not an accident. The athlete who spends additional hours practicing after the rest of the team has gone home may also be more likely to achieve a successful career outside of sports — even though people call him or her an overnight success. When the athlete is called on and excels, it usually happens because they prepared themselves with years of practicing the fundamentals.

You'll find the same discipline applies with students who by the normal standards of their high school or peer group are exceptionally intelligent. They seek out extra tutoring or start associating with other like-minded, academically geared peers, or even seek special assignments from the instructors. It isn't a surprise they end up with the scholarships or are able to remain at the top of the class in college when others become shell-shocked by the increased competition.

Here is another example from my own life. Each morning, I get up thirty to forty-five minutes earlier than necessary to prepare for work. I spend that extra time reading Bible verses, meditating on the Word, writing out particular goals and my daily schedule, and then refocusing on the goals and the schedule in a meditative format. It takes about a half an hour. After I finish on certain days, I do some form of exercise.

Yes, that's thirty to sixty minutes I could use for sleeping. However, I find that my career, my personal life, and all of the attachments that come with them have become much easier for me to pursue — particularly when a crisis comes — by keeping this almost daily habit. It provides a foundation, a focus, and a vision of where you're going, so you find yourself not being derailed anywhere near as quickly. And if you are derailed, you won't find yourself grounded and can get back on track swiftly.

Proverbs 1:8-22

[8] Listen, my son, to your father's instruction and do not forsake your mother's teaching. [9] They will be a garland to grace your head and a chain to adorn your neck. [10] My son, if sinners entice you, do not give in to them. [11] If they say, "Come along with us; let's lie in wait for someone's blood, let's waylay some harmless soul. [12] Let's swallow them alive, like the grave, [b] and whole, like those who go down to the pit. [13] We will get all sorts of valuable things and fill our houses with plunder. [14] Throw in your lot with us, and we will share a common purse." [15] My son, do not go along with them, do not set foot on their paths. [16] for their feet rush into sin, they are swift to shed blood. [17] How useless to spread a net in full view of all the birds! [18] These men lie in wait for their own blood; they waylay only themselves! [19] Such is the end of all who go after ill-gotten gain; it takes away the lives of those who get it. [20] Wisdom calls aloud in the street, she raises her voice in the public squares. [21] at the head of the noisy streets [c] she cries out, in the gateways of the city she makes her speech. [22] "How long will you simple ones [d] love your simple ways?"

How long will mockers delight in disdain? In Proverbs 1:8-19, you'll find a passage that — even though it is ancient and biblical in tone — could be ripped right out of the headlines of today's murder news. It says that lying in wait, mugging, killing, stealing what others have, and basically being an out-and-out criminal and miscreant is an easy choice. However, that is not what a successful, productive, balanced person does.

Proverbs 1:20-22 highlight three other types of people: the mockers, the fools, and the simple. Proverbs refers to mockers, fools, and the simple over and over again as people who are bad or questionable characters we should avoid.

The simple are viewed as the least-harmful group. They live without much thought and are basically too lazy to change. We all have a relative or a friend like this. They're harmless and simple, but we understand they're not really going anywhere unless they change their ways — assuming they're capable.

Fools are smarter, but (in the biblical sense) they make a conscious decision to live by their own wits instead of using God's advice and guidance or other intelligent advice necessary to make proper decisions. Those who feel they can make a living at the roulette wheel or craps table or depend upon a lottery win will likely waste what little money they have on a fool's errand.

Now, the mockers are the worst of all. They don't just ignore biblical advice — they rebel against it. Mockers are considered criminals, muggers, murderers, and thieves. They believe they will get away with their behavior because nothing will happen to them. As we all know, there are prisons full of people who haven't gotten away with their behaviors and actions, and there are graveyards full of people who haven't gotten away with it either. So, how do we apply Proverbs 1 to our life?

You'll find that successful people are readers and communicators. They are always seeking knowledge. Even someone with poor eyesight will seek out knowledge through Braille books or audio books. They are continually expanding themselves in some way that is important to their life — personally, spiritually, and financially. They are living examples that you don't always have to sit in a classroom to improve.

For the sake of comparison, a fool would listen to someone who tells them, "You don't have to educate yourself. You don't necessarily have to be a reader. Just buy my program, and you'll get rich! No reading, no school, no advanced education." I suppose there may be an isolated incident somewhere where something like that may happen. However, we're far better off investing in knowledge that moves us ahead and enjoying the quality of a life we've earned through self-education and expanding our minds whether we have graduated from college or not.

In summary, real words of wisdom are plainspoken and clear. There shouldn't be any confusing language to throw you off track. Sometimes, an individual doesn't understand because the biblical teaching conflicts with their carnal feelings. In such a case, the problem is with the person and not the lesson being spoken. When a decision is to be made, it calls for simple wisdom. There is no sitting on the fence with God's word. Following the teachings and living a wiser existence translates to a better life.

Action Steps on the Life Path

Take a moment to think of a particular area of your life that will improve if you self-educate, read more, improve your process, or apply increased discipline.

What is the area you want to improve?

_____

What actions will you take to improve that area? Name three to five actions with a deadline for each.

_____

_____

_____

_____

_____

_____

What measurable result do you expect to receive?

_____

_____

_____

What is your deadline for completing this improvement?

_____

PROVERBS *2*

The Morality of Wisdom

"Turning your ear to wisdom and applying
your heart to understanding ..."

Proverbs 2:2

According to *Merriam-Webster's Collegiate® Dictionary, 11th Edition,* *moral*[1] means *of or relating to principles of right and wrong in behavior ... conforming to a standard of right behavior ... sanctioned by or operative on one's conscience or ethical judgment <a moral obligation>.* In other words, being capable of right and wrong action isn't enough. By definition, the right thing to do is to take the moral action.

The only way to arrive at the desired or correct destination is to follow the right course. Life is a journey of unknown length. For some, it is long; for others, it seems to end much too quickly. Either way, we must choose a destination and a direction. The assurance of wisdom and wise decision making is that your life is generally better for it. The reason is simple — wisdom's function is to protect and direct.

In Proverbs 2, we'll cover the further benefits of wisdom across moral, ethical, and practical lines.

---

[1] By permission. From *Merriam-Webster's Collegiate® Dictionary, 11th Edition* ©2010 by Merriam-Webster, Incorporated (www.Merriam-Webster.com).

Proverbs 2:1-2

> [1] My son, if you accept my words and store up my commands within you, [2] turning your ear to wisdom and applying your heart to understanding,

These two verses advise you to be still, pay attention, listen, understand, and apply. So many times, we are not listening to advice in a way that allows us to understand it. So open your mind, relax, and listen whether it is with this lesson or any of the lessons that life teaches you.

Numerous times, particularly if someone I am annoyed at tries to tell me something — which, in some cases, is actually good advice — I will simply say, "Mmm hmmm, yeah, I hear ya!" However, what I am really saying is, "The words are entering my ears, but, I have shut myself down. I am not taking in the information." That's not necessarily smart, and this arrogance could lead to bad decision making.

The lesson here is very uncomplicated: merely listen, take in the information, understand, and use it. Think about those situations where you do the same thing that I find myself guilty of. Perhaps you catch yourself "sort of" listening to someone, or you are letting him talk about what is on his mind. Whether you are sitting in a class or listening to a friend or business associate, regard everything the individual says as important information — even if you aren't in the mood to take any advice. Everyone finds himself or herself unwilling to take advice from time to time, but at some point, we need be willing listeners. You may find after all that it will serve you well later. Assume, for example, that you are active in your church or are even a lay leader. If you are not a good, active listener, you'll be less effective in furthering church goals and will no doubt miss out on excellent opportunities to affect positive change. Observe churches you are familiar with that are troubled, and you will find key leadership elements in shutdown mode or missing altogether.

Proverbs 2:3-11

> [3] and if you call out for insight and cry aloud for understanding, [4] and if you look for it as for silver and search for it as for hidden treasure, [5] then you will understand the fear of the Lord and find the knowledge of God. [6] For the Lord gives wisdom, and from his

mouth come knowledge and understanding. [7] He holds victory in store for the upright, he is a shield to those whose walk is blameless, [8] for he guards the course of the just and protects the way of his faithful ones.

Wisdom is an interesting thing. I certainly believe it is a gift from God, particularly as a Christian. Wisdom is a gift that is acquired by paying attention to the details. However, it is almost always activated after a strenuous and vigorous search for it.

I will use a couple of different examples to illustrate my point. For one thing, if you want to be a professional, that generally demands doing the things necessary to achieve a certain status. Master carpenters spend years studying either out of books or apprenticing under someone, continuing to work and hone their craft. People who are not interested in being that level of carpenter or tradesperson can simply dabble in it. In that case, they reach a level of proficiency where they can fix some things around the house. However, they are certainly not acknowledged as master carpenters and are probably not running a business that revolves around carpentry in terms of producing handicraft or artwork.

Here is another example. Let's say that you want to be a business professional. If you want to practice law or become an accountant, you get an advanced degree. That is just the beginning because you certainly have to be intelligent and diligent enough to take the entrance exams to get into a university. However, you aren't an expert just because you graduate. You grow your expertise during the application of the education and the legal principles that you learn from being around other professionals. You continue to expand your expertise while working on different projects, working in the environment, listening for understanding, and applying it to the situations you encounter. There is a reason it is called a "practice."

There is wisdom in sports also. Think about the great athletes in golf, tennis, boxing, martial arts, football, soccer, or basketball. Once athletes reach the professional level, they can perform the basics far better than the ordinary person. What sets them apart as superstars amongst their own group many times is their mental edge. For example, basketball players can run, jump, and dribble with either hand — particularly if they are guards who have to handle the ball. Some people can even shoot with either hand, depending on the distance. What makes them great is practicing, preparing, watching game films, reading the defense, understanding what their opponent is going to do, and interacting with teammates. They just didn't graduate college or high school, step onto the court, and instantaneously become great! Even though you may be able to immediately score, it takes time to learn all the facets of the game. That is why top professionals who seek to be champions in their business — whether it's on a championship team or as an individual champion — are willing to sacrifice to learn and understand. They want to apply what they learn to their given situation. Each one of us can be great in our own way by doing that in our life.

On a personal level, I desire to continue along a path of spiritual enlightenment. I'm pursuing that as something that is good for me — something that I believe in — and hopefully you do also. I have just come to the realization that wisdom is God's gift. It is truly something that God has given us or will give us under certain situations. He doesn't give it to people who are foolish, who squander it, and who are in a continual state of rebellion. Instead, God gives it to those who seem to be diligent, who are seeking it, and who earnestly and strenuously put effort into looking for wisdom, finding it, and applying it.

The best way to go about gaining wisdom is to live your life's purpose. That means that you need to identify your purpose and pursue it vigorously. This will allow you to gain wisdom and apply it in a very energetic, enthusiastic way, and it will make you a better person for it. You may have heard that the pursuit of wisdom comes from pursuing your passion, no matter what your passion may be. I submit to you that passion for something does not provide wisdom. Wisdom is only gained through hard work, commitment, and living your life's purpose.

Think about the last five to ten years and the successes that you achieved over that period. What did you learn from those successes and the challenges that each imposed on your life while you were working on them? I've often found that I learn more from the challenges than the actual success.

Here is an example. After high school, I attended college as an undergraduate full time and worked nights and weekends. After graduation and entering the workforce, I decided to return to school to get an MBA while working full time. It required attending school twice a week in the evening for a couple of hours and then all day on Saturday. I wanted to finish a year ahead of time and even though it was quite difficult at times, I did indeed do just that.

The routine taught me to exercise discipline over myself. I learned the strategies that worked for me personally. That discipline continues to serve me well today. I am able to organize myself for something positive, no matter how strenuous it is. Whether it will take just a few minutes or several years, I know I will come out on the other end of it successful.

I took two or three classes each semester — a big load when going to school at night and working full time. I kept my focus on the classes that semester. However, I kept the long-range goal in mind: to graduate with my degree. It kept me from saying, "You know what? This is too painful. I will never get through it. I'm going to quit now." When all you focus on is the current sacrifice, you see nothing but pain, grief, and agony. It's hard to give up some fun times and not see friends or family. However, taking one class at a time and learning to intelligently set aside time to spend with friends and family, I learned how to balance work, school, and business while securing achievement for my future.

Proverbs 2:9-11

> [9] Then you will understand what is right and just and fair — every good path. [10] For wisdom will enter your heart, and knowledge will be pleasant to your soul. [11] Discretion will protect you, and understanding will guard you.

As a Christian, I look to the Bible to reveal the road map of God's wisdom. We gain wisdom through a continual process of growth. That process means that we continue to make choices — some good; some not so good. You'll find that the good choices will prove themselves as will the not-so-good ones. But always remember that there is much to learn from our mistakes when we endeavor to make the moral, ethical, and wise choice.

I have learned to trust God in all situations. Even when a situation doesn't seem to be going my way, I have to understand and believe firmly that God has an equal or greater benefit coming to me beyond the given situation. It may seem negative at the moment, but I have to trust that something greater is coming to me as I build and grow through that experience. At times, this hasn't been easy; but I always try to stay the course.

> [12] Wisdom will save you from the ways of wicked men, from men whose words are perverse, [13] who leave the straight paths to walk in dark ways, [14] who delight in doing wrong and rejoice in the perverseness of evil, [15] whose paths are crooked and who are devious in their ways. [16] It will save you also from the adulteress, from the wayward wife with her seductive words, [17] who has left the partner of her youth and ignored the covenant she made before God. [a] [18] For her house leads down to death and her paths to the spirits of the dead. [19] None who go to her return or attain the paths of life.

When you think about the adulteress in Proverbs 16, consider that it might not be a woman or even a man. The adulteress could be something that is not good for us. It could be something sinful, illegal, or immoral that beckons — immoral and promiscuous sexual activity, addictions to drugs, alcohol, gambling, or anything excessive such as eating too much food.

Harmless things can start out on the surface being good such as food or a prescription, but overuse can stimulate an addiction and ultimately cause you harm. Even too much pride can lead you down the wrong path. It is good to be proud of yourself and your accomplishments, but there is a difference between being proud of doing good things and prideful arrogance. There is a balance that you can learn to strike, but always be aware that it is much easier to fall into the trap of arrogance.

This is where prayer and meditation become so important. It causes you to look at something greater than yourself to avoid the enticements of temptations such as sexual immorality, pride, and addiction. Just like everyone else, I struggle with resisting activities that are not good for me. It helps to first recognize that the activity is bad and it is not okay to engage in the pursuit — even if someone doesn't see me. One of the greatest tests of who you really are takes place when no one is looking. Resisting or fighting through temptation using prayer, reading the Bible, and meditating on the Scriptures helps me work through it and resist the urge to follow the crowd. It will help you take the high road even when it seems that everyone is cheating at something or taking the shortcut. You've probably heard the phrase, "What happens in Vegas stays in Vegas." Unfortunately, bad behavior on a consistent, repeated basis has a way of being exposed eventually. The fall is great; and the higher position that you have achieved, the longer the fall.

Re-read these verses that we have covered. Highlight those verses that are important or that stick out to you and make notes around them.

Wisdom is a path to walk. If you want to have the best chance to arrive at the correct destination, the path chosen is key. Both Proverbs and Jesus are clear in their direction and guidance. There is no middle ground — only two choices: the bad one that leads to failure and the good one that leads to life. Wisdom is our compass that directs us in our walk with the Creator, the walk with the bad, or the walk with the righteous, just, and honorable.

Action Steps on the Life Path

How do you actively seek wisdom? Name three to five ways you do or should actively seek wisdom. Are you consistent?

_____

_____

_____

_____

_____

Write down three moral or wise decisions you've made. Note the profound effect they had on your life.

_____

_____

_____

_____

_____

_____

_____

_____

How can you duplicate the profound effects in another area of your life that is experiencing challenges? How do you anticipate the effects will exemplify the walk mentioned above?

_____

_____

_____

_____

_____

_____

Think about the last five to ten years. List the successes that you achieved over that period. This exercise should only take about five minutes.

_____

_____

_____

_____

_____

_____

_____

_____

_____

_____

_____

_____

_____

_____

_____

_____

_____

_____

_____

_____

_____

Select three of those successes, and write down two or three pieces of wisdom that you learned from each of those successes.

Success 1 _____

_____

_____

_____

_____

_____

Success 2 _____

_____

_____

_____

_____

_____

Success 3 _____

_____

_____

_____

_____

_____

_____

PROVERBS 3

The Prosperity of Wisdom

"Blessed is the man who finds wisdom, the man who gains understanding,
for she is more profitable than silver and yields better returns than gold."

Proverbs 3:13-14

The interesting consistency in Proverbs and throughout the Bible is that God keeps His promises when we are in His will. When we are following a guide such as Proverbs, we are living a life adhering to biblical direction. When we try to do it our own way, frequently the results are disastrous.

We can learn to live in God's will by studying the Word or reviewing the Bible or material that reflects the true spirit of it. After studying, we must obey and apply the learning to our life. Then, we must give our tithes and offerings while being cheerful and sincere about it as part of our obligation to honor God with the first fruits of our labor.

Remember, this is not a math formula that delivers an expected result consistent with each addition, subtraction, division, and multiplication. Instead, it is a compass that points us in the right direction with an expectation of desired results. For example, the first step is to seek proper guidance in a chosen area (biblical principle). Second, follow the proper guidance when found with faith and conviction. Third, enjoy the blessing of having used your compass (biblical principle and God's will). Remember to use the compass for important decisions that must be planned, prayed upon, and meditated upon such as career choices, marriage, spiritual direction, personal relationships, and sizeable investments.

Take a moment to read Proverbs 3 from your own Bible. As this section further explores wisdom, I'll highlight some characters in the Bible who are generally acknowledged as being wise:

- Joseph was a wise leader.
- Moses was as a wise leader.
- Disraeli was a wise artist.
- Joshua was a wise leader.
- David was a wise leader.
- Abigail was a wise wife.
- Solomon, of course, was a wise leader. His writings are the ones that we're discussing here in Proverbs.
- Daniel was a wise counselor.
- Astrologers are wise learners.
- Stephen was a wise leader.
- Paul was a wise messenger.
- Christ was a wise youth — a wise savior employing the wisdom of God.

For more reference:

- Joseph (Acts 7:10)
- Moses (Acts 7:20-22)
- Desalel (Exodus 31:1-5)
- Joshua (Deuteronomy 34:9)
- David (Samuel 2:14, 2:20)
- Abigail (Samuel 1:25)
- Solomon (Song of Solomon 3, 1 Kings 3:5-14, and 1 Kings 4:29-34)
- Daniel (Daniel 5:11-12)
- Astrologers (Matthew 2:1-12)
- Stephen (Acts 6:8-10)

- Paul (2 Peter 3:5 and 3:16)
- Christ (Luke 2:40 and 2:52, 1 Corinthians 1:20-25)

Proverbs 3 clearly demonstrates wisdom's value across four general areas:

- Prosperity (Proverbs 3:2)
- Love and faithfulness (Proverbs 3:3)
- Acknowledgement (Proverbs 3:6)
- Straight path (Proverbs 3:6)

In regards to prosperity, it's common to see the Hebrew word *Shalom*. It broadly means *wholeness of life* — having good health and harmonious relationships with all the areas of our life in balance and working together. This is general, broad prosperity. Notice that it's not just money — it refers to harmony, balance, and the inner workings of all of the aspects of our life. It means that every aspect is working together in harmony to produce the abundance of a good life.

I remember a time several years ago when I was particularly unhappy with my life. I was making a great deal of money. However, it didn't make up for the problems in my life: living in a relationship that wasn't working, not seeing friends or relatives due to long hours, or spending most of my waking hours with people I did not like or get along with.

Proverbs 3 also discusses love and faithfulness. It is represented as kindness and truth. These are repetitive themes in the Old Testament; however, let's take a closer look because Proverbs 3 is really focusing on unwavering fidelity and constancy.

The second point expressed is unflinching integrity and trustworthiness. Notice the good things that we have in our everyday life. We have no fear of operating in "fidelity and constancy" once we start to notice and appreciate them. The result is better relationships with our spouses, family members, friends, and business associates. Unquestioned integrity allows you to prosper in business and in your personal life while the absence of integrity takes away your peace of mind.

Acknowledgment isn't just about knowing; that's way too easy and transparent. In reality, it is about being aware and having fellowship with others. To have true companionship, you must be aware of yourself and aware of the people that you associate with. Therefore, you're acknowledging by being aware of yourself and the people around you.

For a person of faith, the straight path simply means that God will remove obstacles. It does not mean that you won't experience conflict with them. It also doesn't mean that you will not have to conquer them. However, the supernatural blessing of God will help you remove those obstacles. Someone who is not a person of faith may be amazed at how the things we've mentioned (prosperity, love, faithfulness, and acknowledgement) may work for him or her anyway. It creates a compelling case for faith, doesn't it?

The obstacles encountered when we operate with prosperity, love, faithfulness, and awareness present in our life are somehow removed or limited because of our integrity, fidelity, and constancy. Those are the bedrocks of moving forward in a wisdom-filled life.

Now in Proverbs 3:1-10, there are five critical lessons for living. Each one is presented as a command; but interestingly enough, there is an award or a reward that comes by obeying that command. For example, in Proverbs 3:1, God is saying, "Keep His commands in your heart at all times and throughout your life." You will be rewarded with prolonged life and will bring yourself prosperity for the time that you are alive.

Proverbs 3:3-6

> [3] Let love and faithfulness never leave you; bind them around your neck, write them on the tablet of your heart. [4] Then you will win favor and a good name in the sight of God and man. [5] Trust in the Lord with all your heart and lean not on your own understanding; [6] in all your ways acknowledge him, and he will make your paths straight.

The reward is favor and a good name in the sight of God; but most importantly, it says God and man. These verses tell us to trust in God's direction and not lean on our own understanding. If you didn't need God's direction, you would not need to read this series or know anything about the Bible or Proverbs or spiritual guidance of this nature — you would automatically know what to do. However, those of us who are smart and want to live a more prosperous life seek the guidance of those who are wiser and read the things that will set us on the appropriate course.

These scriptures advise us to trust in God with all our heart. Don't just try to figure it out on your own — acknowledge God's rules, and your path will be straight. Remember what I said before about the obstacles being supernaturally removed in some cases? That is God working supernaturally in the background with you.

Proverbs 3:7

[7] Do not be wise in your own eyes; fear the Lord and shun evil.

When it's all about how smart someone is or how much smarter he is than everyone else, he's already lost. No matter how successful we are financially or in some other aspect of our life, there's always someone smarter or more innovative. There will always be people out ahead of us. The ability to learn allows us to prosper even greater and not live within our limitations or the limitations others set for us.

This also speaks to living poorly. Many times, people think by following the rules or some guide to living such as the Scriptures (in this case Proverbs), we will miss out on something good and fun. Well, if your lifestyle includes hanging out in bars and nightclubs, are you going to miss out on the smoking? Are you going to miss out on the hangover the next day? Are you going to miss out on a "one-night stand" with a stranger? Are you going to miss out on the effect this has on your health (short term and long term), or will you benefit by spending your time with other people heading in a much more positive direction? Think about the negativity that we will attract with the self-destruction of bar and nightclub hopping. I've "been there, done that, and got the T-shirt."

Compare that to spending time with like-minded people heading in the same positive direction that you are by reading this book and implementing the strategies. By being wise in your own eyes, fearing the Lord, shunning evil, doing the right thing, and ignoring evil or improper living, you will be rewarded by bringing health to your body and nourishment to your bones. By avoiding activities that abuse your body such as overindulging in alcohol, smoking, improper nutrition, or lack of exercise, you will live a healthier lifestyle. Abuse only leads to poor health, and we pay a price for that poor health somewhere along the line. However, when you avoid the abusive habits, you will reap the benefit of good health. It will become one more area of prosperity in your life.

Let me be clear about "nightclub hopping." I enjoy dancing, and I particularly enjoy Latin and Swing music. There is nothing wrong with music, dancing, and the fun of meeting friends for an enjoyable evening. Only when you take it over the line and engage in the behavior I've outlined above does it become self-destructive.

Proverbs 3:9-10

> [9] Honor the Lord with your wealth, with the first fruits of all your crops; [10] then your barns will be filled to overflowing, and your vats will brim over with new wine.

The key phrase in the commandment is to "honor the Lord" — or honor the instructions and the commands that He has given you "with your wealth and with the first fruits of all of your crops." A person of Christian faith probably understands that *first fruits* are those gifts on top of tithing or the normal giving. So if you have an extraordinary season as a farmer, businessperson, worker, or in any area of your life, you should give the first fruits of that additional increase and benefit over your normal giving.

Scripture suggests you should sow back into your community. It refers to the immediate community (which should be first) and also the greater community. Giving back and sowing sets specific laws in motion that come back to benefit you. By working together for the greater good — both locally and beyond the local environment — you set positive actions in motion both for yourself and your family.

Most people (and I have been there myself) give what they have leftover to God. It's easy to understand that people cannot tithe when their life is controlled by lack of discipline in the form of debt — consumer debt in particular. This is dramatically more serious than business debt or mortgage debt because most consumer debt sacrifices the future for some pleasure of the present. You'll most likely be still paying for it after the pleasure itself has passed on. At least with a home or a business, the debt associated with it makes sense if you entered into it with sound reasoning. Most likely, you were granted a conventional fifteen or thirty-year home mortgage based on a reasonable expectation that your employment would continue allowing you to make the payment.

Perhaps you use consumer debt to purchase items, such as school supplies, schoolbooks, and appropriate clothing for your family. There is nothing wrong with this practice if you have the discipline to pay it off within a short time. Generally, I recommend you pay off consumer debt within thirty days, but sometimes our budgets require us to stretch repayment to sixty days.

However, you don't need a big-screen television or some other new creature comfort if it will interfere with achieving the progressive increase of your financial prosperity. By lacking discipline regarding discretionary purchases, you can quickly accumulate consumer debt in the tens of thousands of dollars. Instead of delaying gratification until you have the money saved for the purchase, you are increasing the debt. Even if you have good credit, in many cases you're paying a consumer debt interest rate of 14 percent or more. If you have bad credit, you're paying in excess of 20 percent — sometimes in excess of 30 percent. The debt will rob you of your wealth now and leave you in no position to leave a legacy for the next generation.

How in the world is anyone going to be thinking about tithing or giving first fruits if he is running away from his creditors? It just doesn't make sense! The discipline of delayed gratification relieves you of burden. It allows you a life where you sow back into yourself, your family, your local community, and the greater community for the greater good.

Proverbs 3:11-12

> [11] My son, do not despise the Lord's discipline and do not resent his rebuke, [12] because the Lord disciplines those he loves, as a father [a] the son he delights in.

The Lord disciplines those He loves. As a father, He disciplines the son He delights in. The key point here is to honor the Lord with your wealth and do the right thing. If you do that, "your barns will be filled to overflowing and," in some cases, "your vats will brim over with new wine." By accepting discipline without resentment, you're able to benefit in the greater prosperity of finding wisdom, using wisdom, and living through the benefits of wisdom.

Think for a moment of the tabloids. You can't boot up online to look at Yahoo or AOL without seeing some celebrity who has done extremely well financially but whose personal life is negatively splattered across the Internet and the newspapers. They're a total mess. So do you ever imagine trading places with that person? Certainly you want to trade places with that person financially; but do you want to live a lifestyle where you wake up next to a stranger without any recall of how you got there? Naked? Not remembering their name? Fumbling around to figure out how you are going to get home because you're not really sure where you are? Do you want to live a life of regret because you didn't have the discipline to put certain things in motion for yourself and to stay the course and finish the race? Most of us would not choose that path.

In my own life, I wanted to become a Distinguished Toastmaster (DTM) — the highest educational designation that Toastmasters International awards. It requires years of diligence, discipline, and dedication of working toward the designation. It is often recognized by corporate human resources departments as an outstanding achievement.

To reach this level, I had to put a plan together to regularly attend Toastmasters club meetings and deliver speeches both in my own club and in other clubs. I also became involved in leadership projects that helped me advance and broaden my own skills while helping my local club and its members. My achievements helped increase the status of our area, division, and district in the Toastmasters International organization.

Here is the greater lesson: by investing my time in improving my communication and leadership skills, I also invested in my local club. Participation in other clubs helped the division as well as the district achieve its goals. I became a leader in the division and the district by helping other clubs improve. It all comes back to helping yourself by having the discipline to institute beneficial habits for the greater good. However, if you're too busy living a life controlled by lack of discipline and mismanaging important areas of your life, you can't embrace and experience the benefits of self-control. I would never have reached the designation of Distinguished Toastmaster without creating new habits and having the self-control to keep them. Without the new habits and self-control, I would have been continually frustrated by the lack of progress.

Say that you didn't have to earn and save your money to achieve prosperity because you inherited your money or you were able to receive a windfall. Without those important life lessons of creating prosperity on your own, you could basically waste away your life and the money. The folks that you see plastered across the tabloids may live comfortably because of financial success but for every story you read, prosperity there seems to be tainted by self-destruction and dissipation.

You may be tempted to skip the end-of-chapter exercises. You'll find it rewarding to work through this book and complete the exercises as well. Committing you ideas to paper will help you stay on track for improvement. It reminds you of what you need to do every time you refer to it. You'll find out that something powerful happens when your hand grabs a pen, it hits the paper, you write your thoughts, and then read it back aloud if possible. There is something that clicks inside of us.

However, writing things down and repeating things really don't have any value unless you personalize them and put your name on them. Promise yourself that you're going to practice ideas and find meaning in activities even when they seem mundane. Make picking up the kids up from school or doing something a little extra for your spouse or friend seem special to them. See if there is something that you can do in your community to help out or to give back.

Proverbs 3:21-26

> [21] My son, preserve sound judgment and discernment, do not let them out of your sight; [22] they will be life for you, an ornament to grace your neck. [23] Then you will go on your way in safety, and your foot will not stumble; [24] when you lie down, you will not be afraid; when you lie down, your sleep will be sweet. [25] Have no fear of sudden disaster or of the ruin that overtakes the wicked, [26] for the Lord will be your confidence and will keep your foot from being snared.

What is promised here by using good commonsense and discernment consistently? For one thing, your road through life will be safer. Commonsense isn't very common. But with some commonsense, your feet will not stumble. You can go to bed without fear, lie down, and sleep soundly.

Remember what I said about being in debt? If you have personal issues — particularly financial issues — you know the burden of feeling exposed to the risk of losing everything. Perhaps you know the feeling of losing your job or you are way over your head in debt, and it is a weight on your shoulders. When it is relieved and you gain the discipline and wisdom to avoid it in the future, you will live a much better life and certainly sleep a lot sounder.

Focus on the meaning of Proverbs 3:25 where it says, "Have no fear of sudden disaster or of the ruin that overtakes the wicked." If you're deeply in debt and you find yourself living in the difficult times of our nation's economy, you are likely feeling the burden of excess risk. In 2008 and 2009, a number of financial institutions were either bought, went out of business, or had their assets seized. As a result, many people lost their homes. Others lost their jobs because of the financial crisis and could no longer afford their homes and other consumer debt. Most of the personal risk in troubling economic times is connected with credit that is too easy to attain making ill-conceived dreams to easy to chase.

The bottom line is that we're all responsible — whether we're in government, working for a financial institution, or managing our life and our finances — for preparing for a sudden disaster.

If you are buried in debt, you're certainly not saving at least 10 percent of your income for a rainy day such as a sudden disaster, layoff, or even retirement. You're living paycheck to paycheck and, most likely, you're living well beyond your means. You may want to keep up with the Jones' but the Jones' are probably broke themselves. Trying to keep up with others and live beyond your means is a recipe for disaster.

I've been in debt in the past myself and have been way beyond my limits. I learned that sticking to these principles was key to getting out of it. At times in my life, I deviated from the principles and took on too much debt — owing tens of thousands of dollars beyond my mortgage debt. But by doubling down, paying attention, and cutting fat out of the financial diet, I was able to bring things back in line and release myself from the prison of debt.

Proverbs 3:27-32

> [27] Do not withhold good from those who deserve it, when it is in your power to act. [28] Do not say to your neighbor, "Come back later; I'll give it tomorrow" — when you now have it with you. [29] Do not plot harm against your neighbor, who lives trustfully near you. [30] Do not accuse a man for no reason — when he has done you no harm. [31] Do not envy a violent man or choose any of his ways, [32] for the Lord detests a perverse man but takes the upright into his confidence.

The Prosperity of Wisdom

These verses instruct us to help those who deserve it. If you can help your neighbor, help them. Don't tell them to come back tomorrow. It doesn't do you any good to help someone who is suffering today by telling them to come back tomorrow.

The verses go on to advise us to avoid getting involved in plots of revenge against our neighbor. Don't harbor grudges and spend your time trying to figure how you're going to get even. Instead, get even by being successful and moving on! That is the best payback! Occasionally, I encounter people in my professional life who seem to be plotting against me and trying to figure out how they can subvert me. Even though the situation is discouraging, I must keep moving forward — progressing and prospering. It will drive them crazy. Plotting against and subverting someone only hurts you in the end.

Don't use physical or mental violence as Option A, B, or C. Try to remove yourself from situations where violence is present. If you can't protect yourself, look for an opportunity to escape the abuse. Avoid spending time in places where you're inevitably going to come in contact with violent people and behavior. The exposure can't get you anywhere and if you're prone to becoming involved in it, it will come back to bite you in a detrimental way.

Proverbs 3:33 and 3:35

> [33] The Lord's curse is on the house of the wicked, but he blesses the home of the righteous. [34] He mocks proud mockers but gives grace to the humble. [35] The wise inherit honor, but fools are put to shame.

If you're not living a life of commonsense, discipline, discernment, and wisdom, you're shaming yourself. You don't need the Lord to step in to curse you. He blesses the home of the upright. As a person in a relationship with a wonderful woman who is one hundred percent in my corner, I can tell you from personal experience that integrity and faithfulness in this relationship has been one of the best things that has ever happened in my life.

I encourage you to do the exercises and write the verses down on paper. Put your name in the verses, identify the particular areas in your life where you can improve, and note what the benefits of each improvement are.

Keep your blessings in mind as you bring your life in line with these principles if it is not already. Reflect on how being blessed has blessed those around you. As we live a more balanced and abundant life in general, we find better relationships with our family members and friends. We become more able to have to patience and wisdom to diffuse or avoid conflict — particularly in the hostile environment of toxic work situations or bad marriages. Keep in mind this is the more fruitful path but it is not always necessarily the easiest or the one you feel most inclined to pursue emotionally.

Action Steps on the Life Path

Review the scriptures of Proverbs 3 before answering these questions.

Write down each of the commands in Proverbs 3:1-10.

_____

_____

_____

_____

_____

_____

_____

_____

Make a note of three distinct things that you can do to improve your life for each command.

_____

_____

_____

_____

Describe what type of person you could be if you followed the advice in this chapter.

_____

_____

_____

_____

The Prosperity of Wisdom

PROVERBS 4

Wisdom: The Greatest Gift

"Wisdom is supreme; therefore get wisdom. Though it cost all you have, get understanding."

Proverbs 4:7

T he core message of Proverbs 4 is that "wisdom is supreme." In this chapter, we explore why wisdom is supreme and learn how to utilize Proverbs 4 to acquire wisdom. We'll also look at the people who have wisdom and the benefits of having wisdom. As with all chapters in this book, you'll benefit by reading Proverbs 4 before you proceed.

Proverbs 4:3-4

> 3 When I was a boy in my father's house, still tender, and an only child of my mother, 4 he taught me and said, "Lay hold of my words with all your heart; keep my commands and you will live."

These verses refer to a father's instruction. If you meditate on these verses, you will notice it says that a wise person is generally kind and loyal, trusts in the Lord, puts God first, turns away from evil, knows right from wrong, listens, learns, and does what is right. The benefits of this wisdom are a long and satisfying life, favor with God and people, a good reputation, wise judgment, success, health, vitality, riches, honor, a pleasurable life, peace of mind, and protection.

Where you hear wisdom speak, that's the Father's instruction. Later in the book, you'll find that wisdom itself speaks in Proverbs 8 and 9. And when it speaks, people who have wisdom recognize they discover knowledge and discernment; that they hate pride, arrogance, and all forms of corruption; and how they respect and fear God. They speak to giving proper and good advice, and they have commonsense — a recurring theme in Proverbs. It also happens to be a recurring theme in life. Look at yourself and the people you know who don't use it when they should. What do you observe about their results and their life?

Wise people love correction, are teachable, and know God. The benefits they speak to are riches, honor, justice, righteousness, life, and having God's approval. They are constantly reading and learning. Their success comes from understanding.

Proverbs 4:5-8

> [5] Get wisdom, get understanding; do not forget my words or swerve from them. [6] Do not forsake wisdom, and she will protect you; love her, and she will watch over you. [7] Wisdom is supreme; therefore get wisdom. Though it cost all you have, [a] get understanding. [8] Esteem her, and she will exalt you; embrace her, and she will honor you.

So how does someone interact with wisdom? What is Solomon's recommendation? Reflect on your own life. Have you personally experienced how valuing and embracing wisdom has rewarded you? How would it change your life if you pursued and achieved wisdom?

Proverbs 4:1-27 refers to children, listening, and parenting. The references are all in the context of God as parent and you as child. By extension, you may be married and have children. The verses refer to how you're disciplining, explaining, and encouraging them and operating using wisdom. It is clear that one of the great responsibilities of parents is to encourage their children to become wise and to use commonsense. Solomon discusses it even further in 1 Kings 2:1-9. In 1 Chronicles 28-29, it describes David doing just that. Wisdom is something that can be passed from parents to children or from generation to generation. But ultimately, it just comes from God. In the end, it is up to each individual to use it.

If you're given the gift of learning and understanding, you have to apply it to show the value. It doesn't happen on its own. One time, I was watching a television show on a business channel. The host of the show was highlighting teenage entrepreneurs. It was fun to see these young people with very sophisticated ideas — just as sophisticated as adults. The thing that stood out was the running theme of parental support. Either they were there in person or mentioned in very a positive manner. The parents' support, encouragement, and, in some cases, direct involvement was instrumental in the young entrepreneurs' success.

It is dramatically easier for young people to succeed when their parents are supportive and encouraging. If you have children or just young people you are close to, reflect on how you have encouraged them to succeed. Reflect on the people in your life who have encouraged you. We need to surround ourselves with positive people — not those who are dream stealers and future killers. We need people who are dream enablers and goal encouragers. You might find it beneficial to become part of a mastermind group where you meet regularly with people who are like-minded and help hold you accountable to your goals.

Proverbs 4:5-7 says we have to actively pursue wisdom. This requires determination. It's not going to fall out of the sky on you. It is up to you as an individual to go after it, seize it, and use it. Be determined not to abandon the search for wisdom once you begin no matter how difficult the road can become at times. It is not a once-in-a-lifetime action — it is a daily process of making the right choices. Case in point: perhaps you are pursuing an educational goal while you are working in a demanding job and raising a family. If you stay with the company, you understand that you're going to need a bachelor's or master's degree or some type of advanced accreditation. You'll have to determine that you're going to pursue that goal and somehow make the time for it. It will require discipline because it is much easier to come home and turn on the television, grab something to eat, and relax.

There's nothing at all wrong with relaxing after a hard day's work. However, taking the next step sometimes means that you're going to have to delay immediate gratification and sacrifice maybe two or three nights a week to pursue that goal. God approached Solomon because he was doing so well in His eyes and he was also the son of David whose line He promised to bless. He asked him what he wanted because He was going to grant the wish. Solomon asked for wisdom! He didn't ask for a pile of gold the size of Mount Everest, a harem of ten thousand women, or a larger boat. He asked for wisdom — the very thing that he could use to govern well and to live an incredible life that was beneficial to both his kingdom and to himself.

We should all look to activate our faith by incorporating daily prayer and meditation as part of our life. We don't need to pray all day but that certainly would not hurt if you did. However, you may want to start your day out with five or ten minutes of prayer. During that time, review the goals that you have in life as part of that prayer, and give thanks for what is going well in your life and for the ability to map out your goals.

It's good to have three or four major goals. Maybe your goal is to have a good marriage, become more involved in some form of community activity, be more successful in business, or get out of debt. Don't be afraid to ask God for assistance in meeting your goals and remember to thank Him.

Not sure how to pray? I have two suggestions. First, search for *The Lord's Prayer* on the Internet, and pick out the version you are most comfortable with. Say it before or after reviewing your goals or whatever you are praying for. Second, if you are reading a scripture, insert your name into the scripture as if God is speaking directly to you for divine reinforcement.

For example, I might say, "Theodore, take hold of My instructions, don't let them go; guard them, for they are the keys to life." "Theodore, don't do as the wicked do; don't follow the path of evildoers." This is a great way to use scriptures that touch you as a way to better anchor yourself.

Proverbs 4:13-17

> [13] Hold on to instruction, do not let it go; guard it well, for it is your life. [14] Do not set foot on the path of the wicked or walk in the way of evil men. [15] Avoid it, do not travel on it; turn from it and go on your way. [16] For they cannot sleep till they do evil; they are robbed of slumber till they make someone fall. [17] They eat the bread of wickedness and drink the wine of violence.

We all know people who just seem to be in the middle of every negative activity going on anywhere in their general vicinity. Sometimes on the surface, they are very likable. In fact, one of the tools they use to wreak havoc is to be likable by the right type of people — generally their immediate boss or someone in authority. However, they tend to be the opposite to the people they manage or whom they exert some type of control over. As the verse says, "They eat the food of wickedness and drink the wine of violence."

Violent, criminal people generally come to a bad end unless there is some reformation in habit, character, and approach. It doesn't have to end poorly. Certainly some circumstances in life are totally in our control. It's up to each of us to seize the moment and exercise that control.

Think about the people in your life. Note the ones that may not be good for you and the effect they have on the dreams and goals you have. Who is discouraging you? When you say you want to go to college because you want to improve your life or get a better job, they are the people who tell you, "Awww, you don't need to go to college!" "You can't go to college!" "You won't be successful!" On the other hand, they clearly encourage you to follow them on the road to nowhere. Be honest with yourself and identify those people.

On the other side of the fence, think about the people who tell you that you can achieve your dream even though it may be tough. They are the people who will help you get the information together to pursue your dream. Seek out and surround yourself with people who are encouragers.

Unfortunately, we need to clearly understand that even our friends can make us fall. It is difficult for people to accept the fact that the people they hang around with could steer them onto the wrong path. This is particularly true of young people who want to be accepted and who don't want to be confrontational with or be criticized by the group. They are easy prey for negative controlling people. This doesn't mean that we should always be skeptical or suspicious, but we should use commonsense.

You might find that you're being encouraged to engage in self-destructive or criminal behavior at the same time someone else is encouraging you down a different, more positive road. While the positive road may not seem as glamorous or gratifying initially, the positive road emerges as the one that will be the happier, more constructive road to travel in the end.

Look at our prisons! They are filled with people who had great ideas about quick dollars or who were violent and indiscriminate in their activities. Ultimately, they were caught and now spend their time behind bars. It is just not worth it! It is a wasted life. This is the point of wisdom. Decisions that look easy, gratifying, and pleasurable up front may not be the right ones. We must really want to think through how we spend our time and who we spend it with.

Proverbs 4:23-24

> [23] Above all else, guard your heart, for it is the wellspring of life.
> [24] Put away perversity from your mouth; keep corrupt talk far from your lips.

Guard your heart. Our feelings of love and desire dictate to a great extent how we live. By and large, human beings will try to find the time to do the things that we enjoy. These verses remind us to operate with wisdom, commonsense, discretion, and discernment. There is nothing wrong with pursuing a passion; but if your passion as a married person leads to situations where you will become involved in adulterous behavior, run! It might make you feel good initially but will only lead you down the wrong path and cause you great embarrassment at some point.

We aren't hard pressed to find examples of that behavior playing out in real life. We had a recent president who indulged in an indiscretion that was publicly exposed. No matter how you feel about his politics or the politics of the time, that sort of indiscretion led to great personal embarrassment to him, to his family, and to our country. It caused a fracturing of the governmental process because we needed him to be focused on other things. Instead of watching our leader pursue goals in the national interest, he was focused on determining whether he was going to be impeached because of his sexual indiscretion. The decision to move along a short-term pleasurable route in the end made no sense. If we can't do it in the light of day, it probably doesn't make sense. Unfortunately, it is not always easy to do.

Make sure your affections lead you in the right direction, and put boundaries on your desires. You don't have to go after everything you see. Look straight ahead and keep your eyes fixed on your goal. Don't go off track because detours and shortcuts many times will lead you completely down the wrong road to the wrong end.

In summary, we must follow the compass found through prayer, meditation, and Scripture on the principles described here. I believe there is a divine plan for each person, but it is up to us to seek and follow its direction. After all, we are creatures of free will, and we don't have to follow the right path. We should seek guidance by seeking and listening to the right people such as family members, teachers, and peers; learning and using the biblical principles; and using the wisdom obtained to negotiate the turbulent waters of living. Don't let wisdom slip past you or you will let the real "good life" get away. Remember Proverbs 4:13: "Hold on to instruction, do not let it go; guard it well, for it is your life."

Action Steps on the Life Path

Take two or three minutes and make note of actions that you've taken that were not wise.

_____

_____

_____

_____

_____

_____

List two, three, or more things you will do to ensure you will not turn your back on wisdom but instead embrace it. How will taking these actions make you better?

_____

_____

_____

_____

What are some ways that you have been discouraging to either your children or those closest to you?

_____

_____

_____

_____

What are some practices you are going to adopt so you can be encouraging?

_____

_____

_____

_____

Wisdom: The Greatest Gift

Who are some people in your life who are not encouraging to you (dream stealers)? Who may be actively discouraging you from your desired accomplishments? What do they do to discourage you?

_____

_____

_____

_____

_____

_____

_____

_____

_____

_____

Who are some positive, encouraging people you can surround yourself and spend time with? These are dream enablers who can be a part of your mastermind group and will help you understand better how to pursue your dreams more effectively.

_____

_____

_____

_____

_____

_____

_____

_____

_____

_____

Write a short prayer asking for God's assistance and thanking Him for that assistance. For this exercise, you may want to write down three or four major goals keeping in mind the principles covered in the first four chapters. Some of your goals may be to have a good marriage, become more involved in a community activity, be more successful in business, or get out of debt. As we move through this program, there will be opportunities around which to flush out both more strategies and more goals.

_____

_____

_____

_____

_____

_____

_____

_____

_____

_____

_____

_____

_____

_____

_____

_____

_____

_____

_____

_____

_____

PROVERBS 5

Adultery Destroys Your Life

"The evil deeds of a wicked man ensnare him;
the cords of his sin hold him fast."

Proverbs 5:22

In some versions of the Bible, Proverbs 5 is titled "Avoid Immoral Women." It is really a warning against adultery. Although many sections of the Bible may sound sexist by today's politically correct standards, I'm not going to change the genders. I don't want to confuse the reading of it when you refer to the text on your own. Whether you are a man or a woman, I want you to keep in mind that the issue highlighted here is immoral behavior regardless of gender. The immoral woman is actually a prostitute as it is described in Proverbs.

Immoral Behavior

Proverbs includes many warnings against what we would call *illicit sex* today. First, a "prostitute's charm" refers to any type of temptation that will lead you down the wrong path or away from the pursuit of wisdom.

Remember, the goal is wisdom. For people of faith, the goal of this entire collection of lessons is to live according to God's wisdom. Therefore, use these lessons to develop the wisdom of using commonsense and proper discernment.

Secondly, sexual immorality of any type — whether it was 6,000 years ago, 2,000 years ago, 1,000 years ago, yesterday, or today — is still extremely dangerous because it destroys family life by distracting spouses from familial duty. It can even destroy careers. When that happens, it will have a negative effect on the community. If it is pervasive enough, it will have a negative effect on the greater society. Some might say we are living in that cycle now.

You may think of examples of people you know in your own life. To use a public figure as an example, consider what happened to President Bill Clinton because of his immoral sexual behavior. Here was a man who had risen to great heights but his presidency was shaken to its very foundation because of extramarital indiscretion. His sexual immorality got in the way of good judgment and almost destroyed lives and careers. His presidency survived, but the resulting damage to the office could have been horrendous. Look beyond the political realm to sports figures such as Tiger Woods. In the world of entertainment, we witnessed Sandra Bullock's high-profile divorce from Jesse James. Both experienced marriage destruction via adultery. In former President Clinton's case, his marriage miraculously survived.

Third, it erodes a person's ability to love. The continual pursuit of fulfillment in fleeting affairs (visiting with a prostitute in this case) or any illicit temptation is dangerous. As well as threatening the family, it also erodes a person's ability to have an intelligent, loving relationship. Someone — if not everyone — who is involved will become degraded as the whole scenario develops. It turns people into objects and potentially could lead to the transmission of disease, children born out of wedlock, or even unwanted children.

Sexual immorality is totally against God's law. You're going to be hard-pressed to find someone who lives a sexually immoral life, particularly on a continual basis, who is living a happy, fulfilled existence. For example, I saw an interview with a professional wrestler who had become a "born again" Christian, and he was discussing why his life took a downward turn before becoming saved. His comment on his marriage was particularly telling. He basically said he couldn't be on the road for weeks drinking, drugging, and having sex with groupies and then come home and have a normal relationship with his wife. It can't be any plainer than that.

Proverbs 5:3-8

> [3] For the lips of an adulteress drip honey, and her speech is smoother than oil; [4] but in the end she is bitter as gall, sharp as a double-edged sword. [5] Her feet go down to death; her steps lead straight to the grave. [a] [6] She gives no thought to the way of life; her paths are crooked, but she knows it not. [7] Now then, my sons, listen to me; do not turn aside from what I say. [8] Keep to a path far from her, do not go near the door of her house,

Notice it warns against "smooth talkers." These days, that term is used quite a bit, and it can have a flattering tone. However, it is anything but flattering in Proverbs 5. Just remember the phrase "For the lips of an adulteress drip honey, and her speech is smoother than oil; but in the end, she is bitter as gall, sharp as a double-edged sword." The best advice here is to make a turn and go around that roadblock.

Proverbs 5:11-13

> [11] At the end of your life you will groan, when your flesh and body are spent. [12] You will say, "How I hated discipline! How my heart spurned correction! [13] I would not obey my teachers or listen to my instructors.

It's going to be way too late to ask for advice at the end of your life. We've all been there. We really want something — to be in a romantic relationship with someone or to own some object of fascination such as a select model of car, a particular type of fashionable clothing, a choice brand of handbag or watch, or type of pet. Whatever it is, we lose our rationality. The only thing that is going to get "the monkey off your back" is to have satisfaction.

The best time to learn the dangers and the foolishness of going after anything forbidden, harmful, or ill-advised is long before the temptation comes. Resistance is much easier if we've already made the decision to resist. When you have a moral compass, you don't have to worry about the direction your ship is traveling. Prepare for temptations by deciding now, activating the moral compass, and keeping it on alert. It will govern how you will act when you face temptation.

> [15] Drink water from your own cistern, running water from your own well. [16] Should your springs overflow in the streets, your streams of water in the public squares? [17] Let them be yours alone, never to be shared with strangers. [18] May your fountain be blessed, and may you rejoice in the wife of your youth. [19] A loving doe, a graceful deer — may her breasts satisfy you always, may you ever be captivated by her love. [20] Why be captivated, my son, by an adulteress? Why embrace the bosom of another man's wife? [21] For a man's ways are in full view of the Lord, and he examines all his paths.

This provides a clear definition of faithfulness in your marriage. Most everyone has been in a serious, committed, or emotionally charged relationship with someone who got hurt because of infidelity. The verse advises married people to enjoy the spouse that God has given them. The Bible was written in a desert so water is considered precious — a life-giving commodity in sparse supply. In the desert lands, water from a well is pretty much a family's most important possession. Without it, not only will crops not grow, people will either leave the land or die. It is not something that is readily available in abundance. Instead, it is something that is to be treasured when it is found — just like your spouse or the person you are in an exclusive relationship with.

In the Old Testament, it was considered a serious crime to steal water from someone else's well. It was a crime on the level of stealing a man's horse in the Old American West or to have intercourse with another person's spouse. In the Old Testament, it could lead not only to punishment but also to death. Remember the story of the woman brought before Jesus to be judged for adultery? If He had not shown God's mercy, that lady would have been punished by being stoned to death.

Lastly, infidelity is damaging to not just one person's life. The person who leads or allows another person to become involved in something illicit is also endangering the entire family and their extended relationships. It could certainly harm the spouse or the other person in the relationship, but it can affect children and other family members depending upon the circumstances. Without a doubt, immorality as it relates to faithfulness, marriage, and relationships is on the level of stealing one's water in the desert.

The message contained Proverbs 5:15-21 is that couples need to look to one

Adultery Destroys Your Life

another for lifelong satisfaction and companionship instead of looking to external things. That doesn't mean that you don't go to movies, the museum, a party, or some other type of entertainment. However, you should look for fulfillment from the person you're sharing your life with. You want to "take your pleasures at home" and not take them in the street. Your faith says you should rejoice in the blessing that God has given you — the person that you are engaged in a committed relationship with.

One way to rejoice is to show your appreciation. That simple action can pull a relationship closer together. By having an open, sharing, appreciative relationship, you're going to get much more satisfaction out of it.

Again, remember to use commonsense and discernment. Give due respect to the loved one who is in your corner and is a source of comfort, satisfaction, and protection to you. If you are having trouble visualizing this, think back to a time when you had that sort of relationship but for some reason someone's actions led to its destruction. Remember how painful it was? Why indulge that pain when you can avoid it by being in a quality marriage or exclusive relationship?

By not indulging in promiscuous behavior, we keep ourselves free of negative encumbrances and liberate ourselves to live along the divine path our compass is directing us toward. Take, for example, the political costs to a politician's career. Senator John Ensign of Nevada and Governor Mark Sanford of South Carolina had their bright political stars destroyed when their adulteries were uncovered and played out in public. It doesn't matter which political party they belong to because the failings are human, not partisan.

No matter how smart we are or how seemingly easy the situation looks at first, there is always a price to pay when a sin has been committed. In the above-mentioned example, it cost these men their current careers in the near term and possibly greater political ambitions. In both situations, the behavior had gone on for quite some time, and it became ever harder to extract themselves from it. It became a stronger prison for the people involved as time went on. Remember the verse we began our chapter with: "The evil deeds of a wicked man ensnare him; the cords of his sin hold him fast" (Proverbs 5:22).

Action Steps on the Life Path

Some people may think that being in the same relationship is going to get boring or monotonous. Spend five minutes and write down at least five benefits of being with the person you've chosen to spend your life with. How is he or she making your life better?

_____

_____

_____

_____

_____

_____

_____

_____

_____

_____

_____

_____

_____

_____

_____

_____

_____

_____

_____

Don't Get Involved in Foolishness

"Free yourself, like a gazelle from the hand of the hunter, like a bird from the snare of the fowler."

Proverbs 6:5

In some versions of the Bible, Proverbs 6 is called "Lessons for Daily Life." This chapter covers a financial aspect that many of us need to come to grips with — how we handle our finances. Let's not forget that wisdom's compass is actually God's Word. Being such, it exists in our minds and hearts to lead and protect us.

The Word is a lighthouse we need during a storm, but we also need it when the waters are calm. As Proverbs 6:23 says, "For these commands are a lamp, this teaching is a light, and the corrections of discipline are the way to life." Therefore listening to and following biblical principles will keep us from the "snare of the fowler" or, more directly said, out of trouble.

Proverbs 6:1-3

[1] My son, if you have put up security for your neighbor, if you have struck hands in pledge for another, [2] if you have been trapped by what you said, ensnared by the words of your mouth, [3] then do this,

my son, to free yourself, since you have fallen into your neighbor's hands: Go and humble yourself; press your plea with your neighbor!

These verses are introducing us to the danger of debt. In 2008 and 2009, the major, global financial panic and meltdown in every industrialized country including the United States inspired measures to restore fiscal and financial responsibility. It's interesting that several thousand years ago, the issue of debt was just as important as it is now.

So notice that Proverbs 6:1-3 is warning against "putting up security for a neighbor." The modern version of that would be cosigning on a car loan for one of your friends or relatives who doesn't otherwise qualify. If they default on the loan, you are responsible for it. Proverbs supports generosity but not open-ended charity where the amount given and the timing are determined by circumstances beyond your control. Too often, it leads to disaster. This is also covered in Proverbs 11:15, 17:18, and 22:26-27.

The first few verses of Proverbs 6 are not a plea against generosity. Instead, they warn against overextending your financial resources and acting in an irresponsible manner that could launch you into poverty. It's important to maintain a balance between generosity and intelligent, wise stewardship. God wants us to help our friends and the needy, but he does not promise to cover the cost of every foolish commitment that we make. We have to act responsibly so that our families do not suffer. We should not bankrupt ourselves to go on the line for someone else.

There are certain extenuating circumstances. Perhaps a child, spouse, or other family member is the victim of a catastrophic illness. Of course you may have to dig deep into your savings to help them through that period. Hopefully, that period would lead to recovery. I've been there myself when I had to assist with the financial expenses for my mother's illness before she passed on. I was happy to do it. It created a financial challenge for me at the time; however, I wouldn't have had it any other way. Fortunately, I was smart enough with my finances early on to be able to do that.

Lending people money for a purchase is normally a different thing entirely. People have asked me to loan them money so they could pay their credit cards bills. Normally that means they no longer have enough money to pay for their own consumer items. Because they have overextended themselves to the point where even the credit card companies will no longer tolerate

Don't Get Involved in Foolishness

them, of course I said no. It would be foolish to pay someone's credit card bills for consumer items.

The real remedy is for them to contact the credit card companies and negotiate for more time to properly pay it. Borrowing more money from other people is not a realistic solution. I have one rule of thumb in regard to lending someone money for personal reasons: don't lend them anymore than you can afford to kiss goodbye. Don't expect it back because it is likely that you won't see it. That will ease the chance of harboring hard feelings because they placed you in a bad financial situation.

That may sound harsh, but even the credit cards companies — who are known for almost grabbing people and forcing a credit card in their hand — aren't willing to extend credit to people who can't manage their finances. It's just not good commonsense, and it is not good stewardship.

If you don't believe my comment about the credit card companies "grabbing people," next time you travel, notice the counters set up near the busiest points inside the airport terminals where people are waiting for their flights. They all seem to have special promotions designed to have you sign up for some type of credit card. Do you really think they are eager to have you sign up because they love you or care about you?

Proverbs 6:6-11

> [6] Go to the ant, you sluggard; consider its ways and be wise! [7] It has no commander, no overseer or ruler, [8] yet it stores its provisions in summer and gathers its food at harvest. [9] How long will you lie there, you sluggard? When will you get up from your sleep? [10] A little sleep, a little slumber, a little folding of the hands to rest — [11] and poverty will come on you like a bandit and scarcity like an armed man. [a]

Based on these verses, we get the idea that we're not supposed to properly rest or that resting means we're lazy and shiftless. It's actually quite the contrary. What Proverbs is warning against is giving into the temptation of laziness — of sleeping instead of working. This in no way means that we should never rest. God gives the Jews and Christians the Sabbath as a weekly day of rest and restoration, but we should not rest when we should be working. If laziness turns us from our responsibilities, poverty is just around the corner. The Bible uses the example of the ant in the scripture because the ant utilizes its energy and resources in an economically-sound fashion.

Here is another example. I have many activities that happen after work. After having worked all day, I have come home many evenings to work on this book. I was tired, but I just felt revived and rejuvenated by the idea of investing my time in my personal vision and project. I got a shot of adrenaline when it was time to come home and work on the book.

Meetings and community activities such as Toastmasters recharge my batteries too. Of course, I'm tired on the way to the activity. And it's easy to answer the call of the television and dinner; but everything changes once I get there. I get involved in the activities and the commitment, adrenaline, and enthusiasm takes over.

This doesn't mean you should push yourself to the point of exhaustion. Do the things that you're responsible for doing, but when its time to rest, get an appropriate amount of sleep at night. And take advantage of that one day a week where you rest, rejuvenate, and restore.

Proverbs 6:20-23

> [20] My son, keep your father's commands and do not forsake your mother's teaching. [21] Bind them upon your heart forever; fasten them around your neck. [22] When you walk, they will guide you; when you sleep, they will watch over you; when you awake, they will speak to you. [23] For these commands are a lamp, this teaching is a light, and the corrections of discipline are the way to life.

These scriptures talk about raising children. It is natural for children as they grow toward adulthood to become more independent of their parents. The objective is to raise them to be independent adults. However, you don't want to raise children who rebel against authority and to act without commonsense and discernment. As children grow, they should take on wisdom and use it appropriately. Even as adults with adult parents, there is something that we can still learn from our parents because they have been alive longer and have experienced more than we have. So cherish and value the ability to consult the advice of people who are older, and in many cases, wiser.

Don't Get Involved in Foolishness

25 Don't lust for her beauty, don't let her coy glances seduce you; 26 for the prostitute reduces you to a loaf of bread, and the adulteress preys upon your very life. 27 Can a man scoop fire into his lap without his clothes being burned? 28 Can a man walk on hot coals without his feet being scorched? 29 So is he who sleeps with another man's wife; no one who touches her will go unpunished. 30 Men do not despise a thief if he steals to satisfy his hunger when he is starving. 31 Yet if he is caught, he must pay sevenfold, though it costs him all the wealth of his house. 32 But a man who commits adultery lacks judgment; whoever does so destroys himself. 33 Blows and disgrace are his lot, and his shame will never be wiped away; 34 for jealousy arouses a husband's fury, and he will show no mercy when he takes revenge. 35 He will not accept any compensation; he will refuse the bribe, however great it is.

These verses give additional interesting and pointed advice on human nature. They are not talking about lack of desire. They are referring to utilizing wisdom to employ discipline. It suggests using good stewardship of your resources — your body and mind — to avoid desires that will make your life complicated, unproductive, and less useful to you and to those around you. Such negative behaviors can easily lead you to some form of ruin. If you don't believe me, just open your local newspaper to read about a celebrity or politician who is involved in some form of sexual sin or other behavior that prevented a proper, loving relationship and caused their ruin.

Re-read Proverbs 6 and mark the passages that resonate with you. Those are the ones that you should revisit from time to time — especially during times where you feel difficult challenges coming on. Notice that the theme of commonsense, discernment, and wisdom almost doesn't have anything to do with faith. However, faith is a wonderful blessing that you can enjoy while utilizing wisdom, commonsense, and discernment as immutable, universal laws. Those of faith believe in God, and we believe that God is the engine that drives these laws.

Action Steps on the Life Path

If you are in debt, start with these steps.

1. If you are a debt junkie or frequent borrower, stop borrowing immediately.

2. Calculate the true cost of an item you borrow money to own. For example, let's use an item that initially costs $10,000.

Loan amount	$10,000
Annual interest rate	10%
Term of loan (months):	60

   Your estimated monthly payments are $212.47, and you will pay $2,748 in interest over the life of the loan. Is the item worth what you will ACTUALLY pay for it?

3. Don't use bill consolidation strategies to delude yourself into thinking you are handling your debt. When you do this, you aren't reducing debt. Instead, you are only servicing the loans by paying interest and going deeper into debt.

4. List all of your debts on a sheet of paper. Separate the credit cards from your mortgage if you have one. Create a repayment strategy that uses the "drip method" (a little at a time). Pay off the loan with the smallest balance first. For example, you've selected a consumer loan with a $500 monthly payment to focus on paying off. Once it is paid off, take the amount you were paying on it and apply it to the next smallest-balance debt. Avoid the temptation to use the $500 as extra income. Stick to your plan, and put that $500 on debt repayment.

5. If you have a mortgage, pay at least one extra payment yearly. If you feel you won't have the extra payment at one time, then pay an additional amount equivalent to half of the principal portion of your payment each month. You will save thousands of dollars in interest, turn your thirty-year mortgage into a twenty-three-year mortgage, and own your home much sooner.

Don't Get Involved in Foolishness

PROVERBS 7

The Wisdom of Fidelity

"My son, keep my words and store up my commands within you. Keep my commands and you will live; guard my teachings as the apple of your eye."

Proverbs 7:1-2

In Proverbs 7, the title is another warning about immoral women: "Warning against the adulterous." Even though a female will be used as the subject, gender is not important — it's the behavior. In this case, they're using the gender of the female to point out the behavior of a prostitute or someone of immoral character; but it is actually meant for both sexes. You have to take it in the context of the times in which it was written. However, what is more critical is that the first five verses is an emphatic call and reminder to remember the benefits of wisdom and good instruction.

Proverbs 7:1-5

> [1] My son, keep my words and store up my commands within you.
> [2] Keep my commands and you will live; guard my teachings as the apple of your eye. [3] Bind them on your fingers; write them on the tablet of your heart. [4] Say to wisdom, "You are my sister," and call understanding your kinsman; [5] they will keep you from the adulteress, from the wayward wife with her seductive words.

The "apple of your eye" is an old English expression for the eye's center or pupil. The whole body is tuned to protect that pupil from harm, and the eyelids — almost like a reflex — snap shut at the slightest hint of danger. Your tear ducts bathe your eye with a cleansing liquid so that if any irritant enters, it will wash it out. It is almost as if it washes away any stream of danger.

So Proverbs urges you to take as much care of its teachings as you do of your own eye. Let's proceed with some of these teachings.

Proverbs 7:7

> 7 I saw among the simple, I noticed among the young men a youth who lacked judgment.

This verse subtly refers to someone who is naïve or without aim or direction. An empty life is clearly is not a stable life and a naïve person is vulnerable to all sorts of temptations. In this young man's case, even though he has no idea where he is going, the immoral woman knows where she wants him. This is the case with many things that tempt us in life, whether it is of a sexual or criminal nature or it is simply something that is going to veer us off our path.

The lure of easy money is one of those temptations that takes us off of the path. Sooner or later, easy money has a price that must be paid. That price many times leads us to poverty, ruin, or even to jail.

Proverbs 7:10

> 10 Then out came a woman to meet him, dressed like a prostitute and with crafty intent.

Notice the strategy of the woman in Proverbs 7:10. It says she is dressed to allure men.

Imagine that you are trying to make your living in the casino at the craps table, the blackjack table, or the roulette wheel. It's seductive! The money is easy if the turn of the wheel or the throw of the dice is with you. However, the casino is not built on winners, so if you're consistently there, you are actually a loser. Outside of the "house" (casino owners), very few people make a consistent living gambling. They prosper off the gambling losses of its customers.

¹³ She took hold of him and kissed him and with a brazen face she said: ¹⁴ "I have fellowship offerings at home; today I fulfilled my vows. ¹⁵ So I came out to meet you; I looked for you and have found you! ¹⁶ I have covered my bed with colored linens from Egypt. ¹⁷ I have perfumed my bed with myrrh, aloes, and cinnamon. ¹⁸ Come, let's drink deep of love till morning; let's enjoy ourselves with love! ¹⁹ My husband is not at home; he has gone on a long journey. ²⁰ He took his purse filled with money and will not be home till full moon." ²¹ With persuasive words she led him astray; she seduced him with her smooth talk. ²² All at once he followed her like an ox going to the slaughter, like a deer stepping into a noose ²³ till an arrow pierces his liver, like a bird darting into a snare, little knowing it will cost him his life.

The example of a casino doesn't belabor the point of sexual immorality. Think of the lights of Las Vegas, Atlantic City, or any city that caters to a casino lifestyle. Notice how brazen and inviting it appears. When you land at the airport in Las Vegas, you can't even get to the main terminal without passing slot machines. So if you have some time with the slots while you are waiting at the airport, you better have some money to kill there too.

The casinos are designed without clocks and, in many cases, windows either. Instead, there is plenty of food and drink to make it easier for you to linger. If you're in a casino hotel, such as those in Las Vegas, you literally don't have to leave the building as long as you are staying there.

Another design element of these mega-hotel casinos is that you can't leave without passing some form of gaming. You stay, you linger, and you continually lose money. This is one of the ways the house gets paid. In fact, they will give you discounts on rooms, beverages, and food as you lose more money. Think about that! The more you lose, the better they will treat you because casinos make the real money at the gaming tables.

Notice what the temptress does in Proverbs 7:13-23. She invites him over to her place. She cunningly and artfully answers every objection. Then, she persuades him with what the Bible calls "smooth talk." She traps him. To combat temptation, he would have to call upon the full use of God's word, wisdom, commonsense, and discernment. You should not be in a place that endangers you, your livelihood, or your way of life. It can damage your reputation or lead you into poverty. The allure of some quick, pleasurable game can shipwreck us if we do not have the moral compass to navigate those waters.

Proverbs 7:25-27

> [25] Do not let your heart turn to her ways or stray into her paths. [26] Many are the victims she has brought down; her slain are a mighty throng. [27] Her house is a highway to the grave, leading down to the chambers of death.

These verses show us how to protect ourselves. Sin doesn't have to be something so extreme as immoral sexual behavior or gambling. Take for example the overuse of credit cards and frequent borrowing for consumer items. Indulging yourself in luxuries that you cannot afford and that lose value can cause you to fall behind on important payments such as rent or mortgage. It can be tempting to own luxury brands such as Rolex, Breitling, and Armani even when you can't really afford them. Likewise, the lure of a questionable but highly profitable business deal can tempt us as well.

You can take definite steps to avoid sexual sin. First, guard your mind. Avoid exposure to books, pictures, or movies that encourage fantasies that stimulate the wrong desires. Secondly, keep away from settings and "friends" that tempt you to sin. Third, don't think only of the moment. Instead, focus on what that moment's transgression means to your future. Remember, today's thrill may lead to tomorrow's ruin.

Action Steps on the Life Path

Write down the tempting things around you that could steal your future if not properly managed.

_____

_____

_____

_____

_____

_____

_____

_____

_____

_____

_____

_____

_____

_____

_____

_____

_____

_____

_____

_____

_____

_____

PROVERBS 8

The Song You Hear Is Wisdom's Melody

"Listen to my instruction and be wise; do not ignore it. Blessed is the man who listens to me, watching daily at my doors, waiting at my doorway."

Proverbs 8:33-34

Proverbs 8 is named "Wisdom's Call." In the initial stages, it appears as if wisdom is a mothering figure — a woman. Notice in Proverbs 8, how wisdom's call is contrasted to the call of an immoral woman in Chapter 7. However, this time, wisdom is portrayed as a woman who guides just as proper mothering helps us succeed.

Wisdom has been present from the biblical sense since the time of Creation and works with the will of the Creator. If you refer to Proverbs 8:22-35, you'll see the Creator is the source of all wise counsel; and if you follow that counsel, you will find favor. Conversely, whoever ignores His counsel courts disaster. Notice also that in Proverbs 8:36, those who hate wisdom love *death* — a word used in these verses to refer to *bad decision making that results in pain.*

You may see this as a particularly onerous end to someone who hates wisdom. However, as you can see from the events that unfold around you with conflict in the world, the financial crisis of 2008 and 2009 and beyond, wisdom is key because wisdom saves, enriches, and even prolongs our life.

Wisdom is not something that is isolated and kept in a classroom somewhere. It is a tool that we need to apply to our everyday life in a meaningful way. For this reason, we should examine all aspects of our life. From a personal, spiritual, and business perspective, make sure you are operating under the guise and application of wisdom at all times.

Proverbs 8:13

> [13] To fear the Lord is to hate evil; I hate pride and arrogance, evil behavior and perverse speech.

I interpret this verse to mean the more a person hears and respects God, the more he or she will hate evil. However, when people are not motivated by the love of God, maybe they are motivated by sin or evil. Perhaps they are harboring secrets — secrets about what they have done wrong. Whether or not we believe in God or sin and evil, we all have some sense of having done something wrong to someone. Think about the pressure internally that starts to build as lie upon lie has to be created to cover the previous lies and how they lead to a double life. Many people among us live with that burden.

If you are living with secrets, you can make a clean break from sin, bad decisions, or a lack of wisdom by conducting your life and committing yourself completely to the truth by confession and forgiveness. You can use wisdom as a guide to conduct your life. When we live by truth in all aspects of our life, it liberates us. It was very liberating for me when I cast off that type of lifestyle.

Proverbs 8:22-31

> [22] "The LORD brought me forth as the first of his works, before his deeds of old; [23] I was appointed from eternity, from the beginning, before the world began. [24] When there were no oceans, I was given birth, when there were no springs abounding with water; [25] before the mountains were settled in place, before the hills, I was given birth, [26] before he made the earth or its fields or any of the dust of the world. [27] I was there when he set the heavens in place, when he marked out the horizon on the face of the deep, [28] when he established the clouds above and fixed securely the fountains of the deep, [29] when he gave the sea its boundary so the waters would not overstep his command, and when he marked out the foundations of

the earth. ³⁰ Then I was the craftsman at his side. I was filled with delight day after day, rejoicing always in his presence, ³¹ rejoicing in his whole world and delighting in mankind.

These verses reinforce that God and wisdom are present, primary, and fundamental to what life is built on — they are the foundation. By utilizing wisdom, you're utilizing a divine gift that brings you through most circumstances somehow some way. That is a gift that we should not take lightly, and we should exercise it often. If you're interested in developing more around this, you can read Colossians 1:15-17, Colossians 2:2-3, and Revelations 3:14. You'll find that these will enhance Proverbs 8:22-31.

Action Steps on the Life Path

Make note of ten things that work well in your life. Be very specific even if it is only a couple of sentences. Writing these down now will allow you to circle back to this later and spend more time with each of the instances.

_____

_____

_____

_____

_____

_____

_____

_____

_____

_____

Make note of five to ten things that are not working well in your life. Again, be very specific.

_____

_____

_____

_____

_____

_____

_____

_____

_____

Take your list of ten things that work well, and prioritize them relative to their importance in your life. All of us have things that work well in our life. Some have more than others. No matter how many we have, we want to make it a practice to come back to the list again and again to thank God for them.

_____

_____

_____

_____

_____

_____

_____

_____

_____

_____

Reflect on why those things have worked well for you. How you have applied wisdom or considered why it's an ethical or moral activity?

_____

_____

_____

_____

_____

_____

_____

_____

_____

_____

_____

Evaluate the lessons learned from those things that have worked well for you. How can you apply them to some of the things that aren't working as well as you would like?

_____

_____

_____

_____

_____

_____

_____

_____

_____

_____

The Song You Hear Is Wisdom's Melody

PROVERBS 9

The Beginning of Wisdom

*"The fear of the Lord is the beginning of wisdom: and
the knowledge of the holy is understanding."*

Proverbs 9:10

T he theme of Proverbs 9 is "Invitations of Wisdom and of Folly." The
difference between wisdom and folly (foolishness) is the difference
between succeeding or failing. My plan for success has God at its
core on purpose. By doing so, the challenges are not diminished but my
capacity to execute and persevere have dramatically increased as should
yours if you apply yourself.

No belief in God or Christianity is necessary to apply these principles to
your life. However, if you read Proverbs diligently, you will see the
invitation for belief is there. But remember, it is a guide for living and as
long as you treat it as such, I believe its teaching will be as effective for you
as it has been for me.

Proverbs 9:1-2

> [1] Wisdom has built her house, she has carved its seven columns; [2] She
> has prepared a great banquet, mixed the wines and set the table;

The message is not about building a house. The seven columns are a figure of speech or figurative that represent the seven principles of wisdom. As with anything in the Bible, there can be more than one point of view. However, in this case, I read these verses in the sense that wisdom is perfect and complete. Wisdom is the perfect guide to our life even though life will not be perfect. However, if you're not utilizing wisdom as a compass and heading in the wrong direction, you're utilizing folly. Folly in this case relates to foolishness, misdeeds, and bad decision making.

The reference to the number seven is significant. In biblical terms, it represents completeness. So the house — in this case wisdom — represents completeness and perfection of approach. It is the perfect advice, and it has a completeness to it.

Proverbs 9:2 refers to the preparation of the foundation for a fine meal. Likewise, wisdom is the foundation of a woman of character. In contrast, folly would be a prostitute serving stolen food. Very interesting! Folly is that which is ill-gotten while wisdom is that which is fulfillment and completeness. Wisdom appeals to the mind, while folly appeals to the sense of desire for immediate gratification and so often leads us down the wrong path.

Thought, work, and sacrifice (if applied correctly) lead to a much better life. Would you rather plow a field or eat stolen food? The stolen food would probably take less work, but there are consequences of stealing the food — the person you stole it from might seek retribution if he catches you. Life works the same way. You can go along cutting corners, cheating, stealing, and lying, but there will eventually be retribution.

In Luke 14:15-24, Jesus describes a banquet in one of the parables where everyone does not make it to the banquet. Those who did not make it unfortunately were the victims of poor decision making. The choice to apply wisdom to one's life may mean the same thing here. Many people may intend to go to the banquet, but they never make it because they get sidetracked by other activities (folly) that seem more important, interesting, or gratifying at the time. However, in the end and sometimes in the short term, they end up paying a heavy price worth more than the instant gratification or immediate pleasure actually experienced. So don't let anything become more important than the search for, the application of, and the use of wisdom in your life.

Proverbs 9:7-10

> [7] Whoever corrects a mocker invites insult; whoever rebukes a wicked man incurs abuse. [8] Do not rebuke a mocker or he will hate you; rebuke a wise man and he will love you. [9] Instruct a wise man and he will be wiser still; teach a righteous man and he will add to his learning. [10] The fear of the Lord is the beginning of wisdom, and knowledge of the Holy One is understanding.

When I first read Proverbs 9:7-10, I was a little bit taken back by its message. These are powerful verses. Listening to intelligent criticism is the path to wisdom. Wisdom begins with knowing God. However, notice these verses have nothing to do with God or salvation directly. They suggest that the application of wisdom and intelligence directs how we conduct our life. So far personal experience has proven them right.

Are you a mocker or a wise person? Wise people accept and reflect upon criticism they receive. A fool's response to criticism might be to reject it with a wisecrack. However, feedback that others provide can help us avoid bumpy roads ahead. You can seek additional information related to this topic by reading James 1:5 and 2 Peter 1:2-4.

Proverbs 9:13-18

> [13] The woman Folly is loud; she is undisciplined and without knowledge. [14] She sits at the door of her house, on a seat at the highest point of the city, [15] calling out to those who pass by, who go straight on their way. [16] "Let all who are simple come in here!" she says to those who lack judgment. [17] "Stolen water is sweet; food eaten in secret is delicious!" [18] But little do they know that the dead are there, that her guests are in the depths of the grave.

These verses are not meant to be derogatory of women. It is written for biblical times and often in this chapter, wisdom is represented by a woman. Many of the verses illustrate the lessons with the various female forms of mothering, nurturing, and wise counsel. This time, the flip side of that coin is "being brash and ignorant" and they refer to a woman named Folly.

Let's not fool ourselves — sin or wickedness can look very appealing. If you lived in a very poor neighborhood where few of the people you see work or get anywhere in life, but you see the drug dealer, pimp, or gangster is living prosperously, you would probably find yourself attracted to the sinful lifestyle. You would be a fool to say you didn't want what you perceive to be the "successful" lifestyle if the only known alternative is poverty. However, most people realize that things such as proper schooling, access to good living conditions, eligibility for quality employment, and the opportunity to own a business will have more positive longevity by far than living fast and dying young.

This brings certain phrases to mind such as "sex, drugs, and rock and roll" or "La Dolce Vita" (Italian for "the good life") or "fast money, fast cars, and faster women!" The lure of the good life without work and hardship is always there. We read about it and it is glorified in the tabloid media but too often, the human toll ends up not being worth the cost — neglected families, destroyed relationships, lost fortunes, squandered opportunities, bad health, and the list goes on.

Action Steps on the Life Path

Spend five minutes writing down situations where, instead of accepting wise advice, you rejected it and paid a price.

_____

_____

_____

_____

_____

_____

_____

_____

_____

_____

_____

_____

The Beginning of Wisdom

PROVERBS *10*

Wise, Wise Solomon

"Lazy hands make a man poor, but diligent hands bring wealth."

Proverbs 10:4

This lesson is part of the Proverbs of Solomon series. This series covers a broad range of topics. The first section is acknowledged to have been written by Solomon. The next couple of sections were written by other authors but were collected by Solomon. They give people the practical wisdom for good and godly living in every area and stage of their life.

The lesson in Chapter 10 focuses heavily upon the relationship between work, diligence, and money even though it touches on other issues. The Bible and particularly the New Testament encourages caring for those who are poor and suffering hard times. However, there is no tolerance for the lazy and indifferent. They are seen as making their own road hard to travel and, as such, you shouldn't waste time with them. Instead, we should focus on the people who are truly needy. The words "lazy" and "indifferent" not only refer to work habits but also to the way someone handles his debt and opportunities in life.

In addition, as with any blessing, the accumulation of wealth comes with the responsibility of being fair and ethical. You should not use your superior financial position to crush someone.

> [2] Ill-gotten treasures are of no value, but righteousness delivers from death.

Some refer to tainted wealth as wealth that has come from unethical, immoral, or illegal means. Criminal, unethical, or immoral activity always returns to haunt you. Those who choose to engage in it will have to ask themselves if it was worth the price in the end. You can see some examples in the great Wall Street stories or scandals where individuals have made millions — in some cases even billions of dollars — utilizing illegal, unethical, and immoral means to achieve that wealth. Then they have to go through the entire process of public humiliation and probably a prison sentence of some type. They're paying a heavy personal, spiritual, and public price for the tainted wealth. They also lose or severely damage their current and future business career. Even though they may have some money left over after they complete their punishment, most will find it wasn't really worth it in the end. Earning your wealth the honest way may result in accumulating a bit less wealth but will lead to much greater happiness.

Godly living brings the right type of long-lasting happiness. Using sound principles will guide you along the road of the correct behavior — the road that feeds back into longer-lasting happiness. It also allows us to develop our spiritual core to bounce back from the roadblocks that tempt us to take the easy way to tainted wealth.

For example, a public official who is paying extortion money to keep some unethical or immoral behavior quiet is compromised and cannot effectively represent the people who elected him. In 2009, an affair was exposed between Senator John Ensign and a married staffer. Even though they had promised to end the affair, it still continued for some time. When the woman's husband found out, Senator Ensign had to find him a new job to keep him quiet. He also gave the woman's son a job. In addition, he had his parents give her a "gift" of $96,000.

Forget about the illegality and the lack of ethics for a moment — how can someone who is spending his time juggling this type of drama do his job and represent the people of his state effectively? What was most ironic was that a major part of his public persona was being godly and standing for family values. He was often in the forefront vilifying other public officials when they were caught in embarrassing sex-related situations. He subsequently found himself exposed for his own untoward actions.

Proverbs 10:3

> [3] The Lord does not let the righteous go hungry but he thwarts the craving of the wicked.

Proverbs is filled with verses that contrast godly living with a life of wickedness. However, these statements aren't really intended to universally reflect what happens to everyone in every situation. We can look around us and see some good people who are going hungry and experiencing bad things. Likewise, we see good things happen to bad people. However, these scriptures are really intended to communicate a broader, more general truth: the life of a person who seeks God is better in the long run than the life of a wicked person that leads to ruin. Seeking the godly path to wisdom makes perfectly logical sense.

Proverbs is not a formula — it is not one plus one will definitely equal two. You're better off to think of it as one plus one will generally equal two. Remember there are no guarantees or magic formulas in life.

A verse like this assumes that all things are relatively equal in the environment you live — the government, the economy, the people in your community, etc. — and, in general, they are mostly just and operating in a proper manner. When life is thrown out of balance particularly on a larger scale, Proverbs gives you the framework to negotiate the troubled waters. For a biblical reference on this line of thought, see Deuteronomy 24:17-22 where it addresses this issue of a corrupt or negative environment thwarting the plans of people who are trying to live a good and godly life.

Proverbs often describes how God takes care of those who have faith and follow Him. However, being "godly" does not mean that we are like God because we're not perfect. We need Proverbs as well as other biblical principles and faith to guide us. We need help both acknowledging that and utilizing these types of tools to make our life better. As Christians, we have been given the power of the Holy Spirit to help us live a godly life. Therefore, godly people are simply people who love God.

Proverbs 10:4-5

> [4] Lazy hands make a man poor, but diligent hands bring wealth.
> [5] He who gathers crops in summer is a wise son, but he who sleeps during harvest is a disgraceful son.

These scriptures direct us to utilize our efforts to shine as best we can. We have 365 days a year with twenty-four hours full of opportunity to expand ourselves and help those around us. Of course, it's easy to waste time. When you waste time, you're not necessarily doing anything wrong. However, you're letting opportunity — financially, spiritually, and personally — slip through your hands and once time is gone, it can't be recovered. You have to utilize the time you have left.

Analyze the way you spend your time. Recognize behavior and activities where you're not being a good steward of the time God has given you. For instance, oversleeping can waste hours that could be used for productive work. Time is a gift from our Creator that allows us to expand our potential, grow our knowledge, and prosper.

I saw a television show about new entrepreneurs and the newly rich who created business opportunities that had taken them to another level financially. One guy was in the investment banking business and worked on Wall Street in New York City. He lived in an exclusive suburban neighborhood outside of the New York City area that was at least an hour (more if traffic was heavy) from his Wall Street office. They showed him starting his day one morning, getting ready to leave home, grabbing his coffee, and heading out to the car service waiting for him at 6:00 a.m. for the drive to work which turned out to be a twelve-hour day. The commentator said, "Masters of the universe don't sleep in!" That phrase really stuck with me, and it certainly exemplifies Proverbs 10:4-5. If you want to lead a successful life, use the time you have to be the most productive you can be.

Proverbs 10:18-19

> [18] He who conceals his hatred has lying lips, and whoever spreads slander is a fool. [19] When words are many, sin is not absent, but he who holds his tongue is wise.

It's clear from Proverbs 10:18 that harboring hatred toward another person makes someone a liar or fool. When we try to conceal our hatred, often we

Wise, Wise Solomon

end up lying. However, we are always more transparent that we realize. The second part of verse is more straightforward. If we slander other people and end up being proven wrong or being called out on it, then we look like a fool.

Proverbs 10:18 doesn't suggest that we just walk around saying what we might believe to be the truth and letting others know they are wrong or why we don't like them. Instead, it gives us a good opportunity to tap into our spiritual life and admit to God through prayer when we have feelings of hatred that we are lying about and concealing.

Proverbs 10:19 suggests that we should mind our words even when we dislike someone or think he is wrong. It reminds us that we shouldn't be rude and disrespectful. Negativity leads us to a path of ruin because it is immoral, unethical, and, in some cases, illegal. It will suck away the positive things and the godly living that we are working toward.

In contrast, we should learn to handle the negative feelings such as grudges or resentment. Seeking God's wise counsel offers us a method of resolving them by asking God to turn the hatred into love for our fellow man. That will get us much farther than letting the hate fester and grow.

Proverbs 10:20-22

> [20] The tongue of the righteous is choice silver, but the heart of the wicked is of little value. [21] The lips of the righteous nourish many, but fools die for lack of judgment. [22] The blessing of the Lord brings wealth, and he adds no trouble to it.

These verses provide good examples of the proper behavior we should have toward ourselves and toward those around us. Words from a good person are valuable like sterling silver. In contrast, poor advice is worth a lot less than good advice. It is easy to get opinions from people. Sometimes they are telling us what we want to hear, and other times, they are just giving an uninformed or uneducated opinion. Such advice is not helpful. We need to look to people who will speak the truth even though sometimes that truth may hurt.

When I have friends and associates who are having serious, deep-seated, fractious relationship problems, I advise them to get professional counseling. They need professionals who are educated in the methods of helping couples resolve the issues. When I have had relationship issues, I've found counseling was helpful. It gets the two people to the point where they understand each other's point of view, and it provides tools to help them work through their relationship issues. It's a more logical approach than fighting, badgering, or beating on one another with no end or hope in sight.

In Proverbs 10:22, we are reminded that God supplies most of us with the resources and abilities to respond to the needs of others — both personally and financially. Therefore, wealth is a blessing only if we use it in the way that God intended — in a wise, moral way that shows integrity.

Remember Proverbs is not a formula you pull out when you have a challenge or issue in your life and you chant it to make everything all right. We all know people who seemingly are doing all the right things but either can't seem to get ahead or seem to be followed by a hard-luck cloud. Instead, it provides guidance for navigating those tough times so we can learn and grow in the process. Rewards delayed are not rewards denied.

Continue to read one chapter a day. Use the text as a guideline while doing the exercises to transform and stay focused on what is important in your life. For example, I regularly shop at Whole Foods Market (a natural and organic grocery chain) or a similar type of market. Even though there are other non-natural or non-organic-supplied supermarkets nearby, I prefer to shop there. Why? All of the produce and food looks and smells fresh. Their staff members are friendly and can knowledgeably answer questions. There is very little waiting in the checkout line. The prices are reasonable but certainly not the least expensive. I'm willing to pay more for the extra mile of superior service and product. The founder no doubt did his homework before opening his first store, evolved by listening to client feedback, got rid of what didn't work, and continued to innovate. We should all manage ourselves in this manner.

Actions Steps on The Life Path

Keeping in mind the lesson of Proverbs 10:4: "Lazy hands make a man poor, but diligent hands bring wealth." Going the extra mile and overdelivering is the new attitude. How many truly successful people do you know who do more than they are asked to do and, in many cases, do it with a good attitude?

List one to three areas of your life where you feel you are going the extra mile. What are some ways you are doing it?

_____

_____

_____

_____

_____

_____

What is another area of your life where you can go the extra mile? What will it help you achieve?

_____

_____

_____

_____

_____

Wise, Wise Solomon

PROVERBS *11*

Integrity and Righteousness

> *"The integrity of the upright guides them, but the*
> *unfaithful are destroyed by their duplicity."*
>
> *Proverbs 11:3*

A t this point in our lessons, it will be no surprise to hear that God wants us all to be honest in our business activities. Those who are not honest are thieves, pure and simple. It isn't solely stealing that translates into dishonest behavior. Hoarding, selfishness, and ignoring the plight of others are all examples of dishonesty or thievery.

By having integrity and being upstanding and righteous, everyone around you benefits. Your honesty and intelligence will permeate out to your family, friends, and community, but you will benefit most of all. As you read further, you will see that living with integrity is not difficult most of the time, and if done regularly, it becomes a habit.

Proverb 11:4

> [4] Wealth is worthless in the day of wrath, but righteousness delivers from death.

On the surface, this verse speaks to salvation and right living according to biblical principle. However, if you look back at Proverbs 10:2, you will see the principles are still the same. Right living actually saves your life because the principles will steer you on the path guided by wisdom. From a Christian perspective, no amount of money, riches, or wealth gained takes the place of being on the path that God has provided.

Our faith shows us over and over that taking advantage of spiritual grounding is best. However, looking at it from a practical standpoint, wisdom guides our steps for right living. Accumulating wealth and creating riches for ourselves and our families in an ethical way is the best path. When earned this way, there is no price to pay on the back end. Taking a route that is criminal or immoral to make ill-gotten gains will result in some price to pay later. For more biblical exploration on this particular topic, you can review Proverbs 10:2 and also explore Ezekiel 7:19.

Proverb 11:5

> [5] The righteousness of the blameless makes a straight way for them, but the wicked are brought down by their own wickedness.

The truly godly are directed by honesty. However, the wise, intelligent, ethical, and moral are directed by wisdom. It prevents us from laboring under that load of sin or having to pay the price that many pay particularly when they pursue wealth by any means necessary whether ethical and moral or not.

Proverbs 11:7-8

> [7] When a wicked man dies, his hope perishes; all he expected from his power comes to nothing. [8] The righteous man is rescued from trouble, and it comes on the wicked instead.

Proverbs provides universal principles that help us govern our life. However, just being a person of faith doesn't exclude us from trouble. In some cases, it may seem that we get more trouble because we are a person of faith. Even when we follow the right and wise path as we execute our life, we can still run into problems and challenges. However, there always seems to be an exit path where we can avoid trouble, be rescued, or pay a lesser price than those who enthusiastically pursue a negative road in life. The overriding message is that we will not always be able to overcome and avoid challenges, but we will have a compass to guide our life with the principles that make the most sense.

As a Christian, you'll find comfort in knowing that there is salvation at the end of your ordeals. Additionally, the sanity of doing the right thing in a difficult situation somehow always makes life a little better than not doing it. As Proverbs seems to routinely say, the wicked person will fall into his own trap because he makes it and pursues it.

Sooner or later, there is a price to be paid for unethical behavior. The easiest examples were seen in the press during the economic crisis of 2008 and 2009. Many people are paying the price for having pursued the wrong course of action. Some were smaller investors who pursued a strategy of trying to get something for nothing with financial schemes in real estate, the stock market, or some other get-rich-quick venture.

For some reason, they decided not to take a prudent approach. They chose to buy more house than they could afford, gambled, or speculated instead of taking a more measured, intelligent, and well-advised approach to their investment strategies. It is easy to contrast the careless person with the prudent person. The same negative behavior is at work with someone who is embezzling or speculating unwisely with billions of dollars. There is a price to be paid for dangerous behavior no matter what the economic level.

You might ask yourself, "Is it worth it?" I think the people who now face prison time for embezzling millions or billions of dollars or people who have been forced out of their homes they couldn't afford would say no. It doesn't matter what the intentions were — good or bad. A prudent decision is always the right one in the end.

Proverbs 11:9

> [9] With his mouth the godless destroys his neighbor, but through knowledge the righteous escape.

Our words create a trap that many of us fall into from time to time. The ability to communicate can be either a tool to build or a weapon to destroy. If you're damaging and hurting relationships with your words, you're using communication as a weapon of destruction. It is often easier to break something down than it is to build it. Building up may take more time but will also last longer.

Most of us receive much more negative commentary and feedback than we do the positive version. Even though it may be initially easier in the long run, the destruction caused by negativity produces the heavier price to pay. It is always preferable to take a pathway of being more positive when giving feedback and communicating. Even though you may have to be uncomfortably direct and say things that the other person may not want to hear, you don't have to say it in a damaging fashion.

I've been a Toastmasters member for many years. One of the primary lessons that we learn in Toastmasters on the communication educational track is how to listen. Most of us think that Toastmasters is about public speaking. Sure, that's part of it, but Toastmasters focuses on all aspects of communication as well as leadership. An important part of communication between two people or even within a larger group is listening — giving and receiving feedback about what is said.

Communication is a two-way street. Constructive criticism is the best way to provide feedback. Trying to zing someone with a negative comment is almost always unproductive. Unfortunately, most people have no other framework around which to provide positive feedback because they only received negative feedback when they were growing up. People learn by what they see and experience. Remember that building someone up and giving her proper feedback is better than continually trying to tear her down. When someone tears another person down, he ultimately ends up tearing himself down.

Proverbs 11:14

> [14] For lack of guidance a nation falls, but many advisers make victory sure.

A good leader needs wise advisors. He cannot have a group of "yes" men around him who continually tell him what he wants to hear. Eventually, there is a price to be paid for poor counsel. One person's perspective on a situation is normally very limited. No one person can have all of the facts based on just his individual efforts and experiences. Besides that, we all have biases, and humans often operate based on emotion. Put all of that together, and it leads to bad decision making.

Whether you are in a leadership position of a country such as the United States or a leader of a local organization, you have to operate in a certain

Integrity and Righteousness

way. A leader needs to seek wise counsel whether he's the president, a member of Congress, or in the judicial branch. Seeking the wisdom of others ensures that we make better decisions. We have to do the same thing even when we're not leading in a government or company role. It helps to seek advice from trusted and wise individuals in matters of conducting our everyday life with our family, church, and career. Sometimes the wise counsel is not a family member or friend. It may be someone who has a much more objective view of what you are doing because they are not emotionally involved with you.

Proverbs 11:19

> [19] The truly righteous man attains life, but he who pursues evil goes to his death.

The direction here is to live your life as fully as you can each day given the circumstances that you're in. You only get one life. Let's take the matter of health. The proper diet, appropriate exercise, and correct amount of rest cannot be replaced by any type of drug or surgical procedure. You have to maintain a balanced, healthy, physically active life. Without your health, it is difficult to experience a high quality of life. You may want to say it's godly to take a healthy approach to your life, but it's also just plain commonsense.

Moderating your diet doesn't mean that you cannot enjoy a cookie or a glass of wine or other non-destructive indulgence. However, you should not take any type of illegal drug, and you should be very careful of abusing prescription drugs.

Proverbs 11:22

> [22] Like a gold ring in a pig's snout is a beautiful woman who shows no discretion.

It says "a beautiful woman" here but the lesson applies to a man or a woman. Just being physically attractive is not the point of good health. Being physically attractive may mean that people will have a certain positive interaction with someone initially — at least until they get to know him better. However, not everyone who is attractive is pleasant, easy to work with, or any fun to be around.

Take good care of yourself and your body and pay attention to your appearance; however, remember it's what's on the inside that determines how people feel about us. Make wise decisions that are morally and ethically guided first and foremost. If you have been blessed with physical attractiveness or take great care of yourself, that will only serve to your advantage. However, beauty is no substitute for wise decision making.

Proverbs 11:24-25

> [24] One man gives freely, yet gains even more; another withholds unduly, but comes to poverty. [25] A generous man will prosper; he who refreshes others will himself be refreshed.

For clarity, I will cross-reference this with two other Bible verses. One is Matthew 5:7: "Blessed are the merciful, for they will be shown mercy." The other is 2 Corinthians 9:6-7: "Remember this: Whoever sows sparingly will also reap sparingly, and whoever sows generously will also reap generously. Each man should give what he has decided in his heart to give, not reluctantly or under compulsion, for God loves a cheerful giver."

At first reading, Proverbs 11:24-25 seems counterintuitive and does not make sense: "Give freely and become wealthy, be stingy and lose everything." However, it does make sense when you truly live the way it directs. The world we live in says you need to hold on to as much as you possibly can. Coming from a faith perspective, however, we believe God blesses those who give freely of their time, energy, and what they possess without unduly depriving their family. When we do, God supplies us with more so we can give more, do more, and ultimately be more.

More doesn't necessarily mean that you will make more money. Remember, we're talking a balanced life across all of the various spheres — personal, family, community, spiritual, career, and financial. You'll be able to give more of whatever it makes sense for you to give.

Giving provides perspective. If you are only hoarding, your perspective is only you. The world is a much better place when we sincerely reach out and give of ourselves and our possessions to others. Become part of the larger community by being involved and giving in your community.

When I was growing up, I had neighbors who took care of me. If my mother was at work and I needed a meal, I would go see Miss Ella, the nice, little

Integrity and Righteousness

lady up the street. If I needed something else or if I got into some kind of trouble, the neighbors looked out for me. This is a form of giving. Depending upon where we grew up, we all probably have stories of a man or a woman who was always helping others. Think about how well-respected that person was. They may not have had much in terms of wealth to give; but they were able to give of their time and their energy. We remember these people in a favorable light, don't we?

Now, contrast that with people who we remember as mean and tightfisted. Which way would you like to be remembered? Which way would you like to spend your time and your energy? From a personal point of view, becoming more involved in my church and volunteering my time in charitable causes has enabled me to develop deep personal friendships with people that I normally may not have otherwise known.

The quality of those relationships is much more meaningful than the relationship with someone you may meet hanging around in a bar where everyone eventually has too much to drink. You can develop a friend here or there in that way, but think about the friendships that you develop when you work together to do something good for yourself, for them, and for the others around you. There's no substitute for that.

Proverbs 11:29-31

> [29] He who brings trouble on his family will inherit only wind, and the fool will be servant to the wise. [30] The fruit of the righteous is a tree of life, and he who wins souls is wise. [31] If the righteous receive their due on earth, how much more the ungodly and the sinner!

A family is a phenomenal resource if that family is encouraging and accepting and provides guidance to the family members. Family members who bring trouble to the family can destroy its foundation. Family size doesn't matter, but everyone needs to do their part to make their family a better family.

As you notice, people who have families that are not encouraging, accepting, and guiding tend to derail. These individuals will have to find the necessary stability somewhere else. It's possible to do that, but it's a lot to ask — particularly of a youngster growing up. We owe it to young people to provide a giving, accepting environment with a positive stimulus. Whether that's at church, at after-school programs, or with friends and relatives, they need an environment where there is positive reinforcement for good behavior as well as positive reinforcement when they make a mistake to guide them to correct the mistake.

Remember that a family should provide healing, understanding, acceptance, encouragement, and guidance. However, each family member needs to do their part to provide those things. Come to the table looking to make your family a better place to live.

Proverbs 11:30

[30] The fruit of the righteous is a tree of life, and he who wins souls is wise.

A wise person is someone who leads an intelligent and meaningful life. Whether you're going through misfortune or if everything is running smoothly at any given point, remember, nothing runs smoothly all of the time. Hopefully, you don't continually have distress and difficulty. However, it all leads back to making wise decisions and utilizing judicious guidelines.

You'll find a wise person is a more attractive person. I'm not talking about physical attractiveness. A wise person is not only prone to astute decisions; they tend to also be giving people who will sacrifice a bit of themselves for the greater good and to help other like-minded people. People tend to be attracted to those types of individuals.

Perhaps someone is helping others but is not on that path yet himself. Possibly the help he gives and his interaction with the needy will inspire him to take a more giving and generous path. This not only makes a wise person attractive, it also defines good leadership. Remember, you can lead in many different ways, but, sensible leadership generates the best environment for all involved.

As a Christian, take it as your calling to lead as consequential a life as possible because it will demonstrate that you're "walking the talk." You have a chance to live as an example, and you'll benefit by that life across all the different spheres: personal, spiritual, financial, etc. Living a godly life is not something sacrificial. Once you start down the path, it's not a sacrifice to be healthy and to make wise decisions. Ultimately, it's not a sacrifice to make prudent business decisions. It is actually a better way of living than

Integrity and Righteousness

continually looking to cut corners and to do the wrong thing for a quick gain. It is godly to model a life based on wise choices, moderation, prudent decision making.

Proverbs 11:31

> [31] If the righteous receive their due on earth, how much more the ungodly and the sinner!

Contrary to popular belief, no one commits a crime and ultimately gets away with it. There's always a price to be paid for doing the wrong thing — particularly on a consistent basis — and that price can sometimes be very high. It could end up meaning death, prison time, poverty, losing everything, wrecking your health, or all of these. Think about the price to be paid for bad decision making, not utilizing wisdom, and not taking a path that is ethical and moral.

Think about the areas of your life we touched on in Proverbs 11. Make some notes on them, set some goals, and make an action plan. Move ahead with it, and take action. Quite honestly, just because no one witnessed another person doing the wrong thing doesn't mean that the individual didn't get caught. Everyone makes a mistake from time to time. But remember ultimately, when someone continues to do the wrong thing, there is a price to be paid — the price is sometimes very heavy. However, truth, moderation, wise decision making, ethical behavior, and morals will always reap benefits and blessings.

Action Steps on the Life Path

Take two minutes and list up to four people who you would like to improve communication with and why.

_____

_____

_____

_____

_____

_____

_____

Spend two minutes jotting down the names of people you respect whose advice may have proven to be valuable in the past. Don't automatically default to family members and friends. Instead, consider an acquaintance or maybe even someone you don't know personally but have read their wise advice in a book. Don't assume that you have to hang around with someone who has good advice.

_____

_____

_____

_____

_____

_____

_____

_____

_____

Write down some areas where you would like to improve your interaction with the world around you. Specifically, maybe you want to spend more time at your place of worship. Maybe you want to spend more time serving the poor by associating yourself with a charitable organization, making a financial donation, volunteering in a soup kitchen, babysitting, or delivering meals. Highlight areas that resonate strongly with your interests and values. For example, if doing more volunteer work is one of your goals, contact some charitable organizations that cover areas you are passionate about. You can begin to put your toe in the water by serving in some particular way. By serving others, you also serve yourself because you are making the world you live in a better place.

_____

_____

_____

_____

_____

_____

_____

Write down things you would like to see improve in your family or close relationships. Make some notes about what you're going to do to help make it so.

_____

_____

_____

_____

_____

_____

_____

Integrity and Righteousness

PROVERBS *12*

The Partnership of Discipline and Knowledge

"Whoever loves discipline loves knowledge,
but he who hates correction is stupid."

This chapter's lesson centers on Proverbs 12 of King Solomon's Proverbs. Before discussing this chapter's scriptural lesson, let's take another look at the title. Even though the main theme of Proverbs is the application of wisdom — particularly in Solomon's case — you can't apply wisdom without knowledge, and you can't acquire knowledge without discipline.

Although only the first verse mentions discipline, you will notice that almost all of the negative examples in the chapter demonstrate a lack of discipline as well as a lack of wisdom. All of us are taught some form of discipline in life even if it is in a negative manner such as serving prison time.

However, to get the most out of the partnership with knowledge, you must manage your life as if it were a business and hold fast to your priorities, goals, rules, and guidelines. Discipline will encourage you to expand your knowledge and to carry on in a way that will enable you to stay ahead of the game. Discipline challenges you to commit to yourself and to remain committed in times of adversity.

Proverbs 12:1

> [1] Whoever loves discipline loves knowledge, but he who hates correction is stupid.

Going to school and receiving a formal academic or vocational education is critical to success in today's life. If you don't get a formal education, you have to acquire proper training for your chosen field somewhere else. However, like anything else, if you're not willing to learn, you can attend school, listen to lectures, and be tutored for years and yet learn nothing. You can accomplish the goal of not learning, or you can take advantage of the ease of access to knowledge that is available to many of us. If you want to learn new things, there's absolutely no end to what you can study.

The formal setting is a classroom, school, or library. However, many of the best sources are those people who have lived a long time and have experienced and overcome challenges that we have never seen — especially if we are younger than they are. Think of the knowledge that successful people have who are in their thirties, forties, fifties, sixties, and beyond. Imagine the treasure trove of information that they have. In order to take advantage of their knowledge base, we have to be willing to learn. We must rid ourselves of the "I know everything" mind-set. We must avoid the resistance to the discipline of learning and embrace the willingness to accept correction.

In the previous lesson, we learned that sometimes we have to humble ourselves to understand that we don't know everything. We have to be willing to accept correction so that we will get to the end goal of learning what we are seeking to know.

Proverbs 12:3

> [3] A man cannot be established through wickedness, but the righteous cannot be uprooted.

Deep stable roots lead to and reinforce success and stability. Realistically, stability and success come to those who do the right thing, and wisdom helps you utilize those lessons to do the right thing. Sometimes good people make a couple of bad turns in their life, and they have to overcome those struggles. It can be puzzling when bad people seem to be getting ahead.

Particularly if you are operating with a faith-based approach, it makes you scratch your head and wonder, "Well, what am I doing wrong if I'm doing the right thing and it doesn't appear to be working?" You can't dwell on that. If you really look at success of the wicked people who operate in an unethical or immoral fashion, is it really success? When you dig deeper into their success, is everything that has transpired there something to be proud of? Just because we didn't see them pay for their dishonesty, it doesn't mean they won't.

For example, consider a person who continually cheats to get larger and more aggressive tax refunds. That is something that we all have probably been tempted to do. The cheater may become more confident each time and go down that road more aggressively. Sooner or later, the cheater's number will come up, and there will be an audit. Of course, it will then start to unravel in a major way with considerable penalties, stress, and worry. The lack of stability and discipline will lead the cheater to lose any success he gained through dishonesty.

I am not talking about people who have made honest mistakes on their taxes. Clearly, we all make mistakes. When we pay for those mistakes and do the right thing to correct them, we don't have to pay the ultimate penalty. However, someone who is deliberately heading in the wrong direction because it is the "easy way" starts to pay a price whether it's small prices along the way or large, significant prices at some point.

Let's think about it another way. If someone continually ignores family obligations and mistreats those around him but somehow manages to plow ahead and become financially successful, is he really successful? What does it say about his character? What does it say about the people who surround him? What does it say about his own happiness? Can he truly be happy knowing that everyone around him, despite his financial success, has been abused and is only there because they can get something from him or they are paid to be there? He may be wealthy, but isn't that a very lonely, unsatisfying existence? When our behavior is not corrected in some meaningful way, we can head down the wrong path searching for some form of happiness. The good news is we have discipline and knowledge, but we have to apply it with wisdom across all areas of our life.

In essence, continued bad behavior leads to worse behavior, but the reverse also happens with good behavior. Good behavior and wise decisions compound. So, if you are regularly doing the right thing (or at least attempting it), will there be some setbacks? Of course. However, if someone deliberately and continually does the wrong thing, compounding it with larger and larger transgressions along the way, it will result in paying a very steep price at some point. The world is a very interesting place, and the dynamic among people is also very interesting. You cannot do evil and only receive good; but you can do good and receive mostly good.

Proverbs 12:13

> [13] An evil man is trapped by his sinful talk, but a righteous man escapes trouble.

This verse is a continuation of Proverbs 12:3. It means that real success includes practiced personal integrity. You must maintain your personal integrity to have balance and personal success. This verse addresses people who are willing to twist the facts in any contortion possible to support whatever claim or point they are trying to make. They will eventually be trapped by their own lies regardless of what they are trying to accomplish with unethical behavior.

I once had a habit of lying about certain situations. Because of that habit, I ended up paying a huge price with the deterioration or evaporation of some friendships. All in all, some were good, decent people, and they had their faults just like I had mine. However, the lies I told were the ones that destroyed the relationships. I didn't tell the lies to deliberately hurt anyone. Instead, I used them to allow me to continue behaviors in other areas without anyone knowing about it. No matter how good my intentions were, they were still lies. In looking back, it wasn't worth the price.

Telling the truth is a very interesting thing — especially in personal instances. In business, it is too easy to fall into the trap of lying because it seems like everyone else is probably doing it too. It is particularly difficult to avoid if you make a mistake in a toxic work environment. In the past, I have sometimes felt compelled to lie just to protect myself. It was a struggle to get to the point where I just won't do it anymore.

The Partnership of Discipline and Knowledge

Too many are looking for someone to blame, take the heat, or roast for having made a mistake. Clearly those who look to do the finger-pointing forget that if they are pointing the finger at someone else, there are three fingers pointing back at them. This type of condition almost invites you to lie. But beware. It can trap you because the liar has to continue to build upon those lies and continue to cover up. It eventually unravels. It's just not worth it. I have found that if you just stand tall and tell the truth, things will work out in the end.

If I was in a life-or-death situation and telling a lie would get me out of it, I would face the not-so-difficult decision of lying to save my life. However, the vast majority of the lies that we tell are not life-or-death situations. No one is suggesting that you sacrifice your life for something routine in terms of lying. You should save your life, particularly, if you're in a situation where unethical, immoral people involved in all kinds of evil, wicked behavior are trying to harm you. But in the normal course of our personal, spiritual, and business life, we don't need to lie. We sometimes lie to avoid hurting someone's feelings; but we should not use that as an excuse to blatantly lie. I have been associated with people who do that and it is unpleasant at best.

When we find ourselves telling lies, we'll never be in a position to confront someone else who is lying. Liars are not interested in exploring things too deeply. However, when someone makes a conscious decision to stop the lying, they more naturally act in an ethical manner with integrity and character. In fact, you'll find that you can't tolerate liars any longer. No matter how close they are to you, they will have to stop lying, or you will feel compelled to spend much less time with them.

You'll find the plain honest facts are the best defense when accused of something. It is very hard for someone who is continually lying to keep the facts straight — especially in a complex situation. There's no better defense than to tell the truth as you know it and be very straightforward about the information you are rendering. Other people can twist it and turn it around, but if you maintain your stance of integrity by telling the truth, things will likely work out in your favor. I've personally implemented this in the workplace. At times, it can be very uncomfortable but not as bad as being held hostage by a lie or being exposed as a liar.

¹⁶ A fool shows his annoyance at once, but a prudent man overlooks an insult.

If someone insults or harasses you in some way, of course it's natural to want to retaliate. Walking around retaliating against insults — real or imagined — is a draining process. At times, it might make a lot of sense to let something irritating pass. Think about some routine scenarios that you probably have experienced. It may be as trivial as someone staring at someone else. It's possible they may not even be staring. They may be daydreaming. But without considering all the possible reasons, the person being stared at flips out and says, "Ohhh, are you looking at me? Who are you?" As a commuter who takes the train in a big city daily, I see people fighting over seats, inadvertent nudges, or a host of inconsequential issues. Someone may bump into another passenger by accident and all of the sudden, it is World War III.

One morning, I was walking to the train on the way to work. One of my employees called my cell phone regarding an important deal we were involved in. All of a sudden, something hits my heel and I whirl around to find myself confronted by a woman with two young children on either side of her and one in a stroller. She's yelling, "I have a stroller! You're on your phone talking! I yelled, 'Stroller!'" I will not lie; my first reaction was to give her a piece of my mind. She was trying to pass me on the side of the walk with almost no room when she could have easily gone around me on the other side with room to spare. Then I looked at a maintenance worker who was off to the side, and he made a facial expression to let it pass and not say anything. He brought me back to Earth, and I kept going on my way leaving her to yell at her kids. Looking back on the event, she was obviously late to get the kids to school or the sitter and on to whatever her schedule held that day.

Arguing with a stressed-out mother and her three children on the sidewalk during rush hour would have been a bad way to expend energy I needed for a long, hard day at the office and in front of clients. The next time you run into one of these irritating, stress-inducing, but ultimately unimportant confrontations, take a deep breath, and ask yourself, "Is that a really good use of my energy?"

Think about other occurrences where you read about people who were shot

The Partnership of Discipline and Knowledge

because they "dissed" somebody? It isn't worth a lifetime in prison because someone thought somebody insulted them or even for something equally as trivial. If I'm in a life-or-death situation, that's a different story and not routine by any measure. The routine slights and annoyances that are going on in life are not worth a brawl, fight, or shooting.

Let's think about people who are quick tempered in the workplace. We work with them forty or more hours each week. We report to some of them and supervise others. Any conversation beyond hello and three minutes of chatting causes their voice and their blood pressure to rise. Those are symptoms of someone who has other issues. Many times, these dysfunctional people are taking steps to agitate the people around them.

When I'm insulted, annoyed, or harassed at work, I've learned to stop and take the time to decide *how* or even *if* I'm going to respond. I try to remember that I'm being paid to interact with people at the office in a positive manner. I'm not there because these coworkers are my friends, I grew up with them, or they're family. Instead, I'm getting paid to do a job and work with them to accomplish the goals of the company. Therefore, I would rather not spend my day worrying about who is insulting me and if I should take further action. That's what we have human resources professionals for. We have other avenues to handle it that are perfectly legitimate and ethical. Sometimes a workplace is so toxic that none of that makes any sense or anyone can remedy it. At that point, you have to take some further action which, in select cases, may involve getting legal help or resigning.

Proverbs 12:19-21

> [19] Truthful lips endure forever, but a lying tongue lasts only a moment. [20] There is deceit in the hearts of those who plot evil, but joy for those who promote peace. [21] No harm befalls the righteous, but the wicked have their fill of trouble.

Proverbs 12:21 is a very general statement and it can be considered a broad truth but not a universal one. However, I remember an author named W. Clement Stone who was often quoted saying there is a greater benefit in all trouble that might befall you. All godly or faith-based people — people who are just plain and simple doing the right thing — who have trouble can be harmed. However, they're able to see opportunities in their problems, move past their troubles, and take advantage of those opportunities. The people who are broke, busted, disgusted, twisted, and bitter stay there in that ugly place and don't move ahead. They hold that grudge. The evil in their hearts eats away at them and doesn't do them any good. If you work with people like that, you need to develop the capability to get past your anger as quickly as possible so you can move forward.

Do you remember that we spoke about gaining knowledge and being disciplined? Only fools just continuously boast about themselves and brag about how much they know. There is nothing wrong with quiet confidence. It's okay to keep your opinions to yourself. It's also okay to offer an opinion if someone asks you for it. However, you don't have to do a filibuster. Keep it simple, answer the question, interact with other intelligent, knowledgeable people, and exchange information. Just don't be a braggart.

Make proper use of your possessions whether they are mental or physical. "Waste not, want not" takes on a new meaning when you're on the ethical, moral, and wise path. Make sure that you are appropriately utilizing and managing whatever talents and possessions you have. Remember, everything you have at your disposal is a blessing. Make the best possible use of it, because that is the way it will most likely be the most beneficial to you.

The Partnership of Discipline and Knowledge

Action Steps on the Life Path

Take five minutes and think back to the people you previously listed whom you consider to give valuable advice. Add to that list one or two people who could be beneficial in helping you accomplish your goals and objectives in your personal, spiritual, or business life.

_____

_____

_____

_____

_____

_____

_____

_____

Are there areas of your life where you are telling lies? If so, decide when you are going to begin telling the truth in those areas. How will you be rewarded for taking that step?

_____

_____

_____

_____

_____

_____

_____

_____

_____

The Partnership of Discipline and Knowledge

Further Thoughts on the Partnership of Discipline and Knowledge

"He who ignores discipline comes to poverty and shame, but whoever heeds correction is honored."

Proverbs 13:18

This chapter also deals heavily in promoting self-discipline. Many of the examples touch on handling money or wealth, but the lessons discuss all areas of our life. Think for minute about the time period in which these teachings were written. There was no social safety net and technology didn't exist to make everyone's life better.

Take for example an advancement like air conditioning. It's a modern convenience we've come to expect in our homes and buildings. It benefits everyone who comes in contact with it not just the person who owns the air-conditioned building. It's a standard in our society today but in biblical times, their life was simple, and even primitive technology in terms of personal comfort was only afforded to the wealthy. For those who were not disciplined with their earnings and wealth, they could literally endanger their survival. In those times, people could literally starve or die. If you were homeless, it meant you slept outside because there was no public shelter to go to. Those were such different times compared to today when some people consider poverty to be the inability to upgrade their car or home. You would be better off looking to some of the third-world areas such as Darfur to understand what it means not to have access to any resource.

Proverbs 13:3

> [3] He who guards his lips guards his life, but he who speaks rashly will come to ruin.

How many times have we had events going our way, and then we decided to add that little extra blab here or there — adding something on or talking too long (in sales, we call it "talking past the close") — and unraveled a lot of good work. It causes what we're trying to accomplish to come apart. Even though this is a short verse, it says something incredibly insightful about self-control. When people have not learned to control themselves, they're most likely not controlling what they say either.

Clearly words can do much harm when used inappropriately. Self-control starts with our mouth! Stop and think before you react or speak. When you can control this small bit of yourself, it will become a powerful tool as you move forward in utilizing and applying wisdom to all aspects of your life. A great deal of our life is spent interacting with others; therefore, inappropriate use of language, out-of-place conversations, and excessive gossip all demonstrate a lack of self-control and are issues you can control even if you can't control the environment. Participating in those activities can kill a career and personal relationships. We must exercise self-control when we speak.

Proverbs 13:6

> [6] Righteousness guards the man of integrity, but wickedness overthrows the sinner.

Despite the religious overtones, intentionally attempting to live an intelligent, blameless life safeguards us. Being blameless doesn't mean we are always correct. Instead, it means that we endeavor to make wise, ethical decisions when faced with important choices. All of our choices (good and bad) set events into motion that can be visually represented by a boomerang — our decisions can come back to us and land easy or hit hard.

Further Thoughts on the Partnership of Discipline and Knowledge

For argument's sake, I don't think there is anyone who can point to a life of consistent lying, stealing, cheating, murder, and mayhem and prove it brought good results for the people involved. Case in point, when the occasional gang war flares up — whether it involves street gangs or more traditional organized criminal groups such as the Mafia — notice the increased rate of homicide. When people are embedded in that life, it sets events in motion that bring destruction. Most rational people recognize that lifestyle is not the correct way to live. But aside from that, living a criminal or unethical way of life and routinely engaging in destructive activities will reap destructive results eventually.

Remembering this helps me actively choose to avoid lying or engage in an activity that lacks uprightness. Instead, I try to conduct myself in an exemplary fashion to the best of my ability. Of course, being human, I have made mistakes, but they eventually brought me to this point after much soul-searching and missteps. Like many others, some of my actions have caused destruction when I have acted inappropriately. Once I recognized what I had done was wrong, I corrected that behavior. It's interesting to watch people who are not engaged in the suitable behavior and see events unfold that punish them for their damaging activities.

Proverbs 13:10

> [10] Pride only breeds quarrels, but wisdom is found in those who take advice.

Do you ever find it difficult to say "I apologize" or "I was wrong"? If you're a typical person, sometimes those words can come with great difficulty. They are like molasses oozing along — not setting a speed record getting out. At this stage of my life, I am much better at saying those words as well as recognizing when I have been incorrect. The source of this inability, truthfully, is pride. There is nothing wrong whatsoever with being proud of your accomplishments or being proud of the way you conduct your life. However, it must be mixed with humility. We have to be able to say, "I was incorrect," or "I need your help." We have to be willing to admit our mistakes. Humility is not a negative human trait, and it does not mean we should be a doormat. It simply means we should look to be modest or respectful when appropriate.

Proverbs 13:13

> ¹³ He who scorns instruction will pay for it, but he who respects a command is rewarded.

The inability to ask for advice or accept intelligent criticism limits us. Someone can steamroll ahead in life up to a certain point depending upon God-given ability, native intelligence, and personality. At some point though, if you are not taking the advice of wise counsel — of people in your life who can share their experiences so you can expand your knowledge — you will never really achieve the success that you're capable of.

Proverbs 13:17

> ¹⁷ A wicked messenger falls into trouble, but a trustworthy envoy brings healing.

There are a couple of different ways to look at this verse. From Solomon's perspective, a king with a large empire needs to rely upon people to inform him about what is going on. The people that are informing the king — the businessperson, manager, or general counsel — need to be reliable. Have you heard the phrase *GIGO*? It means *garbage in, garbage out*. If you have bad advice or information from bad messengers, you will make bad decisions. They will cause your business and personal relationships and your ultimate success to break down because of the incorrect information — no matter how well-intentioned your decision might be.

Let's take an example from the business world. Say a manager who is based in one city supervises the activities of managers in other cities. If that manager is not getting good input from his direct reports, he will experience a breakdown in communication, teamwork, performance, and morale. A supervisor cannot rely upon gossip and off-the-cuff conversations — especially from people whose personal agendas don't contribute to the success of the area they serve. Toxic people who are trying to promote themselves by being in the middle of negativity can cause a terrible breakdown. It is easy to fall into the trap of counting hearsay as evidence in a long-distance management relationship unless you are really confident in the people that you have chosen for your team.

A manager also shouldn't "shoot the messenger." A supervisor relies on the people who report to him to give him important information — good and bad — and it deserves careful consideration before acting upon it. Just because a manager doesn't want to hear bad news, doesn't mean he should punish the person delivering the data. We have to be very careful to make sure that our system for gathering information is both reliable and appropriate. Good decisions rely on truthful input provided by the people around us.

Proverbs 13:20

> [20] He who walks with the wise grows wise, but a companion of fools suffers harm.

All of us need advice, and we often go to our friends for it. Some of those people might be friends we associate with in a community activity, or they might be business partners or colleagues. We gravitate to friends or acquaintances we like and respect. Generally, we are looking for helpful, unbiased advice. That is why we have to choose friends and acquaintances wisely. The good thing about friends is they are often like us and agree with us — that is probably why we're friends.

There are going to be situations where you need to rely on the input of people who aren't necessarily close to you. Seek out people whose work, opinions, and values you respect and admire. Sometimes you need input that is not colored by the bias of friendship. It is easy to surround yourself with people who think alike and ultimately arrive at the same decision. A leader who surrounds himself with "yes men" will never reach his highest pinnacle of success. We need valid, intelligent input that may differ from ours. Challenging thoughts hone our intellect.

When seeking advice, choose people who have a wide breadth of experience — people who have lived their life and walked the talk. If you're a young person, it may not necessarily be a person who is in your age group. It may be someone older and wiser. They can give you intelligent advice about situations even though they may not be up on the latest video game or online activity. Relationships and human nature haven't changed so much even though the medium of our interaction has changed.

For example, think of how Bill Gates and Warren Buffet met. Here is a case where you have people in two different professions. Warren Buffet is a professional investor who is at least two decades older than his friend. Bill Gates helped usher in some of the profound changes of the desktop age. He is generally acknowledged as being brilliant. Bill's trusted advisors urged him to contact Warren. Why does he need to chat with Warren? This was initially Bill's attitude. Why do I need to talk to him?

When they met, it was supposed to be a very short meeting — a meet and greet. They ended up talking for several hours. They realized they not only had a lot in common, they learned they could help each other. Warren had a lot to offer in terms of business advice to Bill. Conversely, Bill had much to offer as it related to high tech. In addition, Bill and his wife run a charitable foundation that eventually would help disburse their own money and money from other philanthropic-minded individuals and organizations as well as Warren's for the benefit of mankind. Their casual meeting launched a relationship that led them to become business associates and close friends.

This is why you shouldn't count out someone just because they don't think, act, and look like you. Seek out the widest possible breadth in your circle of acquaintances and friends that can be of value as you move forward in life. Everyone will experience the value as you exchange ideas and advice that help you become better, wiser individuals.

Proverbs 13:23

> [23] A poor man's field may produce abundant food, but injustice sweeps it away.

This verse is not intended to take poverty or injustice lightly. Instead, it is a signal or call to action. From a personal perspective, I became active in youth charities and educational initiatives. I don't have enough time to do all of what I would like to do, but I think formal education is critical in these times. I believe that everyone, despite their social or economic challenges, should have access to self-development when needed. Advice often comes in the form of informal schooling or training that helps someone move along the path that they are trying to travel. That advice can be delivered through organizations such as a church.

I also support charitable activities that serve elderly people. Even though I cannot always get physically involved, I can certainly write a check. Some people say that is not enough, but money used wisely to solve issues is still a very good thing. Think about this verse as a call to action no matter what cause you serve.

You may be able to enrich your life and help the organization by volunteering your time and supporting it financially. Pick the cause that you're most passionate about, and get involved physically and financially to the extent that your time and financial resources allow. Helping those who are disadvantaged benefits everyone when it empowers the needy to become active, contributing members of society. I have taken it as a call to action.

Proverbs 13:24

> [24] He who spares the rod hates his son, but he who loves him is careful to discipline him.

This brings back the old "spare the rod, spoil the child" adage. This verse is not about corporal punishment. It is instead about discipline which takes many forms. When we do not discipline our children, we're not helping them grow into responsible adults. Children who are allowed to run wild with a minimal amount of discipline in the home don't learn to exercise restraint. Eventually the greater world disciplines them. By the time that happens, it might be too late to make the child a responsible member of society. In its worse case, the child could land in harm's way, end up in jail, or experience a lifetime of failed dreams or lack of capacity to make proper decisions to expand their abilities.

Proper discipline is a balancing act. You don't want to be so hard on children that you beat the creativity out of them. They need guidelines around which they can operate and still be creative, have fun, and grow toward adulthood. It provides them the framework around which to make wise, intelligent decisions. Ultimately, they will be responsible for their decisions. And, of course, just because you've done the best you can doesn't mean that they are always going to follow the guidebook that you have laid out.

The same works when dealing with people in general. We all need discipline whether the discipline is involves our health and proper diet or exercising correctly. For professionals, this can affect our ability to advance in our career. Maybe that career path means becoming an entrepreneur. Learning proper discipline early in life prepares someone who wants to be self-employed with the ability to follow that path. It may mean completing certain courses and seminars, practicing for long hours, and working diligently. Whatever it may be, discipline trains us to do it consistently.

Even creating a book such as this requires allocating the time, being very disciplined about adhering to a writing schedule, and pushing forward.

So discipline is key for us whether we're children or adults. We need to exercise discipline along with wisdom to get the proper output. We don't want "garbage in and garbage out." We want success, therefore, quality input is required.

Further Thoughts on the Partnership of Discipline and Knowledge

Action Steps on the Life Path

Write down five areas of your life where you could exercise better self-control over what you say.

_____

_____

_____

_____

_____

Write down five instances where you "spoke past the close" or you spoke inappropriately and it harmed a person or a situation.

_____

_____

_____

_____

_____

Spend five to ten minutes writing down and evaluating important life decisions you've made over the last twelve months. In each of those decisions, determine what role wisdom and integrity played. Did it affect the outcome of the decision?

_____

_____

_____

_____

_____

_____

_____

_____

Time yourself for three minutes and write down some instances — personal or business — when you've been wrong but were too proud to admit it. Was it harmful to your relationship with those involved?

_____

_____

_____

_____

_____

_____

_____

_____

_____

What are some charitable activities or organizations you would like to support that you're passionate about? Note whether you can devote personal time or money to each activity or both.

_____

_____

_____

_____

_____

_____

_____

_____

_____

_____

The Sensible Thinker

"The simple inherit folly, but the prudent are crowned with knowledge."

Proverbs 14:18

Scorn and ridicule are the weapons of the fool. There is only one problem as Proverbs 14 so aptly points out: foolish behavior ultimately hurts the fools and those who listen to them the most. Fools aren't able to find wisdom even when it is staring them in the face. The worst type of fools are those who scorn. Because of their arrogance, they cannot humble themselves enough to accept the input to learn or do better. They know it all; just ask them. This is not God's way and it is not the intelligent way either. The wise recognize the fools and the damage they can do and move on. Learn from their example.

Proverbs 14:4

⁴ Where there are no oxen, the manger is empty, but from the strength of an ox comes an abundant harvest.

A clean stable means there are no animals. In the context during the period this was written, that meant you were broke. Having to clean up the stable because you have healthy oxen is a good problem to have. This simple verse has a strong message: inventory the people in your life. A farmer has less hassle without oxen because there are no droppings on the stable floor to clean up. However, good, strong oxen provide value to the farmer when it comes to harvest.

We want to make sure that we have strong oxen in our stable — that we are surrounded by the right people. Our life will most likely be a reflection of the six people closest to us. Even though it can be challenging to find and create quality relationships in life, the harvest is worth the trouble.

Are you surrounding yourself and spending time with the right kind of people? Evaluate your personal life, family, and friends. With friends, you can make a choice about whether you spend time with them. With family members, you may need to spend less time with those who are not healthy contributors to your existence.

It's also important to surround yourself with people who enhance your spiritual life and inspire spiritual growth. Evaluate the quality time you spend at your place of worship. Having a strong spiritual core is key to living the right kind of life.

The business world is a tricky one. You'll find you have to concentrate harder on how you conduct yourself because of the pressures of the work environment. At times, you will have more friends in the workplace than other times. You may find some workplaces where you will have to work with hostile people. Regardless, you have to operate according to your moral compass. You must make wise decisions, show character, and operate out of integrity. Whether it's personal, spiritual, or business, operate according to the highest moral standards. In addition, you'll find it valuable to invest quality time building relationships with the people you supervise.

In the spiritual and the personal spheres of your life, you'll find you have much more leeway with how you spend your time and who you spend it with. Each circumstance is different, but you can normally exercise that freedom of choice and verify you're spending time with the right type of people.

Proverbs 14:6

> [6] The mocker seeks wisdom and finds none, but knowledge comes easily to the discerning.

Mockers never seem to have a good word about anything. When you are trying to do something right and you are headed in the right direction, the mockers arrive with good old negativity. They pull you down and try to make the worst out of a good situation.

Mockers don't ever find wisdom unless they make a decision to change their mind-set. In fact, they really don't seek wisdom in a serious fashion. Instead, they are looking for the negative and what could and should go wrong. If there's nothing wrong, they will find something wrong for you! They consider themselves realists.

Wisdom comes to those who are applying it by using God's word in their life and seeking out godly counselors and advisors. The most godly people in your life may not be the people sitting next to you in a house of worship. Wherever you find them, the message is sent through them if you are willing to listen.

Strive to live your life according to the big three: wisdom, integrity, and proper character. To do this, you'll find it difficult to spend time with mockers and succeed. You can work with them; you can be related to them; and you might even pal around with them. However, you can't spend all of your time with them if you want to be successful. For example, I worked with a receptionist who had been doing the exact same tasks day in and day out for approximately fifteen years. Once I got to know her better, I realized how much she bad-mouthed the company and the people that worked for it. The office was relocated to a place that wasn't as convenient a commute for her. When this happened, she took her miserable attitude to an entirely new level of complaining, negativity, and uncooperativeness.

Here we have an individual who had been doing a relatively low-level job, but it an important one for any company office. The receptionist is the first face to clients and visitors. However, in this case, she was clearly not doing her job and was openly subverting the company's effort to make a successful transition to the new space. Additionally, her computer skills were poor. Instead of "thanking her lucky stars" she had a decent job during a period of economic downturn, she was cursing her own blessing!

Sometimes all of that mocking is worth a laugh. Learn to recognize people who will scoff when you want to be a top performer in your chosen profession. They will tell you that you can't be or that what you want to do can't be done. If you're going to finish high school, they are the people who ask, "Why are you doing that? You don't need it." If you're going to go to college, they say, "You can't do it. It can't be done. Why are you doing that?

There are no jobs anyway." God forbid that you want to go beyond college. They'll say, "You can't get the job you are looking for. You can't become a dentist." They will hold you back under the guise of friendship, family relation, business relation — whatever relationship they come under. They will always have a reason you shouldn't get ahead. Mockers are dream killers who say things like "You can't," "No one can," and "People like us can't." You can't change them if they aren't willing to change. Let those types of folks go until they are willing to work on themselves. If they can improve their negative attitude, you can welcome them back into your life

I remember setting up a Toastmasters club, and a senior manager was discouraging employees and other participants who were interested. This person had no power to stop the club from forming. Instead, he was a mocker with the power over the weak-minded people who were willing to follow the least-intelligent advice. Be on guard. We all have them in our life. Identify them and weed them out if you can.

Proverbs 14:12

> [12] There is a way that seems right to a man, but in the end it leads to death.

Some things are too good to be true. If your friend tells you that his venture doesn't take a lot of time or effort to make a lot of money, investigate closer before you get involved. Generally, those types of scenarios end up in disaster somewhere along the line. Take gangsters for instance. Very few hoodlums and gangsters retire of old age. They are generally killed or in prison long before retirement. And if you're making a choice because it doesn't require you to do anything, that is generally what you're going to get back — nothing in, nothing out.

The lottery player's mentality is, "All I have to do is buy a ticket and then when I win, I'll get rich." People with that mentality aren't saving any money. Even if they win, they typically don't have any skills to manage it or utilize the resources. That is why so many lottery winners go broke. We need to carefully evaluate choices that seem to reap rewards too easily.

Something that requires more sacrifice on your part is likely to reap a greater reward. You might decide to go to night school and allocate an hour each morning or evening so you can complete your coursework within a certain amount of time. That hard work will provide a better guarantee of reward than a scheme that requires ten minutes a day to make a $100,000 a year. You have to build a foundation for that type of income stream to come in. You certainly aren't going to become rich if you've invested no effort.

If someone chooses to overextend herself on credit because she can borrow from one credit card to pay another credit card, she will eventually exhaust that option because she has become accustomed to living on credit. If she continues the cycle, she will run out of money for the future. If you evaluate choices, make the intelligent choice, use good character and wisdom, and operate out of integrity, generally good things will follow.

Proverbs 14:29

> [29] A patient man has great understanding, but a quick-tempered man displays folly.

It may appear that some people with bad tempers get ahead in life. And make no mistake — some bad-tempered types do prosper. However, it is much easier to get along with someone who controls their emotions. It is difficult to handle someone who has a bad temper and regularly acts out in a state of rage. You will find it empowering when you avoid that type of person in your personal or professional life. Otherwise, you spend your time dancing around other peoples' moods on a road to nowhere.

If your "friend" has an explosive nature, you'll find yourself doing whatever is necessary to fit in with his mood just to be his friend. "People pleasing" is a lot of work. It's easier to be friends with someone you share a natural connection with whose good attitude makes it effortless to be friends.

Let's think about how this applies in the workplace. We've all gotten "flamethrower e-mails" that just set fire to everything they touch. They are generally long and easy to write. They are also not received well by the recipient. In those conditions, the sender would have been better off to deliver the information by phone. Often those e-mails don't portray us in our finest hour. In addition, it is an electronic document that people can forward to others and keep for posterity. It will come back to haunt the sender sooner or later. It is even worse than just having a face-to-face argument with someone because the details are saved in a permanent way.

If you get angry, don't write an e-mail and send it immediately. Sit down and relax until you've had time to think about it. If you do write that angry e-mail, save it to your draft folder and don't send it. Writing your thoughts can help you get your negative feelings off your chest and help you clarify why you feel the way you do. Being angry is not productive and can destroy relationships!

I am not the kind of person who runs around ranting and raving. Believe it or not, I have interviewed for a couple of jobs where they wanted to hire someone who did. I just find it counterproductive to be like that. It's better to stay calm in difficult situations. It doesn't mean that you don't get upset, but most employers expect employees to maintain control when faced with adversity and think through their actions as they interact with people.

When you deal with someone who needs to holler and scream, you'll find it empowering to tell them that you won't listen to them until they calm down. Once that happens, you'll be happy to interact with them. Sometimes that doesn't go over very well, and you will need to make a decision about whether that is the kind of workplace you want to be part of.

Be that as it may, angry, rage-filled people are hard to be around. They can inspire decisions about how we spend our time personally, spiritually, and professionally. When we don't have choices about who we spend our time with, it helps to learn some techniques for dealing with difficult people. When I am really disturbed about something, I will stop to read a passage from the Bible, pray, or review some of my personal goals that I keep with me. This helps me decompress a little bit, and generally I come out of it within a very short time. A few quiet moments can reveal a little different perspective.

We are not always going to be in a position to do that. Sometimes we are confronted and, just like anyone else, we react to the moment and voices get raised. Life is not perfect, but take the opportunity to stop for a second and think through your reaction to an event or person. Many times, whatever the other person is spiraling off about has nothing to do with you. They are acting out something that has come from somewhere else. Don't let them draw you in. Stay focused on what you're looking to do, particularly in a business environment. Think through your responses and interaction. I have reacted both ways and found that flying off the handle rarely works in the vast majority of instances.

The gift of wisdom and its intelligent use is beyond value. Working diligently and smartly in business is a good thing but just as we are what we eat, we are also very much like the people we spend time with. Spending time with do-nothing big mouths can't help but rub off on us. Spending time with those who forever dream without action rubs off on us. But spending time with intelligent, motivated people who are moving ahead rubs off on us too. Understand where you want to go and hop a ride with others heading in that direction.

Action Steps on the Life Path

List the people in your life who are closest to you. Do they have integrity?
Do they have a moral center? Do they take care of the responsibilities in
their life? Are they concerned about moving ahead in life? Are they doing
anything about it? Are they supportive of your dreams and goals?

_____

_____

_____

_____

_____

_____

_____

_____

_____

_____

_____

_____

_____

_____

_____

_____

_____

_____

_____

_____

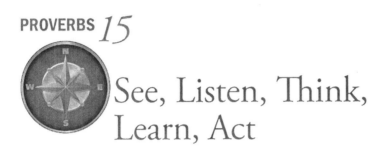

PROVERBS *15*

See, Listen, Think, Learn, Act

"He who ignores discipline despises himself, but whoever heeds correction gains understanding."

Proverbs 15:32

This lesson will center on Proverbs 15 of the Proverbs of Solomon. It covers several points concerning knowledge and discipline. However, the very first verse deals with a common but often deadly error: speaking before we think. Our mouths often act way ahead of our brains. Words can be beautiful and a magnificent way to express ourselves. They can also be a great way to demonstrate a generous spirit of conciliation when engaged in conflict with others. By taking the high road, you'll increase the chances of a peaceful resolution.

As is the case with most good advice and especially the teachings of Proverbs, we need to have a good heart and not come from a place of bitterness. You don't have to be a doormat and get walked on to take the high road. Taking the high road means being strong enough to yield when sensible but strong enough to know when other approaches may make more sense. It is not a process for the stupid or undisciplined.

Proverbs 15:1

[1] A gentle answer turns away wrath, but a harsh word stirs up anger.

Have you ever argued with someone in a whisper? I have tried that on occasion in a public place or maybe a theater. Maybe it was with a spouse, close friend, or family member. Perhaps the subject was ridiculous or personal. Do you ever notice how difficult it is to argue with a lowered voice or a whisper? It is more frustrating than what you're arguing about because you can't use the volume to reinforce your point. However, keeping your voice down can keep matters from getting dramatically worse or embarrassing everyone involved.

It is understandably difficult to answer gently if someone is yelling and screaming at you unless you stay calm. If you can maintain a calm exterior, it will eventually lower the volume of the conversation. It is just way too difficult for an angry person to scream and yell when he doesn't get the feedback he needs to do it. Unless the angry person has no governor on his emotions, he's going to eventually ratchet it down so that he finishes up at the calm person's level. He just can't sustain the intensity without the opposing angry feedback. An angry person needs the other person to holler, yell, scream, and lose his temper right along with him.

You can apply this technique in all areas in your personal, spiritual, and professional life. Regardless of the other person's attitude, you want to maintain control as much as possible. This doesn't mean that you will never get angry, but you need to plan how you would handle the situation before you have such an encounter. Harsh words, raised voices, and the emotion of the moment leads people to say things said that can never be taken back no matter how sincere the apology. This technique is particularly useful when handling angry exchanges with family members and friends — the group most vulnerable to angry words.

Think how handy this practice could be in dealing with businesspeople who fly off the handle. Don't let them draw you in to their anger. Stay calm and focused on the task at hand so you can get it accomplished. It is interesting how situations will often work out to your advantage simply because the other person spiraled out of control. Good behavior gets noticed in adverse situations. Negative behavior doesn't get anyone anywhere, and it does not build good client relationships, bridges, or alliances.

If you have a problem with anger, take a different approach next time you feel like stoking up your "flamethrower" to go at someone. Step back for a minute, take a deep breath, and don't write that angry e-mail. If you need to write it, save it to draft and put it away instead of sending it. Maybe writing your feelings in a journal will improve the way you feel about the situation. Before you interact with someone, measure your tone and take it easy. Once you've calmed down, decide whether it is worth the trouble. You might find it isn't.

Proverbs 15:3

> [3] The eyes of the Lord are everywhere, keeping watch on the wicked and the good.

This verse can be interpreted in many ways. For our purposes, I am going to look at it this way: sometimes bad things happen to good people but, in the end, things seem to work out for the better. Christians need to have faith that somehow the evil and horrendous acts in this world will somehow unravel toward a good ending.

The world that we live in now — despite the wars, chaos, and economic upheaval —is a better, less-brutal, less-coarse place to live in than ever. That does not mean that it's perfect. What it does indicate is that somehow, some way — despite all of the incredibly evil things that seem to periodically flare up — we just seem to lurch forward based on the energy of the good in us that ultimately wins out. In the end, most people want to do the right thing. They want to have a better life. For most people, evil is not an inherent part of their character that is in full control at all times. If it reveals itself at all, evil is a very small part of what we exude or act on.

There are other people — some who are in leadership positions — who unfortunately take actions that produce and expand negative events happening in this life. In a historical context, the obvious examples are Hitler, Stalin, Pol Pot, and other such dictators and rulers. Just look at the last hundred years of *ethnic cleansing* (more properly called *genocide*) in parts of the world such as Europe and Africa. Sometimes the adversity turns up in the form of natural disasters such as tsunamis, earthquakes, and volcanic eruptions. Even though the results — whether natural or man-made — are catastrophic, the good always emerges. Nature always recovers from the destruction.

All people are natural beings regardless of how much technology we create for ourselves. It's this gift that helps us make a better world and live more comfortably than any generation before us. It is the reason we end up better despite the pitfalls that we experience along the way. We just need to remember that God has a plan, and part of this plan can lead us to toward a good ending despite the horrendous things that may go on in our life.

Think about a time of adversity in your life — a divorce, layoff, or economic calamity. We've all experienced something that was catastrophic on a personal level. If you were able to stay positive and focused, keep yourself moving in the right direction, and take the right actions, you probably came out on the other side of it better for the experience. Maintaining a positive approach allows you to continue working. If you can put one foot in front of the other toward the right goal, good things end up happening.

Proverbs 15:14

> [14] The discerning heart seeks knowledge, but the mouth of a fool feeds on folly.

What we put into our minds is just as important as what we put into our stomachs. In fact, it's even more so, because our minds affect what we put into our stomachs. One of my success rules is "Successful people are readers!" You should read one to four quality books or equivalent written works (substantial periodicals, for example) per month if you are on a self-education program. Choose books that add value to your life in some way — an inspiring story, an autobiography, maybe an economic or historical book. There is nothing wrong with reading something light to relax; but try to invest in reading material that will provide education and inspiration, and put the right stuff in your mind. Consider creating a reading list of ten books to read over the next ninety days or so. Review best-seller lists in the *New York Times* or on BarnesandNoble.com or Borders.com to put yours together.

If you are not a fast reader, consider investing in a speed-reading course. There are different options that cater to a variety of budgets. Do what you need to do to increase your reading speed so you can maximize the time you set aside for self-development. That may mean giving up some of your television time or making wiser choices in the television you watch. If reading isn't your thing, get audio books from resources like Audible.com and iTunes.

See, Listen, Think, Learn, Act

There is now an incredible amount of quality television that is both educational and entertaining like the Science Channel, the History Channel, the BBC, PBS, and National Geographic. There is quality business news that doesn't have the hysterics or political commentary that some other stations focus on. Programming from news sources such as Bloomberg (www. bloomberg.com) provide much more unfiltered information so that you get more of the straight economic data and reporting.

I have nothing against some of the other stations, but too many stations operate under the philosophy of "if it bleeds, it leads." Local news stations tend to use sensationalism to draw viewers but don't focus on quality. You need to police what you watch. Turn it on, get the weather, scope out the local morning commuting update, and then turn it off.

Many television networks provide educational programming on topics such as home decorating, fitness, and cooking. Maybe you're doing a house project and watching some of the shows may help fine-tune some decisions that you will make. I learned quite a bit this way for a redecorating project. Some stations have a tremendous amount of health information on them. There's a lot you can watch on television without wasting time on empty frivolous programming that won't add anything to your life. I have nothing against those shows and obviously there is a market for them or they couldn't afford to stay on the air. However, if you are going to be successful, you can't waste time on that kind of television.

Case in point, I talk to many people in business about what they watch. Everyone you meet is not necessarily a titan of industry, but it is interesting to see the people that power ahead don't seem to watch silly programming on television. That's not to say that an occasional diversion is not a good thing for us all, but a steady diet of it is bad. Just like too much sugar which will cause tooth decay, too much empty programming will cause mental decay. A strong desire to learn and seek knowledge so that you can leverage information really is a mark of wisdom and of a successful person.

By the way, if reading still presents a challenge, listen to audio books and courses while on the go. You can turn the time you spend sitting in traffic or on a crowded train into your own classroom.

¹⁵ All the days of the oppressed are wretched, but the cheerful heart has a continual feast.

A positive mental attitude is one of the keys to a happy, productive life. It isn't any secret that positive people tend to do better. Unfortunately, many people are raised in a negative atmosphere. Instead of being encouraged and empowered, they spend a lot of time in school or at home amongst peers or family members who tell them they can't accomplish goals or steer them in a direction away from positive goals.

My parents wanted to make sure that I went to college. Who knows what may have happened if they didn't reinforce that? I have talents that I didn't explore that may have led me in a different direction. Those talents might have required less or no college, but life is always better if you end up with a decent education, and that education isn't always in the classroom.

Sometimes when we have talents and dreams that lead to other areas outside the norm, people try to discourage them. It is harder to stay the course when you are a young child who is influenced by negative adults. But you have to be strong and believe in yourself. Understand where you're going and what you're going to do. As you get older, that belief will become stronger because you fought through the adversity. When it becomes your own truth learned through your own experience, somehow it becomes stronger.

Make sure your mind is filled with positive reinforcement for your life. My three main life areas are personal, spiritual, and business. I worked very hard to get out of that negative mode and create a positive psychological mind-set. One of the little tricks that helped me along the way was to spend more time thinking about things that I like. Sometimes we spend too much time thinking about what we don't like and that creates a negative part of our life. Focus your attention on things you like. Sound simple? It is. You just have to actively decide to do it if you aren't already.

Every time a negative, self-defeating thought enters your mind — "I can't do it. They can't do it. It can't be done. I'm no good. I'm never going to be able to get this" — I want you to stop and say "No" to the thought. It might help you to include a physical motion like tapping the side of your head, hitting your chest, pinching your leg, or simply actively repeating your goals aloud or silently. I repeat silently, out loud, or just mouth the words of my five main goals. In fact, you may just want to say the first one several times. If another negative thought creeps in or you find yourself "going negative," repeat the second goal three or four times.

Get into the habit of interrupting yourself when negativity emerges. It is much more difficult to be negative when you're interrupting it by repeating something positive that you desire. And don't forget to put a smile on your face while you're doing it. Feel good! It is difficult to feel bad while you are smiling and focused on something enjoyable.

Proverbs 15:17-19

> [17] Better a meal of vegetables where there is love than a fattened calf with hatred. [18] A hot-tempered man stirs up dissension, but a patient man calms a quarrel. [19] The way of the sluggard is blocked with thorns, but the path of the upright is a highway.

Doing the right thing isn't always the easy initial choice but most of the time, it seems to reveal itself ultimately as the right choice. It takes courage to be the upright one. However, the alternative is hatred, dissension, laziness, and lack of true success. Those problems end up becoming greater than actually making any decision that leads to the greater good.

Doing the right thing has worked for me even though its hasn't always been easy. Like everyone else, it was a long and winding road to get here. No matter how good the wrong choices feel at the moment, they will never lead you to where you should go — especially when you compound decision after decision based on wrong choices.

Proverbs 15:22

> [22] Plans fail for lack of counsel, but with many advisers they succeed.

Seek out advisors who provide useful and valuable advice. They should be people of knowledge who would have your best interest at heart. This verse refers to people who are myopic — those who have tunnel vision. It's different than being single minded and pursuing your purpose. When people become myopic in pursuing their purpose, they shut out sound advice and neglect to see the things that are going wrong around them. To overcome it, they may need to shift course momentarily to get to where they ultimately want to go. We must make sure that our minds are open to new options and new ways of looking at things that can help us reach our goals fairly. We need people who can help us fulfill our vision and widen our perspective.

We are using wisdom and commonsense when we seek out people who are knowledgeable, beneficial, or willing to help. Networking uses the same principle. Networking is about collaborating with others so you can help each other. Search for the right kind of advisors and build a network of people who can be beneficial to you on your journey and who you can help in return.

Proverbs 15:28

> [28] The heart of the righteous weighs its answers, but the mouth of the wicked gushes evil.

I wanted to end on this verse because it ties neatly back to where we started with arguing and hot-tempered behavior. We should think very carefully before we speak, and that doesn't mean taking an inordinate amount of time between each sentence. Instead, practice giving feedback and interacting with people in a way that is not harmful or hurtful but is instead supportive. If you're around people who are negative or who are enemies, that's even more reason for you to think carefully before you speak. That is what a wise person would do. So use wisdom, stay on track, and don't let words just flow forth because they can end up being traps that ensnare you.

Considering the title of this chapter, let's give the last word to Scripture: "He who listens to a life-giving rebuke will be at home among the wise. He who ignores discipline despises himself, but whoever heeds correction gains understanding. The fear of the Lord teaches a man wisdom, and humility comes before honor" (Proverbs 15:31-33).

See, Listen, Think, Learn, Act

Action Steps on the Life Path

Write down two to five events from your life that you feel are defining moments. Were they good or bad? What made them good or bad? What was the positive benefit that eventually emerged?

_____

_____

_____

_____

_____

_____

_____

_____

_____

_____

_____

_____

_____

_____

_____

_____

_____

_____

_____

_____

Spend no more than five minutes writing out your five main goals. Repeat them to yourself at least once after you have written them out. Use this format:

> "I, [your name], am a or have achieved (desired position or goal) and being this or having accomplished this allows me to ..."

Repeat each goal out loud five times once or twice a day.

_____

_____

_____

_____

_____

_____

_____

_____

_____

_____

_____

_____

_____

_____

_____

_____

_____

_____

_____

_____

_____

_____

PROVERBS *16*

The Mouth and Mind Partnership

"The wise in heart are called discerning, and
pleasant words promote instruction."

Proverbs 16:21

This lesson covers Proverbs 16 of the Proverbs of Solomon and discusses the importance of our thoughts. The word *think* means *to consider, reflect, reason, and ponder*. We become what we think about and dwell upon. Our thoughts shape our behavior. Think of the people we know or have heard about who just kept thinking about the wrong things until they found themselves in a mess.

So what are you thinking about most of the time? Are you thinking ethically and morally? Having a mind fixated on negativity leads to anxiety, worry, emptiness, and restlessness. You have to understand that the body always wants to satisfy its flesh and desires without regard to good or bad.

Place yourself around positive people who are headed in the right direction. It will make it easier for you to train your mind for the positive and speak to it. Making your desires plain and spoken is jet fuel for their realization.

Proverbs 16:1

> [1] To man belong the plans of the heart, but from the LORD comes the reply of the tongue.

Our theme throughout Proverbs is wisdom, and our mission should be to apply wisdom to every aspect of our life. Proverbs 16:1 is not suggesting that we don't make plans because God's will is God's will. We should make plans, but we need to make them according to God's will. This simple verse suggests that we use our good judgment and seek intelligent counsel to make an intelligent plan. We accomplish this by speaking and listening. Speaking is a gift we use a lot but unfortunately, we think too little before using it. Listening is also key, however, as it makes our acquisition of knowledge possible.

When you make discerning, ethical decisions based on the lessons and wisdom you've learned from your education and experience, you are naturally going to increase the probability of having a good result. Applying wisdom isn't always an exact formula for success, and we'll encounter challenges along the way. However, taking the right action will normally yield a suitable result. Things won't always work exactly as planned; however, events overall will work out according to your abilities and circumstances. Even our challenges will prepare us for our next steps so we finish stronger than we started.

Proverbs 16:2

> [2] All a man's ways seem innocent to him, but motives are weighed by the LORD.

As the old accountant used to say, "If you torture the numbers long enough, they will say anything that you want them to say." People are the same way. We can rationalize anything that we do and make ourselves out to be the hero or the victim, depending upon which angle represents us best. But that's not how we should operate our life. Instead, we should make savvy plans.

Later in this book, I will go more deeply into goal setting and planning; but remember, our goal is not to prove ourselves right. Our intent is to put an intelligent plan into action, use the wisdom we have acquired, and then ask ourselves these questions to verify:

- Does it make sense?
- Will this plan work? Is my life set up in such a way that it will work? If not, what do I need to do? What changes do I need to make in order for this plan to come to fruition?
- Do I have a positive mental attitude toward myself and my life? Or am I one of those "You can't do it. I can't do it. It can't be done" people?

Next, ask these questions to weigh your plan and see if it is in God's will.

- Is the plan in harmony with God's written word?
- Will the plan work under real-life conditions?
- Is my attitude pleasing to God?

Beware of the negative people who see the downfall in every plan. In many instances, they call themselves "realists" but in reality, they are people lacking self-confidence. They are always looking for an excuse so when things go south, they're "covered." They are the victims.

When you carefully create a plan, it shelters you from the negative people because you have thought through the contingencies.

To initiate your solid plan, you'll first want to list the steps in it. For instance, say you want to buy a house. Here are some steps you would take:

1. Start researching neighborhoods.
2. Start researching brokers and lenders.
3. Start saving a certain amount of money per month to cover the cost of a down payment or acquiring a house.
4. Evaluate if you can take on a home that requires work — a "fixer upper." Ask yourself if you have the skills or money to do the work in a timely and realistic fashion?

Once you've written down the steps, ask yourself if your plan is reasonable and how long it would take. If your goal is to buy a half-million dollar house and you make $50,000 a year, you may want to rethink this goal in the short term. You could give yourself one year to work on it, and then revisit the type of house you should be in based upon cost. Miracles don't happen every day, but they do happen. Maybe you will end up able to afford the home you want at that point! In the meantime, put together a realistic plan to buy a $150,000 house, and make sure that you're doing the things necessary to acquire it within a reasonable period of time. The best plans are based on commonsense and real-life conditions. With a little more searching and diligence, you may be able to find a home you want that is in your price range.

Proverbs 16:3

> ³ Commit to the LORD whatever you do, and your plans will succeed.

Successful plans are rooted in commitment. Clearly there are different ways to commit ourselves to any plan. However, we can fail if we do not commit our plans to God. Some people will commit their work only superficially and will profess they are doing a project for God's sake; but in reality, they are doing it for themselves. It's important to be realistic and truthful with yourself about why you're doing something. Some will give God some control of their interests only to take the control back when things stop going the way that they expect — either they want to do it their way or they simply forgot they had started out trying to do it God's way. God's way will get you where you ultimately need to be — not necessarily where you ultimately thought you wanted to go.

Still many others will commit to a task but not really put themselves into it one hundred percent — and then they wonder why it didn't succeed. It's important to strike a balance. We need to trust in God as if everything depended on Him — because it does. Wouldn't it be a lonely, large, frightening universe if the only thing you could depend on was yourself? Think of something very, very specific that you're involved in right now. Have you committed it to God? Do you have real faith that you will succeed?

God expects our full commitment on those plans we commit to Him also. If we're fully committed to what we're doing, what's the likelihood that we're going to succeed? But if we don't have a strong sense of commitment, our chance of success drops dramatically. When I fail to achieve certain goals and reflect on the experience, I normally find that I didn't make an intelligent plan, act in faith, and see it through to the end.

At one point in my career, I was very motivated to get a Masters in Business Administration. I went to school two evenings a week and all day Saturday while I was working full time. I finished my MBA a year ahead of time and was close to being an A student. After that, I thought I was committed to getting a doctoral degree. I even went to class but, quite honestly, I really

The Mouth and Mind Partnership

wasn't quite committed. I would love to have a PhD, but I wasn't passionate about it and willing to pay the price to earn it. Eventually, I admitted my lack of commitment to myself, and I put my energies to work in other ways. Don't try to fool yourself, and don't expect to fool others. If you are motivated to give one hundred percent to something, then do it. Otherwise, you may want to find a different project to devote your energy to.

Proverbs 16:4

> 4 The LORD works out everything for his own end; even the wicked for a day of disaster.

This verse does not mean that God has created some people to be evil. We clearly do not have the capability of fully understanding God's plan, and it is puzzling that He uses the evil activities of some people for good purposes. For a reference point, see Genesis 50:20: "You intended to harm me, but God intended it for good to accomplish what is now being done, the saving of many lives." Because we believe God is infinite and we are not — no matter how intelligent we believe ourselves to be — we will never be able to understand God completely. However, we have to accept by faith that God is not the cause of evil or wants evil in the world for evil purposes. Instead, He is using it to better our life when it appears.

Despite struggle, mankind somehow moves forward and becomes better. Somehow, the life we lead becomes better notwithstanding the pain and suffering in many parts of the world. And the world is a better place to live in than ever — and even where it isn't good, we know there is a better, more enlightened way that exists. Our technological changes have been beneficial for the planet. There is a lot of awareness of our environment and all types of knowledge and capabilities that have come from progress.

And, along the way, there have been many evil or wicked people. The obvious ones that comes to mind are historical figures like Hitler, Mussolini, and Stalin. But look at the benefit that came in the aftermath of their reigns. The world became a better place — not just for Europeans but for many other people as well. The breakdown in European power led to many countries shaking off the shackles of colonialism. Yes, there was pain and suffering along the way; but once again, because man's nature is inherently good, the greater good always seems to move toward making the situation better. Thankfully, mankind does not always act in concert with those impulses inspired by someone who is engaged in evil activities.

We need to rely on God to help us overcome the evil-mindedness in us and in others. The world is a better place if our attitudes are pointing in a positive, spiritually grounded direction.

Proverbs 16:5

> [5] The LORD detests all the proud of heart. Be sure of this: They will not go unpunished.

I'm fond of this saying about a prideful person: "They're the smartest person they know." Anytime anyone thinks that the only good answer is his or hers, that's already a problem. No one person has all the answers. No matter how successful someone is, when he positions himself in that manner, he is setting the conditions for a downfall. And like any fall, the higher you go, the harder the fall is.

I once worked with someone who did not like me. I'm not sure why because I didn't have any history with them. Who knows what his motivations were. However, in watching his behavior, he seemed to project negative energy, and he was always frowning. I'm not sure if that was a protective mechanism or it was his way of trying to exert control over his environment. He only seemed to smile when he was talking about himself. It was dysfunctional and a bit bizarre. The environment was toxic, and this person was financially successful despite making it a miserable place to work for a high number of employees.

It's not possible to constructively lead ourselves or others if we have a bad attitude. People depend on us to lead by example and give them the best we have to offer. Look at the areas of your life. Are there any areas where you are being prideful, being a know-it-all, giving people a hard time for no reason, picking out people to bully, or somehow demonstrating to others that you're smarter, better, or more important? Negative, prideful behavior is destructive to other people and prevents us from taking in important information and filtering it properly. We don't process it properly because we're busy looking for information to justify what we already think. We cannot make a wise decision if we're filtering it inappropriately so that we can be right.

There is nothing wrong with being proud of accomplishments, your family, and the good things that you do, but prideful behavior is never helpful.

Proverbs 16:7

> [7] When a man's ways are pleasing to the LORD, he makes even his enemies live at peace with him.

We all want other people to like us. The problems come when we are willing to do anything for people to like us. Remember that God tells us to put our energy into pleasing Him and not into pleasing our neighbors. So what's the old phrase? "Make peace, not war?" Good neighbors tend to be people who are easier to get along with and try to make peace when there is contention. They're busy making the environment around them much more attractive and easier to be in as well as pleasing to God.

Proverbs 16:9

> [9] In his heart a man plans his course, but the LORD determines his steps.

Have your priorities in order. You can't do everything so don't try. Instead make choices. You must decide what's really important and what isn't. Take some time to consider the direction of your life.

When your mind is focused and directed, you begin to accomplish what you are seeking. It doesn't matter if it's bad or good. But if you are directed by biblical teaching, you will position yourself for success. You'll have wisdom, discernment, insight, and the ability to pursue meaningful goals in balance with ethical and moral content. The focused, God-inspired mind has access to the tools to achieve abundance and prosperity in every area of your life, but it is up to you to use those tools properly. Don't let another day pass by without engaging in prayer and meditation on its direction.

Just when we think we are "all that and a bag of chips," life throws cold water on us and ruins the celebration. Enjoy the good times and learn from the bad times, but don't let your emotions go too far one way or the other. Stay centered, and enjoy the positive events in your life without the arrogance.

Proverbs 16:18

[18] Pride goes before destruction, a haughty spirit before a fall.

If you are going to interact with people of differing points of view in a negative and caustic manner, you will lose friends and may not able to effectively influence people. Sometimes, what you don't say or how you say what you do say is more important than the content.

Irritating, niggling, and nagging are no no's in the communication game. Be civil and pleasant to win the war. Don't worry about getting the verbal upper hand in a skirmish or showing others how smart you are. Wisdom and humility form a good partnership.

Proverbs 16:21

[21] The wise in heart are called discerning, and pleasant words promote instruction.

There is some very powerful advice in this verse. Remember as you grow both in wisdom and the application of it, part of your duty is to be encouraging and constructive toward others. You heal the broken hearted with words of encouragement, not condemnation.

In this chapter, we have discussed quite a bit regarding speaking, listening, planning, and doing. However, let's end with the reminder that our Creator is the creator of all things and all wisdom and proper use of them stems from Him. Nevertheless, as we plan our way through prayer and meditation, let God's will direct our steps. Our responsibility is to study, think, evaluate, and make up our mind. By keeping our actions in concert with scriptural instruction, the righteous purpose will be pursued and manifested by our actions, thoughts, and speech.

Action Steps on the Life Path

Once you go down the road of an insincere relationship, you'll find it takes a lot of energy to keep up the false front and continue doing things so the other person will like you. You're better off going to find a real friend instead.

Note relationships where you are doing anything possible to be liked — in other words, being a "people pleaser." Are there any relationships where you have special conditions or unrealistic expectations that you shouldn't have of the other person?

_____

_____

_____

_____

_____

_____

_____

List the projects you are involved in. Maybe you have ten; maybe you have two. Which projects are you passionately committed to?

_____

_____

_____

_____

_____

_____

_____

_____

_____

Examine one major area of your life that you invest time in such as your business, personal, or community life. Make a list of the things associated with that area you are involved in and are not passionately committed to.

_____

_____

_____

_____

_____

_____

Productivity will skyrocket when you are working on something you are passionate about. How can you reallocate your time so you're pursuing the things that you are fervent about?

_____

_____

_____

_____

Do you struggle with pride in any area of your life? Take a few minutes to journal about those areas where you can eliminate pride from your life.

_____

_____

_____

_____

_____

_____

_____

_____

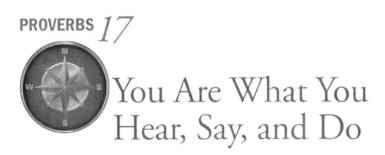

You Are What You Hear, Say, and Do

*"Even a fool is thought wise if he keeps silent,
and discerning if he holds his tongue."*

Proverbs 17:28

Growing up, I always thought it was odd the when the doctor asked me to stick out my tongue to see if I was sick. As an adult, I can see how the tongue can help reveal physical illness, but it can also reveal mental illness. Mental illness? Yes. When I say mental illness, I'm referring to corrupted thought, speech, and action. Words can be used to manipulate and destroy, or they can be used to bless and heal. The only question is which purpose are we choosing our words for?

The most obvious transgression is lying. Knowingly listening to gossip and lies while enjoying it is just as bad as telling lies. By engaging in gossip, you are encouraging bad behavior. You are also likely to repeat it in some form. How? One telltale sign of liars is that they enjoy listening to other liars. Therefore if you are listening to and enjoying gossip, you are showing approval and willing participation. Proverbs 17:4 says, "A wicked man listens to evil lips; a liar pays attention to a malicious tongue."

Proverbs 17:3

> [3] The crucible for silver and the furnace for gold, but the LORD tests the heart.

It takes intense heat to purify gold and silver. Similarly, it often takes the heat of trials and tribulations for a Christian to be purified. Of course, you don't have to be a Christian to understand this concept. In fact, a gentleman named W. Clemens Stone and his contemporary, Napoleon Hill, observed that there was always a seed of a greater or equivalent benefit in every challenge or trouble that we have. In many ways, this echoes the wisdom of Proverbs 17:3. We can learn from our trials and tribulations. We grow when we can celebrate our challenges and "enjoy" the price along the way — even though the price is sometimes painful. It clears out anything that gets in the way of complete trust in God's way.

Purification in this application refers to learning. In the process of dealing with life's challenges, God shows you what is in you. The challenges, trials, and adversities introduce you to who you are and who He meant you to be. If you come through those trials and adversities without becoming bitter but instead becoming better, you will see great benefit. By learning from the lessons and applying them to other parts of your life, you will be able to conduct yourself with integrity and character.

During tough times, I've grown to realize that my faith shepherds me through them. I'm not really sure how anyone can operate without faith and a belief in something greater than themselves. I need faith to operate beyond those difficult circumstances when it seems impossible to make it through to the other side on my own. Sometimes we are involved in events and circumstances that just seem so overwhelming that they dishearten us. However, if you have something greater than yourself to believe in that shepherds you through no matter what happens, it always reinforces your belief that somehow you're going to come out better on the other side of the trial. The more it works, the stronger your faith becomes. This is an exciting state to be in.

Proverbs 17:5

> [5] He who mocks the poor shows contempt for their Maker; whoever gloats over disaster will not go unpunished.

There are few things as negative and cruel as making fun of someone less fortunate. Unfortunately, many people do it because it makes them feel good to be more successful than someone else. What is it inside of those people that compels them to ridicule and make fun of someone who is less fortunate? Most would feel sympathy for that person or take some action to help him. Clearly, someone who would do that has serious issues.

Mocking the poor is really mocking the God who made them. No matter how innocent is seems, mocking the weak, different, or less fortunate or putting others down just for the fun of it is ridiculing God. What good comes out of bullying the less fortunate or defenseless? People who engage in this type of behavior need to ask themselves if they would consider making fun and putting down the Creator. Instead, we should focus our energy on helping all of God's people and glorifying Him.

Proverbs 5:17 also speaks to bullying. Why does bullying someone make the bully feel good? Scientific study has shown that bullies experience a certain amount of remorse in some cases when they torture someone. However, their pleasure center is also stimulated and they get some pleasure out of it. I will bet you anything that pleasure is related to something they lack in their own life. Bullies need to examine themselves. They should consider what is really bothering them that is causing them to pick on others.

Proverbs 17:8

> 8 A bribe is a charm to the one who gives it; wherever he turns, he succeeds.

Solomon is not condoning bribery in this verse. If you go on to Proverbs 17:15 and 17:23, you will see this is not the case. He is simply making an observation about the way the world operates. Bribes may get people what they want, but the Bible clearly condemns using them. Refer to Exodus 23:8 and Matthew 28:11-15 for more information. Make no mistake; what is said here is merely an observation about the use of bribery and its place in the world. It is not condoning it in any way, shape, or form.

> ⁹ He who covers over an offense promotes love, but whoever repeats the matter separates close friends.

Lack of forgiveness not only separates close friends, it divides all relationships. If you have been through a divorce as I have, you've seen that lack of forgiveness on top of whatever transgressions occurred contributed to the inevitability of the divorce. Rarely are there such extenuating circumstances that lack of forgiveness does not play into it. As a result, this proverb says that we should be willing to disregard the faults of others and that forgiving faults is necessary to any relationship.

No one is going to please you all of the time, nor should you expect them to. They can't make you happy. Only you can make you happy and do the things that make you happy. You have no obligation to stay in a bad relationship, but sometimes it takes time to get out of it. Say, for example, you work at a place where there are a lot of toxic people. But until you are able to remove yourself from a toxic situation through other employment, you'll have to avoid being drawn into the noxiousness.

On a personal level, it is very tempting — especially in an argument — to bring up all the mistakes the other person has ever made. However, true love tells us we need to keep our mouths shut. It is difficult though because it is so easy to look backwards. Remember Lott's wife in Genesis 19:16-33? She and Lott were told to leave without looking back. Instead, she looked back and turned into a pillar of salt.

Stop anchoring in the past and embrace your future. When you're having disagreements, try not to bring anything into an argument that is unrelated to the topic being discussed. Bringing in additional issues is only going to fuel the fire and stoke things to a level that flames out of control. The actions will get out of hand and then the confrontation will become something dramatically worse than its origin. Instead, talk though situations as calmly as possible, and don't exaggerate the situation by bringing in transgressions and past misdeeds. Save them for the appropriate time. Concentrate on being as level-headed as possible and all your relationships will dramatically improve.

Forgiveness is a recurring theme in all of the work that I do. I have struggled with it and made a tremendous amount of progress. Life is much better because when we do not hold grudges and engage in vendettas. We don't have to carry the memory of the person on our back who did something wrong to us, a family member, or a friend. It was bad enough to have the experience once, why would we need to continue to carry it around? Forgiveness is not just about the person who mistreated or failed us. It is really about you being a healthier person.

Proverbs 17:17

> [17] A friend loves at all times, and a brother is born for adversity.

Ask yourself, "What kind of friend am I to other people?" There is a vast difference between knowing someone well and being a true friend. The greatest evidence of genuine friendship is loyalty. According to I Corinthians 13:7, being available to help in times of great personal distress or struggle is what is going to make you a friend. You may not know the person you're helping very well, nor do you have to in times of emergency. Too many people are fair-weather friends. We need to be available to help others during the good times and bad. This action has meaning because it isn't easy to do and demands the personal sacrifice of time.

You should be cautious of the fair-weather friends in your life. Just because someone knows you doesn't mean they won't turn on you. One moment they are patting you on the back and laughing with you; and the next moment, they are telling someone you're the worst person to ever walk the earth. Be careful to avoid those people because they will cause you to have unhealthy, nonproductive thoughts, and a continual focus on them will stimulate unhealthy, unproductive behavior. The theme of Proverbs is wisdom, and part of growing our wisdom is developing discernment about the people we surround ourselves with.

Do you have fair-weather friends — the people who are around during the good times but who aren't available when the times get tough or when they're not getting what they want out of the friendship? They view relationships as disposable, and they move on. Really assess your loyalty to friends and theirs to you. Be the kind of true friend that is encouraged in the Bible. You never know who your friends are until you get into trouble.

Proverbs 17:22

> ²² A cheerful heart is good medicine, but a crushed spirit dries up the bones.

We like to be around someone who is cheerful and greets others warmly in a welcoming manner with encouragement and enthusiasm. That type of person will have more friends and be able to head down the road of developing better relationships.

Medical studies have shown that when you laugh, it increases your number of T-cells, which raises your immunity level. Laughter is good for your health as well as your outlook. Humor is a gift from heaven, so enjoy it. Remember, it is okay take God seriously, but don't take yourself too seriously. Learn to laugh at your limitations while you work on improving them.

Proverbs 17:24

> ²⁴ A discerning man keeps wisdom in view, but a fool's eyes wander to the ends of the earth.

I am all for having big dreams, but it's easy to set unrealistic goals. In this verse, Proverbs is pointing out the folly of chasing fantasies — having eyes that "wander to the ends of the earth." To set realistic goals, we need to understand how to best align our goals with God's will and our skills, desires, and true wants. We need to spend time looking inside ourselves and understand what we really want.

If you want to own a $100 million business, you'll need to make sacrifices and do the things necessary to create a business of that level. If you build it from scratch, you'll need to study what others have done to get there. However, if being at home with your family so you never miss birthdays and PTA meetings is also a priority, you may find that you can't achieve both.

You'll discover that you need to make choices and strike a balance that is realistic. And you can't do it based upon what everyone else is doing or wants you to do. You have to do what makes sense in your life. Wisdom, honesty, patience, and love need to be balanced against other needs. Goals that are realistic for your life may not seem as exciting as a list of goals that revolve around being part of the super rich.

Being rich can provide a lot of material comforts, but it doesn't always provide happiness. Look at someone like movie actor, Owen Wilson. When he attempted suicide, he was an A-list actor who had been in several successful films. He's just one example of how having financial and career success without balance is not enough to make a person happy and secure. I'm not here to judge him; but that should serve as an example that we can do great harm to ourselves if our life is not in balance — no matter how good the successful parts are.

Proverbs 17:27-28

> [27] A man of knowledge uses words with restraint, and a man of understanding is even-tempered. [28] Even a fool is thought wise if he keeps silent, and discerning if he holds his tongue.

These verses highlight several benefits of being silent. Like me, you probably have spoken too much or out of turn at some point. Sometimes, we say too much and it either doesn't help the situation or gets us in trouble. Consequently, when we don't have anything worthwhile to add, the best policy is to be quiet. It also provides the opportunity to listen and learn — a trait of wise and knowledgeable people. Remember to pause, think, and listen so when you do speak, you have something important to say.

In Toastmasters meetings, we have a role that is related to this idea even though, on the surface, it doesn't seem to be. That role is called the "ahh counter" or grammarian. That person counts the filler words the speakers use. They look for empty words and phrases such as "ahh," "uhm," "you know what I'm saying," and "the bottom line is."

People often use filler words and phrases because they are trying to think about what they're going to say next. Instead of simply being quiet and taking a moment to pause, they fill it in with a word or phrase that is often more distracting than silence. Sometimes silence is more powerful than any word we can use. It's been good practice for me because I didn't realize I had filler words until they were counted. I worked on it because of my Toastmasters training, and it improved my speaking because I am not filling the room with words that make no sense and add no value.

Sensible people keep their eyes glued on wisdom. So wisdom is a recurring theme in Proverbs. Take a look at this, then, take a look at yourself, and act appropriately. Start to take action in a way that will be beneficial to improving your use of wisdom.

Action Steps on the Path of Life

Write out the verses we discussed in this chapter, and give them serious thought.

_____

_____

_____

_____

_____

_____

_____

_____

_____

_____

_____

_____

_____

_____

_____

_____

_____

_____

_____

_____

_____

_____

_____

_____

Consider the tests and challenges you encounter in your life. Are you overcoming them and coming out better on the other side? If not, what can you do differently to learn and grow from them?

_____

_____

_____

_____

_____

_____

_____

Take something that is currently challenging you and ask, "What can I do to gain greater benefit from this experience?" If it is something traumatic like a divorce, consider what you can do to become a better companion in the future. What can you do to better recognize certain negative characteristics in yourself or certain types of people that may not be healthy for you to have a relationship with? Jot down three or four of these ideas and refer back to them.

_____

_____

_____

_____

_____

_____

_____

_____

_____

_____

What are some reasons that you think bullies pick on other people? How might they resolve those issues?

_____

_____

_____

_____

_____

_____

_____

What type of friend are you? What types of friends are you looking for? What kind of friends do you currently have?

_____

_____

_____

_____

_____

_____

_____

People have to tiptoe around those who are always snarling and unhappy. Grumpy people find themselves unhappy and without many friends. What are some possible reasons they could be unhappy? Are they being disagreeable with people because of things that are happening in other areas of their life?

_____

_____

_____

_____

_____

You Are What You Hear, Say, and Do

Do you find yourself as one of those grumpy people on occasion? If so, write down why you feel unhappy. What are some things you can do to improve the issues and your attitude?

_____

_____

_____

_____

_____

_____

_____

_____

_____

_____

_____

Why do people speak when they don't have anything to say?

_____

_____

_____

_____

_____

_____

_____

_____

PROVERBS *18*

The Mouth of a Fool
Is a Hole Full of Trouble

"A fool's lips bring him strife, and his mouth invites a beating."

Proverbs 18:6

Fools can't handle or learn from wisdom primarily because they can't focus on the important issues before them. God's instruction gives us the tools for proper decision making, but a fool rejects them and acts instead by feeling and desire born of fantasy. If you recognize when you are around people who speak before thinking, who will not listen to intelligent advice, who are always speaking about what they are going to do but never get started, and who lie about or besmirch the reputation of others, then congratulations, you are now able to recognize a fool. You are also able to recognize the kind of person you don't want to become.

This lesson is taken from Proverbs 18 from the Proverbs of Solomon. Like every chapter in this study, I recommend that you read the proverb before we dive into the study.

Proverbs 18:8

> [8] The words of a gossip are like choice morsels; they go down to a man's inmost parts.

In our weakness, we like to listen to rumors and gossip. We can easily find ourselves drawn to gossip magazines, columns, and news sources that specialize in rumors and gossip that may or may not have some basis in truth. It's interesting to peek into other peoples' private life where we normally can't see them, isn't it?

We should strive to resist rumors and gossip because they don't serve us. By definition, rumor and gossip may not have anything to do with the truth. It may simply detract from it, add to it, or inflate it. It may be based in truth but it starts to morph into some form of lie or negativity. Here are the definitions from *Merriam-Webster's Collegiate® Dictionary, 11th Edition.*

Rumor[2]

> 1: talk or opinion widely disseminated with no discernible source
>
> 2: a statement or report current without known authority for its truth
>
> 3: talk or report of a notable person or event

Gossip[3]

> 1: … companion, crony … a person who habitually reveals personal or sensational facts about others
>
> 2: rumor or report of an intimate nature …

Take, for example, two girlfriends gossiping about another girlfriend's husband. They may think she needs to leave her husband. They need to tend to their own life since he's not their husband, it not their relationship, and they are not walking in her shoes. They may not have all the details and could be spreading information that isn't true. Plus, it would hurt the girlfriend to know that her life was under such public scrutiny. That's a conversation best handled face-to-face if it's that important. Besides, friendships between two people have to be based on conversations deeper than gossiping about other people as if they were on a talk show.

I once worked with a woman who would periodically call with gossip about people in the office that I worked in. Oddly, she didn't even work in the same office I worked in — she was several states away! It made me suspicious that she would spend that kind of energy telling me about things

---

going on in an office she almost never visited. I guess if someone talks with enough people and gathers enough gossip, she can put some pieces together and make a story out of it. On top of that, this person never said anything good about someone without adding "but" on the end following it with something negative. For example: "He is smart, bright, and works hard, but he is negative and condescending." Notice how the positive was cancelled by the negative?

Subsequently, if I say Jane is a fantastic person, but she sleeps late, her hair is not always in place, and she dresses poorly, I am really saying that Jane's really not such a fantastic person. Be very careful about the "buts" in your life, whether they are in human form or verbal form. Stay away from even the most innocent-sounding gossip because it helps no one.

Gossip is a waste of mental and verbal energy and can affect our ability to make objective decisions. When encountering these situations, use your moral compass and your wisdom to consider all the facts. We must be honest with ourselves — are we letting personal feelings of like or dislike color our judgment instead of taking in the real information available? For example, say you manage a small group of people and you have to rank them for a bonus. Are you giving a higher ranking to someone you've heard good things about even though he isn't getting the job done over someone you've heard bad things about who performs noticeably better. Think how much better your decisions are if you have factual information.

Proverbs 18:11

> [11] The wealth of the rich is their fortified city; they imagine it an unscalable wall.

If I was writing this book during a strong economic climate, the lesson might have been a little different. However, I'm writing this in 2009 and 2010 when we have just left a horrific period in terms of diminished personal financial investments, failed real estate investment deals, bank failures, and a record number of people being put out of work. We haven't seen anything like this since the Great Depression in the 1930s. Add to that the schemes and scams that aided the tumble of the financial firms. Hence, it has become clear that wealth is not the strongest defense. If you think that, look at the people around you who have lost their retirement income or have seen it dramatically reduced to two-thirds or three-quarters of its original value.

Wealth is fleeting. Knowledge and wisdom are solid. The whole point of going through this transformation process with Proverbs is to gain wisdom and understand how to apply your knowledge to your situation. In the process, it helps you become more effective so you can make the world around you a better place.

In tough economic times, even hoarding money doesn't help because if the government is not able to stimulate the economy in certain ways, things can become dramatically worse. Remember, the U.S. dollar is only as strong as the government's desire to back it. It is not backed by gold or any other kind of precious commodity. It is backed by the will of the United States government and the people. If the official mechanism of the United States government decided, for whatever reason, it did not make sense to support the currency you currently have, it would have no value. So truthfully, the value that you can control is what is between your ears — the wisdom, ability to apply your knowledge, your moral compass, willingness to act ethically, keenness, and awareness of new sources of income beyond the job. You must keep your eyes open for new opportunities and trends.

So think for a minute about some of the exercises from previous chapters that led to you visualizing a better life. Think also about the things that you really love doing — that you're passionate about. Are there any of those that could use your creativity and lead to another stream of income?

Lastly, you have God to depend on, and God's power is never lost. God is always dependable and that security and safety comes from your prayer life, belief, and faith. Do not lose that. Continue to meditate day and night on that foundation so that it strengthens you as you fight these battles that life inevitably throws at you.

Proverbs 18:13-17

> [13] He who answers before listening that is his folly and his shame. [14] A man's spirit sustains him in sickness, but a crushed spirit who can bear? [15] The heart of the discerning acquires knowledge; the ears of the wise seek it out. [16] A gift opens the way for the giver and ushers him into the presence of the great. [17] The first to present his case seems right, till another comes forward and questions him.

These verses are truly a road map. They are guiding us to get the appropriate information before answering questions or making decisions. We need to have an open mind and be open to new ideas. We need to listen to both sides of a story so we can figure out where in the middle the truth actually lies.

When we do anything other than this, we open ourselves up for making grievous mistakes and errors in judgment or even worse, relying on gossip and innuendo to make decisions. Do you remember we started out talking about gossip? Gossip is a prejudicial view of things based on incorrect or insufficient information when it comes time to make a decision. We don't want to put ourselves in that position because it shows lack of wisdom, intelligent decision making, and character in many cases. This is particularly true for people who operate like that on a personal level where they hold grudges, pursue vendettas, and base their worldview on the way they want things to look which may not be accurate. It is critical that we get all or as many of the facts as possible before we act.

Proverbs 18:22

> [22] He who finds a wife finds what is good and receives favor from the LORD.

Even though it's written from the man's point of view, this verse says that marriage needs to be something that is treasured and enjoyed — not another burden. As someone who has been in a bad marriage that ended in divorce and is now in a quality relationship, the difference is plain as night and day. Having someone in your life who is a confidante, who is supportive, who you can share a laugh or a tear with is critical to your well-being and makes you well-rounded. However, until you find that type of person, you should actively seek this type of relationship.

Never settle for populating your life with negative, toxic people who will eventually sidetrack you from where you're trying to go in life. It's better to spend a little more time alone than to spend time with people who are destroying your dreams — I like to call them "mental vampires" because they suck the blood out of your life's vision. For a little more research on the topic of marriage, take a look at Proverbs 12:4, Proverbs 19:14, Proverbs 31:10-31, Proverbs 5:15-19, John 2:1-11, Ephesians 5:31-33, and Genesis 2:21-25.

As you continue in this study, make notes regarding the elements of your marriage that you would like to improve along with those that you appreciate because they are good. It is human nature to concentrate on the things that aren't right, but we also want to reinforce the things that are working well.

Proverbs 18:23

> [23] A poor man pleads for mercy, but a rich man answers harshly.

Regardless of our financial position, we should never look down on someone because of the amount of money that they may or may not have. I support several charitable causes; some are faith-related and some are not. I chose to support them because I understand first hand what it's like to run into some hard luck. I don't always have tolerance for people who have made and continue to make choices that make their luck worse. However, I haven't walked in their shoes, and I will not judge them.

Remember, no matter how much money anyone has, people are people. I will say that when I see television interviews where wealthy people are talking about poorer people or — to use some television lingo — "working class, poverty class, middle class." For some, it's easy to see their arrogance and condescension. It is clear they are looking down on the people who are economically below them, and they need to change their behavior. It makes me angry because there's not that much difference — particularly during tough economic times that can propel someone who was worth millions of dollars to being broke — between being wealthy and dropping to the "lower classes." We all have to remember that it's not the money but the blessing that we received that is the gift, and how we use it truly makes us rich.

Proverbs 18:24

> [24] A man of many companions may come to ruin, but there is a friend who sticks closer than a brother.

Everyone gets lonely at some point. Sometimes people feel disconnected or cut off from other people. We can be around a lot of people but still feel isolated. Sometimes it can increase the feeling of isolation to be around a lot of people who are enjoying one another when you're out of the mix. We all need close friends who are confidantes in good times or bad. It is better to have one real friend than many friends who are superficial acquaintances who really don't care about us. We need to cultivate relationships where we take the time to truly get to know one another.

The Mouth of a Fool Is a Hole Full of Trouble

Take a good look at who is around you. You should see people who need your friendship; and in return, you should need their friendship. Think about the places where you've made your closest friends. I have found that I've made some very good friends through church or other charitable activities. They are people I would not have met any other place. However, we found so much more in common through our interests. Our positive activities helped us forge stronger associations. They became close, caring friends who supported me when one of my parents passed away.

To form stronger relationships, find places where you can go regularly to serve. Not only are you serving where other like-minded people serve, but you are seeing them more frequently. It creates a bond between the volunteers. You could volunteer in a church, soup kitchen, neighborhood cleanup, or school project. There is something positive about being part of an initiative where everyone is headed in same direction.

You'll probably meet some people that you would rather not see. However, you'll always benefit when you work toward a common mission with good people who share common interests and positive energy. And listen carefully to those you spend time with. If you don't value what they have to say, why are you with them?

Never underestimate the power of words. Whether they are used for good or for evil, they can affect millions of lives. For example, Abraham Lincoln's "Gettysburg Address" and Martin Luther King's "I Have A Dream" speeches show the positive side of the coin. Now think of the damage done by evil leaders such as Hitler, Stalin, and Pol Pot. Don't forget that speech is a gift when used correctly, but it is a curse when used for evil. We have the ability to use it for both purposes; therefore, we have a choice of which path to take.

Proverbs 18:21

> [21] The tongue has the power of life and death, and those who love it will eat its fruit.

Our ability to speak is like our ability to breathe — we don't notice it unless it is taken away from us. The power of words themselves is also taken for granted unless they affect our life in some dramatically good or bad way. Our ability to communicate far beyond any other creature in the animal kingdom makes us unique and, no doubt, is part of the reason we are the dominant species on the planet.

Think of a courtroom, the United States Congress, the news media, movies, songs, books, or a leader addressing followers. Words are what make these places and events dynamic and powerful. The ability for ever-more complex but useful communication is wrapped around our ability to speak and understand. Communication can be auditory, oral, and ophthalmic. If you are blind and use Braille, then tactile communication becomes your mode of speaking. Four of our senses can be used to allow us to "speak."

Our words as parents and guardians shape the life of our children and those under our care. Our words or communication on a broader stage can bring peace or war. Think of all the great conflicts; without exception, there is a never-ending verbal and written justification for waging or engaging in war whether right or wrong.

Every well-known dictator (and even those who aren't well-known) engages in demonizing "the enemy" who, in most cases, turns out to be people who can't defend themselves from the aggression. Remember Rwanda in Africa? The Hutus verbally dehumanized the Tutsi to the point were 800,000 people were slaughtered. The same thing happened with Serbia, Croatia, Bosnia, Southeast Asia, the Taliban, and Al-Qaeda.

Stalin, Mao, and Hitler were masters that took the practice to levels unseen since their time, thank God. In fact, in his *Books That Changed the World,* Robert B. Downs stated that 125 people died for every word in Hitler's blood-drenched, sociopathic ramblings of *Mein Kamph.* Death and life are truly in the power of the tongue. Be careful who you listen to and what you say.

The Mouth of a Fool Is a Hole Full of Trouble

Action Steps on the Life Path

Are there areas in your own life where you are gossiping or not getting all the facts required to make a good decision? If so, spend two or three minutes writing about what you need to do to stop gossiping or get the correct information.

_____

_____

_____

_____

_____

_____

_____

Write down the names of your true friends.

_____

_____

_____

_____

Write down the names of people who are just acquaintances.

_____

_____

_____

_____

_____

What are some differences between your true friends and your acquaintances?

_____

_____

_____

_____

_____

_____

_____

What are some positive places in your community where you can regularly serve with people who are headed in a positive direction? It could be a church, your children's school, a soup kitchen, a community cleanup, or other volunteer activity.

_____

_____

_____

_____

_____

_____

_____

_____

_____

_____

_____

The Mouth of a Fool Is a Hole Full of Trouble

Reasons for Wealth and Poverty

"Listen to advice and accept instruction, and in the end you will be wise."

Proverbs 19:20

Proverbs 19 is from the collection of the Proverbs of Solomon. Proverbs would seem to be in conflict with its view of the poor and the rich if you only take the instruction at face value. However, as with any divinely inspired work, we must look for and understand the subtleties to grasp the deeper meaning. People who start out poor or rich by birth have no initial control over their condition. Conversely, some are poor because they have made decisions counter to accepting intelligent instruction and doing hard work.

Proverbs speaks to those who expand upon their condition and experience gained through hard work and education as noted in Proverbs 19:20. Whether you are living in a poor or rich environment, to experience abundance under your particular circumstances, you must do the best with what you have.

Proverbs 19:1

> [1] Better a poor man whose walk is blameless than a fool whose lips are perverse.

Our goal should be to lead a life that minimizes the amount of blame that can be attributed to us due to negative behavior. The reality is none of us are free of blame, but attempting to live that way only makes our life better. If it was easy and we knew the correct path all the time, we wouldn't need to study books and guides such as the Bible and Proverbs. But minimizing the negative impact that your life has on others is a valuable tool, and it is also one of the real concepts of true wealth along with wisdom.

Wanting to have it all right now leads us down the path to making bad decisions based on poor judgment and then suffering the negative consequences. I will do anything that I'm called upon to do to be successful except something that is immoral or unethical. It doesn't mean that you can't be a tough negotiator or a hard-nosed businessperson. However, it does mean ultimately if you're not being unethical, immoral, or personally toxic, you will end up being fair and operating ethically within the given situation. Cheating on taxes may not seem like a big item, but continuously making negative, unethical decisions will build up until the transgressions evolve into a lifestyle.

We need to carefully examine any behavior that leads us to cheating, stealing, refusing to give when it's appropriate, or being selfish and negative. Even the best of us commit errors in our life where we can examine behavior and look to correct it if necessary. Read and meditate on the Word, operate according to its principle, and set your priorities straight.

Proverbs 19:2

> [2] It is not good to have zeal without knowledge, nor to be hasty and miss the way.

I am definitely guilty of haste and, as a result, I have had to do major work in my life. I have made bad business investments and decisions. I've also loaned money because of a hasty, greedy attitude. Accordingly, I have stepped up my enthusiasm to remain positive and motivated.

Consequently, I stopped trying to be a one-man, people-salvage operation

Reasons for Wealth and Poverty

for people who had lack in their life. An example of someone who has lack is a friend who wants to borrow money or get you involved in his business idea; however, he has never shown any industriousness to move forward without someone giving him money that he consequently wasted. Those people always have a get-rich-quick business idea, but they just need you to give them some money to get it going. Regardless of whether they are a friend or family member, loaning them the money just results in a major disappointment. Instead, I help the needy through my charitable activities and support altruistic giving through the church and recognizable institutions (faith-based and non-faith-based). For me, they are a better channel of philanthropy.

We all are guilty of moving through life way too fast sometimes and then hurtling straight into the unknown. Sometimes that unknown turns out to be really ugly. One example of this is marrying someone without getting to know him or her. Love at first sight may work in the movies, but it frequently doesn't in real life.

More extreme examples of hasty, ill-advised decision making include getting involved in negative sexual relationships, gangs, and drug abuse. In the case of drugs, the decision might seem fabulous at first, but it seems a little bit less fabulous each time. As a result, the abuser has to take a little bit more each time to get that same effect. In the end, the abuser — or "junkie" — is not taking the drugs to feel good but instead to keep the pain away.

Even going into a career without evaluating whether the career or its environment is really suitable for us can be considered hasty. We have to ask if it is helping to fund the vision or the passion that we are pursuing? Are we simply taking a job that pays a lot of money instead of pursuing a passion or a personal vision?

Whatever decision you are making, take a good strong look at what you're getting ready to embark upon. Take a deep breath before taking action. It's important to do a little homework before you make important decisions in your life. You don't want to go down the wrong path regardless of whether it involves a personal relationship such as marriage or pursuing and staying steadfastly engaged in an unfulfilling, displeasing career strictly for the money. If you must work strictly for the money, make sure it will fund or lead to the career you are pursuing. In other words, it should fuel your vision and not your dysfunction.

Proverbs 19:8

> [8] He who gets wisdom loves his own soul; he who cherishes understanding prospers.

People who really care about appropriately conducting themselves do the things necessary to operate in a judicious manner. They care about themselves in the appropriate way, want to make the world around them a better place, and want to be a better person for their friends and family. They are willing to take the time to leverage knowledge with appropriate wisdom that can make those things happen.

Proverbs 19:11

> [11] A man's wisdom gives him patience; it is to his glory to overlook an offense.

When someone comes to you for guidance, don't try to "talk them to death" with advice. First, listen and let them emotionally unload without going on the defensive. Feelings are not always logical. So at first nod — even if you are not in agreement — hold back on your own possible feelings of resentment and anger as they can make you unintentionally inflame. Listening indicates you care about the relationship and value the friendship.

Proverbs 19:16-17

> [16] He who obeys instructions guards his life, but he who is contemptuous of his ways will die. [17] He who is kind to the poor lends to the LORD, and he will reward him for what he has done.

Proverbs 19:16 is talking about the Ten Commandments which are introduced biblically in Exodus 20. Obeying the word of God is something that preserves life. Disobedience is destructive. Proverbs 19:17 introduces the concept of being kind to the poor — better known as *loving your neighbor as yourself.* Loving your neighbor doesn't just refer to the person across the fence from your house. It also means tending to the needs of the poor, dispossessed, and defenseless wherever they may be. In the New Testament, visit Matthew 25:31-46. It shows how Jesus and God identified with the poor and dispossessed.

When looking at the Ten Commandments, notice the first three or four items in terms of loving God above all else, not worshiping false idols, keeping the Sabbath holy, and not taking the Lord's name in vain. These are things that lend themselves to the spiritual. Let's just think about the commandments in the practical sense for a moment.

For instance, consider these practical context of keeping the Sabbath holy. Think of the workaholics you know — people who are working seven days a week. Are they healthy people? There might be an occasional person who is somehow able to work seven days a week without taking a vacation or needing to take time off for his family or himself and still maintain his health. I don't personally know of any.

Everyone needs a rest day. Working five or six days a week is plenty of stress on the body. The body and the mind need an opportunity to recover. This is what the Sabbath is for. Not only that, but you need a day of rest so you can reconnect and re-engage with God and spend time contemplating the lessons from God's teachings as they are presented in the Bible. In other words, you need to spiritually recharge your batteries.

The commandments are really smart ways to live amongst your neighbors and stay out of trouble. Let's explore some more commandments:

- Honor your father and your mother. This is a good thing no matter what issues you have with your parents. The majority of parents are not perfect; but if they gave you life and took reasonable care of you, be thankful and forget about the other stuff. It's a tremendous responsibility to care for another human being. Be grateful someone owned up to that responsibility.

- Adultery. Whether that adultery is in a marriage or in a committed relationship, it doesn't get you anywhere but into more unconstructive situations. It does not work to bring the damaging influence of peripheral romantic relationships into your committed relationship.

- Stealing. We're not talking about grabbing an apple or a piece of bread because you're starving and near death. Nor are we talking about those extreme cases where people take things because they are in desperate straits. Instead, we're talking about stealing things because of want or desire. Regardless of how bad someone wants something, shoplifting is still a crime. Taking something from someone's house while they are visiting them is criminal. Cheating on taxes is criminal. No matter what excuse someone comes up with for stealing someone else's property, it is still engaging in criminal behavior.

- Lying. There are all kinds of lies. We don't have to be involved in unscrupulous behavior like adultery and theft to find ourselves needing to cover up discretions and protect ourselves. Even those little "white" lies where we are trying to keep from hurting someone's feelings with the truth are still lies. Some people just lie to shade the truth and make themselves look or sound better. If you lie in court, that's perjury and it's punishable. It seems logical that we can get away with a lot of other lies though, doesn't it? However, continued non-stop lying is a self-perpetuating way to get into trouble. It also can eventually destroy relationships. I've gotten caught up in lies and damaged important relationships in my life. In a couple of cases, they caused permanent damage.

- Envy and jealousy. Don't covet your neighbor, your neighbor's wife, or your neighbor's property. In biblical times, wives were viewed more as property. Envy is viewed the same as stealing in God's eyes. Forget about coveting someone else's property or achievement — you can create your own opportunity. Learn from others but focus on what you can do to achieve your own dream life.

Proverbs 19:23

> ^{23} The fear of the LORD leads to life: Then one rests content, untouched by trouble.

I'm not suggesting that if you say, "I'm afraid of God," you are going to be safe and secure and nothing bad is ever going to happen. Fear of the Lord doesn't always keep us protected from trouble in life. Evil and bad things happen to people who love God. This verse is not a promise that you will be protected. Instead, this is more of a general guideline — an all-purpose way of looking at your devotion to God's word — because if the world was a place where everyone followed God's word, you would be safe from trouble. Use this verse as instruction relating to your personal responsibility, how you interact with the world around you, and how you utilize and meditate on the power of the Word. When we allow fear of the Lord to shape how we conduct ourselves, we find it easier to operate ethically and morally. The world is a place that provides opportunity for you, but you will periodically run into roadblocks and speed bumps. Fear of the Lord will provide the framework to overcome those obstacles.

Reasons for Wealth and Poverty

Remember, this series is not a formula for perfection. It is a formula for negotiating life and getting the most out of life while weathering the storms that inevitably come up.

Proverbs 19:25

> [25] Flog a mocker, and the simple will learn prudence; rebuke a discerning man, and he will gain knowledge.

I do not know one single person who cannot accept constructive criticism that performs up to their ability. Remember, criticism in and of itself is not negative — it's just feedback. If a person is not taking good advice, it indicates their mind is not open, therefore, they are probably not living a prosperous, balanced life. They may be able to eek out success in one avenue, but they can't achieve it across their professional, personal, and spiritual lives.

We should welcome well-intentioned, constructive criticism. To grow, we need to be able to process information about our behavior. The only way we can discern valid criticism is by listening carefully for the message.

Let's end this chapter with the advice that most of life's challenges are dealt with in biblical teaching. Proverbs 19:27 says, "Stop listening to instruction, my son, and you will stray from the words of knowledge." Listening to instruction regarding practical living makes perfect sense and will work toward your good.

Proverbs is not a step-by-step manual like those that you might buy to learn how to invest in real estate, trade stocks, get an Internet date, or any of the other parts of modern life. What it will do is give you the tools to discern the wisest and best choice to make for all concerned.

Action Steps on the Life Path

Write down three to five troubling areas where you want to make changes in your life. If you improve those areas of your life, in what way will your life be different?

_____

_____

_____

_____

_____

_____

_____

Take ten minutes to create a plan to tackle one of those areas. First, create the goal. Next, develop the steps that it will take to get there. Finally, come up with a time line associated with each of those steps.

For example, your goal might be to lose twenty pounds. The steps might include walking thirty minutes each day, writing down all the food you eat, and cutting your daily intake to 1,500 calories. Other steps might include taking the stairs to your office instead of the elevator or adding a weight-training routine to your schedule. Your time line could include a start date for each of those steps and also certain weight-loss markers. A goal is not reached without all the steps and habit changes that support the goal.

_____

_____

_____

_____

_____

_____

_____

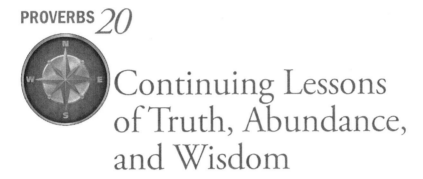

PROVERBS 20

Continuing Lessons of Truth, Abundance, and Wisdom

"Gold there is, and rubies in abundance, but lips
that speak knowledge are a rare jewel."

Proverbs 20:15

This chapter focuses on Proverbs 20 from the Proverbs of Solomon. In it, you will read verses that seem at first to be haphazard, but the message is consistent with the chapter title. Truth is one area the chapter touches on. Truth is not just retelling an event as it happened. It is also fulfilling responsibilities, completing commitments, and being trustworthy. Faithfulness has always been a rare quality whether in biblical stories or everyday life.

Another area this chapter touches on is wisdom. The best reinforcement tool for wisdom is failure, and failure prevents arrogance. If everything you did was a success, not only would there be no living with you, but you couldn't help anyone who had to overcome struggle because you had never experienced one. Failure is God's way to provoke us be introspective and reflective. As Proverbs 20:30 says, "Blows and wounds cleanse away evil, and beatings purge the inmost being." Our life is a test but one we can pass and enjoy along the way.

Proverbs 20:3

> [3] It is to a man's honor to avoid strife, but every fool is quick to quarrel.

A person who is truly confident does not go about bullying and looking for fights. At various points in our life, we have more confidence than others. Depending upon our early experiences as children, we may have to build that confidence up through trial, error, and experience. That is a normal part of growing up. However, someone who bullies others is troubled.

Fighting and picking fights are symptoms of negative internal issues that need attention. Obviously, this is not a productive use of time, whether the fighting is physical or verbal. Many times, the verbal fighting is even worse because of the cascading negativity that it brings with it. Some people might learn their lesson quicker with the physical fighting — after a couple of beatings, they start looking for ways to change their behavior. It doesn't work for someone to start fights just because he thinks he is bigger and stronger than someone else. Eventually, someone will give him the pain he was looking to give someone else.

Resourceful intelligent people look for ways to avoid fighting and retaliation. Retaliation never accomplishes anything. Look at areas such as the Middle East where they have endured centuries of continual fighting amongst various groups. The fighting only stops after everyone sits down and decides that it doesn't matter who got in the last punch. Only then, do they move ahead and attempt to negotiate their way out of it, which then leads to an era of peace. Holding on to grudges and vendettas never works for anything but increasing weapons sales.

To look at it from a more definitive point of view, one of the characteristics of a fool is someone who seems to find it very difficult to stay out of trouble. People of wisdom and character who understand how they should conduct themselves ethically and morally seem to avoid these pitfalls more times than not.

Consequently, you need to ask yourself, "Which kind of person am I?" Do you need to initiate trouble to prove a point? Do you fly off the handle

Continuing Lessons of Truth, Abundance, and Wisdom

quickly? Are you holding grudges? If someone offends you, do you find yourself still wanting to get back at them after the incident has long since passed? Do you need to retaliate? Are you planning ways to retaliate later, or are you more into immediate retaliation? If so, you are heading down a dangerous road. It isn't healthy to carry the negative energy required to lash out against someone. Are you hurting someone as a result? Or are you hurting you?

I had a grudge against someone from the time we were pre-teens. I didn't like him, and he didn't like me. I can't even remember what the issue was. However, I remember seeing this person ten or fifteen years later. When I saw him, we just passed and waved to each other. It was odd because I felt the old negative energy come in, and I had to stop myself. I thought to myself, "I'm in my late twenties (or thirties) now. Why am I angry about something from ten to fifteen or maybe more years ago when I can't remember what prompted it?"

It was an eye opener for me that I could still be angry at this guy. It just seemed ridiculous to gather up negative energy against someone I see maybe once every decade — about something that I wasn't able to recall. If it sounds stupid to you, that's because it is. I was being a fool by even extending myself in this manner. Who knows what kind of person he is as an adult. I would hope that he is better than he was as a teenager and, thank goodness, I'm a better person than I was back then.

Do you have areas of your life where you're carrying grudges — either on purpose or not, but maybe just the negative energy is still there? If so, you need to disperse that energy. Forgive yourself, forgive them, and move on. Everyone is most likely at a different place and time than they were years past. Live in the present. We must stop living where we can't make any changes. We can't change what happened in the past, and we must move on.

Proverbs 20:4

> ⁴ A sluggard does not plow in season; so at harvest time he looks but finds nothing.

Do you remember the old saying, "If you don't prepare properly, you will fail your failure test." Unless you are just blessed with only having to read through something once to "ace" a test, you will have to study and work at it. If you don't plan properly for a financial crisis, then you'll end up broke most likely, and you won't have any money when you need it. There are some who believe that planning shows a lack of faith in God. However, having faith in God does not mean that you cannot or should not anticipate and prepare for certain needs in the future.

I remember I was listening to the sermon of a well-known preacher. She said carrying around extra money in your wallet showed a lack of faith that God would look out for you. Even though her messages were very good and helpful and her ministry did a lot of good work, I disagreed with what she was saying here. As with anything else, you just can't blindly accept what other people say because we are all capable of being wrong — whether someone is anointed to speak God's word and principles or not. This preacher's message made no sense to me.

I keep a little extra cash in my wallet and some in my pocket (just in case I lose my wallet) for emergencies, but I don't go to extremes. If I'm stuck somewhere, I would like to be able to get a meal and get in out of the rain. Sometimes things happen and you need a few extra dollars on hand. There is nothing that says that God does not want you to anticipate any of your future needs and does not want you to prepare for them. It does not show lack of faith. In fact, you're actually going against God's word by not anticipating your needs — whether it's retirement needs or some other type of planning.

There are things that you need to do that are very specific to living in the world. A faith-based person needs to make sure he is putting his faith in God first; but that does not relieve his responsibility of proper planning. If someone doesn't believe in planning, why even send children to school if God is going to take care of them and we don't have to worry about them? We don't want to be overly concerned to the exclusion of our faith about worldly things; but we do need to properly plan for the future and educate ourselves so we can be successful. In short, the person who is too lazy, silly, ridiculous, and foolish to plan or act responsibly shouldn't expect God to show up. That's not the point of biblical principle. God will do His part, but we're also expected to do our part.

For instance, say that you need to look at your credit report because the last time you saw it, there were some things you needed to take care of but you hadn't yet. It's worth the trouble to do it now because you may want to make a major purchase in the future. If you have credit problems, you may have to pay a higher interest rate or worse yet, be denied the loan.

It's easy to procrastinate on life's irritating little details when they are not urgent or have a deadline — no matter how important they are. Look at your life and make note of three to five things that you can take care of in the next thirty days that have been sitting on the back burner. Once you determine what they are, I think you'll realize that addressing them has nothing to do with faith or God or anything else. It has to do with cleaning out your personal closet. As the author and motivational speaker Brian Tracy says, "Eat that frog," and stop procrastinating.

Proverbs 20:9

[9] Who can say, "I have kept my heart pure; I am clean and without sin"?

Sin is one of those words that has a charged element to it. Much of how we view it comes from how we were socialized in childhood and whether we were raised as a Christian or in another religion. One of the barriers that interferes with moving ahead in life and prospering in the personal, business, and spiritual spheres is that we hold ourselves back through self-defeating thoughts and actions.

Lets explore the definition of *sin*[4] from *Merriam-Webster's Collegiate® Dictionary, 11th Edition*:

1 a: an offense against religious or moral law b: an action that is or is felt to be highly reprehensible <it's a sin to waste food> c: an often serious shortcoming: fault

2 a: transgression of the law of God b: a vitiated state of human nature in which the self is estranged from God

For me, sin also means deliberately turning our back on something that is ethically and morally clear for the sake of convenience or momentary pleasure. Hence, we are committing offense against or transgressing the law of God and the temporal authorities depending upon the crime. We all have sinful thoughts and actions; and we all need to continually cleanse our

---

[4] By permission. From *Merriam-Webster's Collegiate® Dictionary, 11th Edition* ©2010 by Merriam-Webster, Incorporated (www.Merriam-Webster.com).

minds of these things. I'm thankful that my relationship with God allows me both to forgive others and forgive myself, therefore allowing God to forgive me.

If I would like to confess what I do wrong, I confess out loud and make active note of actions not following that principle. It allows me to highlight my behavior. In doing so, I am basically putting myself in a position where I'm called to account for things either on a personal or a group level. Under the right circumstances, it can serve as a way of continuing to modify behavior according to the teachings in this book. I also listen to recordings of sermons and spiritual teachings as learning and reinforcement tools.

Some may use some form of counseling to accomplish the same thing. Be very careful with counseling that you don't go into "rent-a-friend" mode. If you do decide to move ahead with it then consider using only a licensed professional counselor instead if you are truly having personal or relationship issues. It can provide the proper forum in which to address your issues. If you do not have a spiritual relationship with a faith-based advisor, I would encourage you to develop one.

Proverbs 20:23

> [23] The LORD detests differing weights, and dishonest scales do not please him.

This unmistakably refers to a merchant "loading the scales" in order to cheat customers. Dishonesty can be a very difficult sin or transgression to steer clear of — especially when it is convenient, self-gratifying, or self-enriching. Ultimately, it is self-defeating.

Some people find it easy to be pious and holy when the spotlight is on but may not follow the right path when they are out of sight. Some may think it might not hurt anyone to "load the scales" a little bit here or there, but it does over time in a cumulative manner. Moreover, the corrosive dishonesty affects people at the center of who they are. They end up being able to justify to themselves why it's okay to commit bigger crimes. Initially, it is difficult for people who fall into that pattern of dishonesty to clean up their act, but it is possible.

Wise people do the right thing even when no one is watching and when it isn't easy or convenient. I haven't always been the best that I can be, and

I'm still trying to be better. Leading a life based on judicious principles is a journey. Are there any areas of your life where you are not being as honest as you should be? Have you promised something you have not provided? Think about those areas of your life in need of improvement. Then, prioritize them and start to take a look at how you can best turn things around. Be honest with yourself.

Proverbs 20:24

> [24] A man's steps are directed by the LORD. How then can anyone understand his own way?

Sometimes you need to just let things unfold around you and continue staying focused on where you want to go. After over twenty years of working in business, I have been in work situations where I wasn't happy, wasn't treated fairly, or something else was wrong. Sometimes we go through things and don't understand why we're going through them. We may think the event is unfair and there will be massive amounts of negativity associated with it. However, we need to go through those tough experiences because they are making us better and smarter. Perhaps you were reprimanded unfairly, singled out for punishment when you did nothing wrong, or given the worst assignment. When we have faith, we learn to understand that sometimes we have to endure the hardship and inequity of the trouble as it will lead us to an improved place.

Proverbs 20:25

> [25] It is a trap for a man to dedicate something rashly and only later to consider his vows.

This verse warns us to not make promises unless we intend to keep them. It is very easy to promise to do something, and then back off on it later after thinking it through. Unfortunately, that is being dishonest. Now we may have good intentions and we're not necessarily intending to be deceitful, but it is still being dishonest. Don't make promises until you've thought about what you're promising.

In Judges 11:30-31, Jephthah said to the Lord, "If you give me victory over the Ammonites, I will give to the Lord whatever comes out of my house to meet me when I return in triumph. I will sacrifice it as a burnt offering."

The first thing he saw was his daughter. Talk about a rash promise! It's better not to make rash promises than to not to keep them. Think through the ramifications of your promises before you make them. Jesus says in Matthew 5 that God doesn't want you to make promises you don't intend to keep because God understands that promises can be very difficult to keep particularly if they entail great sacrifice.

So remember, just making promises along the way and then determining whether or not to keep them based on convenience does no one any good. Stop, think, and then make your promise ... or not. Proverbs 20:6 says, "Many a man claims to have unfailing love, but a faithful man who can find?" People who outshine the crowd keep their word. They are reliable and can be counted on to do what they say they'll do when they say they will do it. So they surpass others in the crowd because people of integrity are rare in our society.

Action Steps on the Path of Life

Review some areas of your life that you want to improve. Are you doing enough in the financial area — maybe in terms of saving for retirement or an emergency? Also, take a look at your personal life. Are you maintaining a healthy lifestyle? Are you spending enough time with your family? Are you executing on your family responsibilities? Take a look across the different areas. Don't spend a huge amount of time on one area. Rather, write down the ones you feel are most important so you can come back to flesh them out later.

_____

_____

_____

_____

_____

_____

_____

_____

_____

What are three to five things that you have been procrastinating on that you can take care of in the next thirty days?

_____

_____

_____

_____

_____

_____

Take a look at your interactions with the people in your life. Are you being as involved in your marriage or committed relationship as you could be? Are you being as honest at work as you could be? Are you being as sincere in the other relationships in your life as you could be? Anywhere you're involved with other people, evaluate whether you are being as ethical and moral as you could be. Have you promised that you would do something but haven't? Do you consider promising something that you haven't done to be lying when you don't complete it? Make note of those areas where you can do better.

_____

_____

_____

_____

_____

_____

_____

_____

_____

_____

_____

_____

_____

_____

_____

_____

_____

_____

_____

_____

PROVERBS *21*

Doing the Right Thing Is a Blessing

"He who pursues righteousness and love finds life, prosperity, and honor."

Proverbs 21:21

To make the correct decision in a given circumstance, we have to recognize the correct thing to do. A fool may not know how to use wealth properly — particularly in the case of a dissolute individual who inherited his money. Fools have no true appreciation of the value of what they possess, so they cannot make the right choices concerning it. Never having felt the pain of financial lack or poor financial decision making, they can be of no active value in helping others do the right thing. Today's lesson comes from Proverbs 21 of the Proverbs of Solomon. In this lesson, you will see foolish, wealth-destroying behavior highlighted in the teachings.

Proverbs 21:1-2

> [1] The king's heart is in the hand of the LORD; he directs it like a watercourse wherever he pleases. [2] All a man's ways seem right to him, but the LORD weighs the heart.

Even though the principles of Proverbs are principles of using wisdom, acquiring knowledge, and using those principles to direct your life, it is important to have an ethical and moral compass in making decisions. Those of faith believe that God is in command of everything. The important thing to realize is that no one person is an island. There are effects that go on outside of ourselves that most recognize as unexplainable except by the hand of a supreme being.

We make a point of following certain directives and utilizing certain principles in these lessons, but let's not forget that there is more to life than just ourselves. Whether you are the dishwasher or the emperor, there are powers at work far greater than just you and your particular wants and needs. Even when we are able to put ourselves in a situation where we're in control, events in life may happen to take us out of that control and remind us that we are just flesh and blood.

Proverbs 21:2

> [2] People may be right in their own eyes, but the Lord examines their heart.

Think about actions you or someone you know have taken that could be insincere. For instance, let's just take a fairly routine custom. When Christmas comes, don't we all expect a gift? In fact, there are not many pleasures better than receiving a gift you like from someone that you like. In reverse, I would like to think that there are not many pleasures greater than giving a present that shows appreciation to someone that you like. However, isn't there something unsettling, distasteful, and insincere about receiving a gift from people who feel they are obligated to give us presents but who also expect something in return?

I'm grateful when people give me anything — particularly if it took energy and expense. However, I would like to have received it because they wanted to give a present and not because they have an ulterior motive. I have been guilty of doing that and perhaps you have been too. It's particularly prevalent at work where exchanging gifts is expected. It's wonderful to give a gift to a child, because even though they might expect a Christmas gift, they genuinely appreciate the fact that someone gave them something. It is heart-warming to see them so wrapped up in the joy of Christmas. We experience the opposite effect when we see someone acting with insincerity.

I used Christmas as an example because it has become a very commercialized

Doing the Right Thing Is a Blessing

holiday and has moved away from much of its original meaning. It's important that we examine our actions and motivations. If we are being insincere, we must strive to evaluate why. Think through some of your important work or personal relationships where you might not be conducting yourself in a sincere manner. Is there some reason you're forcing yourself to be untruthful in your interaction with them? Sometimes we end up in that position because their behavior causes us to react that way to them.

It's important to learn to recognize it and evaluate the motivations for our actions when we find ourselves in this position. We need to ask ourselves, "Is it critical that I act this way? Am I manipulating or being manipulated for self-gain that has no greater good to it?" This is a tricky question, but we need to be as honest about our interactions with other people as we can. Think about the associations that you have in your professional or personal life and the people that you spend time with. Ask yourself, "Am I doing the best that I can do? Am I being as truthful and sincere as I can be in my interaction with them?" It's important to examine these situations because God is not pleased with insincerity. He knows our hearts and is not pleased when we do good deeds only to receive something from someone in return.

Proverbs 21:3

> ³ To do what is right and just is more acceptable to the LORD than sacrifice.

We give in many ways. People in ancient times offered a sacrifice. Today, we donate money or volunteer time to our church or charity. If we are only doing it solely to get something back from God, He knows we are being insincere. God knows our heart — and He judges us based on our heart and not on our actions. If we are doing things to win favor with those around us, our motive exposes itself over time. Remember the old adage coined by Abraham Lincoln: "You can fool some of the people all of the time, and all of the people some of the time, but you can not fool all of the people all of the time." If you are around people on a continual basis, it eventually becomes apparent if they are deceitful in their interactions with you.

Proverbs 21:5 and 21:20

⁵ The plans of the diligent lead to profit as surely as haste leads to poverty.

²⁰ In the house of the wise are stores of choice food and oil, but a foolish man devours all he has.

Proverbs 21:5 speaks to the faithful completion of whatever task we take on. And completion in real life is a great accomplishment. Being workers who diligently and competently do what we need to do and are interested in executing our responsibilities faithfully does not necessarily come naturally to all people. It's a result of character development and, in some cases, upbringing. In other cases, the upbringing was flawed, but the character was developed in other ways.

It's not good to look for shortcuts when taking the longer road will provide more benefit. For example, if someone is fifty to one hundred pounds overweight, she can take diet drugs and lose the weight in a reasonably small number of weeks. However, that puts a strain on her system and can endanger her life.

In this case, the longer road is a slower, safer weight-loss plan that produces longer-lasting results. It requires adjusting eating habits by eating smaller portions, avoiding processed foods, and eating more fresh fruits and vegetables. Additionally, she could start an exercise program that may begin with walking or other low-stress, calorie-burning methods. Then, she could work her way up to running, cycling, or weight lifting. Instead of losing the weight so quickly and running a great risk of gaining it all back because her habits haven't changed, she loses two or three pounds a week to achieve her goal in six to nine months. The benefit she gains on the long road is new habits she crafted that create a lifestyle where she keeps the excess weight off naturally. Using the quick method most likely leads to a yo-yo effect of regaining and losing and regaining the weight.

Shortcuts are often inefficient in the long run as the previous example illustrates. In addition, not thinking through shortcuts can persistently lead us down paths we don't want to go down. The direction they lead often prevents us from making wise choices. Because we're trying to find a shortcut, we're not gaining the knowledge from doing the work diligently.

Examine how you perform your tasks and work. Are you putting yourself into it? When we put the most into it, we often find ourselves in a position to demand the most out of it. Think of someone who is lazy or — to use the proverbial term — a sluggard. Isn't it much more difficult for the sluggard to take a stand sincerely? Imagine if such a person would demand that he deserves a raise at work. He would have to be in a state of denial or massively delusional to make such a demand of the company. To do so would basically place him in a job-threatening position. At the least, he risks the embarrassment of being told how incompetent he truly is. He will probably find out how differently his supervisor views his performance.

Proverbs 21:20 speaks about saving for the future. The person who navigates through life looking for one shortcut after another does not have the future in mind. Just look at the way that we live now in a world of easy credit that has put many people in bankruptcy, the desire for easy money, and the infomercials that sell products that provide the two-day work week. All we have to do is buy the latest system or join the latest get-rich-quick scheme, and the wealth is ours instantaneously! Now, that is not to say that investments that require timing and savvy don't periodically yield a fast turnaround of profit. There is nothing wrong with this as long as they are legitimate and legal and they do not hurt other people. The problem comes when someone tries to make a living by continually looking for a fast buck — a shortcut — and when people stop asking questions about their suspect methods.

When we think of this topic, some of the great scandals of 2008 and 2009 come to mind — the Bernie Madoff investment scam, the Stanford investment scam, and the "robber baron" behavior of many of the CEOs of the companies needing "bail-out" money. A great number of wealthy people were willing to invest their money but were not willing to investigate the investment opportunity thoroughly enough.

I'm sure Mr. Madoff did not tell his wealthy investors that he had a dishonest scheme. He must have painted a picture of a reputable company and presented statements to investors. However, any intelligent perusal of statements and the books would have revealed his illegal activities. I'm basing this on the news reports from responsible periodicals that did just that after he was caught. Evidently, that financial oversight was not in place and intelligent business people under normal circumstances would have known better. I guess the money kept coming, and they stopped asking questions. Eventually, the last sucker buys. When suckers stopped buying, the house of cards started falling.

So the lesson here is to use the diligence that you apply at work or in whatever endeavors you're engaged in, and understand that credit is something to be used extremely wisely. Using consumer credit for creature comforts that produce no gain makes no sense. This is why I recommend that if you are going to have long-term, extended credit, it needs to be based around an investment (such as your home) that makes the most sense. At least with a home, you have roof over your head.

Remember, when you spend all you have, you're spending more than you can afford. A wise person always puts money aside for the hard times when things go wrong. Things will always happen such as the economy declining or investments going down.

Proverbs 21:31

> [31] The horse is made ready for the day of battle, but victory rests with the LORD.

Preparing for life is like preparing for battle. Probably like you, some days I have gone to work feeling like I was preparing for battle. When we prepare for life, it means we do the things necessary to live. A lot of people say, "Well, God will provide," or "Somehow it will work out," and that's true up to a point. But God's provision doesn't absolve you of your responsibility to do what is necessary to move forward. God blesses plans that are in His will — not no planning at all.

If you want to become a physician, you need to go to school. You need to learn to read, write, and interact in a classroom situation, take care of patients, and do the end work, calculations, and research necessary. Someone can't do all the things required to become a physician if she never gets an education or drops out of high school. If somebody wants to serve the greater good in the legal arena, he must decide that watching hours of game shows and court TV makes no sense. Instead, he must choose to study to become a lawyer and benefit society by helping others as an employee of the court system.

Even though we believe that God controls the outcome, it does not take away our responsibility to do what we need to do to prepare for the future. If you do your part, then God will aid you to accomplish the purpose. Making the necessary preparations will allow you to accomplish the mission that you set forth. If you want to go live comfortably in a foreign

Doing the Right Thing Is a Blessing

country, then you need to learn the language and the customs. If you aren't independently wealthy or retired and living on savings, you'll need to figure out how much money you'll need to live abroad and how you'll pay your expenses there.

Preparing for battle — preparing for life in today's times — comes back to working as diligently as you can. It also means not taking on excessive debt and credit that will end up controlling your life. As Proverbs 22:7 says, "The borrower is servant to the lender."

Think through your needs for your future plans. If you want to be a successful certified financial planner, you'll need to get the necessary training and certifications. If you already have the certifications and are working in that role, you'll need to build a healthy client base. If you want to be a successful salesperson, you'll need to develop skills and strategies to grow your business. If you're an independent business owner, you need to acquire the skills and tools necessary to be a successful entrepreneur, grow your business, and serve your customers.

We all know people who are certain that the only reason they are not successful is that it is everyone else's fault. When they have that point of view, they stand a good chance of failing. In order to turn themselves around and prepare for the future, the first thing they need to do is to get rid of the "stinking thinking."

Let's sum up the chapter by reinforcing that successful people do the right thing because they have acquired and use wisdom to manage their personal life, family life, community associations, and their money. In regard to their finances, they learn to live on less than they make, and they properly invest the difference. They make a budget so they will know where their money goes and conscientiously plan if they decide they want to invest it in a different direction.

Action Steps on the Life Path

"Preparing for battle" is much like writing an award-winning novel. You probably don't start out as a great writer. You build your expertise through practice and study. Likewise, the novel isn't written in one sitting. It is written a page or more a day and most likely follows an outline that details the plot. There will also be many edits along the way. And many writers are also speakers so they must get training to speak to groups. Some join a Toastmasters Club to develop the skills.

What are some ways that you can prepare for battle so you can move forward in life? Are there some places you can conserve money? What could you do at work to advance? Do you have any professional development needs that you could address through special training or coaching? Think through this exercise carefully. Your life is worth it.

What are some non-essential consumer items you'd like to have? How can you save money for those rather than putting them on a credit card?

PROVERBS *22*

What the Wise Have to Say

"Humility and the fear of the Lord bring wealth and honor and life."

Proverbs 22:4

Today's lesson comes from Proverbs 22 of the Proverbs of Solomon. As I re-read this chapter — in particular the first five verses — it suddenly dawned on me that when we follow proverbial and biblical wisdom, we take full responsibility for our behavior while being guided by our Creator. I'm mentioning it because it's a rare occurrence to find people who are willing to take complete responsibility for their actions. In fact, quite the opposite seems to be true. Everyone at times feels as if he or she is a victim of something or someone.

You've heard excuses and complaints. The government isn't doing enough. It's too big and is doing too much. The concept is too abstract. It's the parents who are at fault. I attended the wrong school. I wasn't popular. It's society's fault. There's no need for anyone to feel bad for not taking responsibility for his or her life because we can find people to blame anywhere and everywhere.

Proverbs 22:1-5

> [1] A good name is more desirable than great riches; to be esteemed is better than silver or gold. [2] Rich and poor have this in common: The LORD is the Maker of them all. [3] A prudent man sees danger and takes refuge, but the simple keep going and suffer for it. [4] Humility and the fear of the LORD bring wealth and honor and life. [5] In the paths of the wicked lie thorns and snares, but he who guards his soul stays far from them.

There are many lessons we can apply to our life in Proverbs 22:1-7. Proverbs 22:1-4 contain general observations that reiterate that fear of God (listening to His Word) leads to wealth, a good name, and a long life. If you think about the world in which these verses were written, they would have been really applicable to an obedient Jew or Israelite living in Solomon's time. However, those lessons are still relevant today. Acquiring wealth, particularly according to the biblical principles, is very desirable. If used properly, wealth affords comfort and security that poverty does not. Additionally, it allows you to benefit your community financially.

In a non-economic sense, your honor or your good name is a form of wealth. One reason that people instinctively attack someone's good name to discredit them is because they understand its value. The attacker instinctively knows that breaking down someone's honor can be a means to turn other people against them in hopes that those people will change sides.

The last part of Proverbs 22:4 speaks to life. Most of us would all like a long, healthy life. Those of us who are living according to the biblical insight and knowledge of Proverbs — a clean living regime and the discipline associated with that — can generally expect to live a healthy life unless there are extraordinary events that interfere with our health. But even when this happens, our immune systems are strong and help us to fight the battle.

We should make a practice of looking forward. Proverbs 22:1-4 point toward living a better life, thinking ahead, and not living in the past. Time and again, we approach our life as a file cabinet — looking backward while trying to live forward. Instead, we should be thinking forward. The file cabinet should only be used for storing lessons learned — not for attempts to recreate the past as we move into the future. We are always looking for a brighter future. We have the guide map and the compass already, but we need to have the good sense to use them. The discipline of acquiring knowledge and using it wisely according to proverbial wisdom is the success formula. In fact, it's the method I use.

Proverbs 22:6

> [6] Train [a] a child in the way he should go, and when he is old he will not turn from it.

At a recent men's spiritual retreat, one of the main philosophical questions that we wrestled with was "How should we raise our children?" Much of the program also centered on being a good role model. Eventually, the discussion turned to "How do we protect them from harm?" We want to protect our loved ones and our children from harm, but we probably can't prevent them from making mistakes! We can only provide them a road map. As adults, we decide along the way whether or not to use it. You can only put them on the road — you cannot live the road for them.

This verse is not about protecting your children from making a mistake. It serves as a guide to parents who should be discerning about the capabilities, strengths, and weaknesses that God has given each child. Notice faith is the foundation. Good parents should take in account the strengths and weaknesses of their individual children as they apply the teachings.

Whether you have children or not, you may serve as a role or behavior model to children you encounter — whether you know it or not. Some we influence only briefly, but our effect can be profound. Likewise, we need to realize the influence that other people can have on our own children. Spend time with your children so you are the most influential person in their life. Talk to teachers, other parents, relatives, and grandparents because they are tools to help you better understand and develop the individual capabilities of your children. Children, of course, have self-directing tendencies and a will of their own. However, while they are under your care, you must seize the opportunity to guide that self-will and stop it if it becomes self-destructive. You can't outsource the task of being a role model to athletes and celebrities. It's the parent's job.

Being good parents and being involved in our children's life doesn't mean we need to watch everything they do every second. As a parent, caring for their needs often means working to financially support their requirements, and that necessitates being away from home. We can't always be there, which is the reason we teach them the difference between right and wrong along with teaching them good decision-making skills.

We should avoid trying to make choices for our children where they can make their own choices. Different ages are ready to make different choices. They can start with the smaller, easier choices and gradually learn to make bigger ones as they mature. This practice ultimately gives them the ability and the power to wield intelligent decision-making skills. Through practice, they understand how to process the knowledge and the evidence of the world around them and wisely come to a decision. In most cases, the decision will be a wise one and will move them forward in their development. Sometimes they will make mistakes, but they will grow from them as they recover from errors in judgment.

Proverbs 22:7

[7] The rich rule over the poor, and the borrower is servant to the lender.

This scripture does not mean that you should never borrow money. However, it serves to caution us against unnecessarily borrowing money. It is best to utilize cash and save to purchase everything — particularly if you have uncertain financial circumstances or you're undisciplined with credit. Even for big-ticket items such as a home, you will benefit from waiting until you have saved enough to put down a more substantial down payment. A conservative fifteen or thirty-year mortgage for a reasonably priced home is a legitimate reason to borrow money.

Are you thinking about buying a new big-screen television on credit, purchasing new furniture instead of steam cleaning your current set, or replacing the perfectly good, working set of appliances you have now because you don't like the way they look anymore? Avoid the temptation, and save your money so you can pay cash — if you really need to have an extravagant item. Consider spending more time doing something besides watching television shows and commercials.

This scripture is guiding us toward intelligent stewardship and management of our financial resources. Credit is not a benefit unless it is used wisely. Be very careful when you borrow money whether it's a credit card or an outright loan. When we use it, we become a servant to the person or institution that we are borrowing from.

Proverbs 22:12-16

[12] The eyes of the Lord keep watch over knowledge, but he frustrates the words of the unfaithful. [13] The sluggard says, "There is a lion outside!" or, "I will be murdered in the streets!" [14] The mouth of an adulteress is a deep pit; he who is under the Lord's wrath will fall into it. [15] Folly is bound up in the heart of a child, but the rod of discipline will drive it far from him. [16] He who oppresses the poor to increase his wealth and he who gives gifts to the rich — both come to poverty.

These verses speak to knowledge — specifically the way that we gather information, apply it to how we live, and speak truthfully. It also highlights discipline, determination, and the ability to work and seek God's direction.

Many times, we will see people who don't do the right thing who seem to be prospering. However, if you study them long enough, you will find out that consistently going down the wrong path does not lead to a long, healthy, or balanced life. Those around them will not find balance and prosperity either.

Sometimes we make excuses that seem like a good way to deal with issues. However, excuses paint us in a bad light if they make us look lazy, inattentive, disorganized, or untruthful. I can remember children giving me excuses about why they did not complete assignments or why they misbehaved while I was watching them. Sometimes we correct them when the issue arises, and then other times, we just think, "Oh my goodness, I just don't have the energy to deal with this right now," thus making an excuse for not correcting the situation. As mature adults, we can even find ourselves making up ridiculous, incredibly fantastic excuses about why we didn't complete a task or address an issue which will lead to some kind of punishment.

I've learned that making a habit of telling the truth about the situation versus making an excuse prevents or reduces the punishment. It just takes the everyday situations, bad decisions, and mistakes that happen and puts them into perspective. Sometimes when we make excuses, it makes things worse in the end because the situation goes on longer without being addressed. When we find ourselves making excuses to cover circumstances or a lie, we should instead try to admit it and address it as soon as possible so it does not become a burden.

I have spent many years in sales and sales management. We have to forecast what business we're going to bring in on weekly, monthly, and annual basis. Executive management, of course, wants as much business as possible as soon as possible. If our forecast was not large enough and did not meet expectations, they got on our backs about it. On the other hand, if we forecasted a certain amount of sales and the company based their projections on that expectation, we were in trouble if the projected business didn't come in. It would have been better to create a realistic projection than to put the company in jeopardy later on. Legitimate mistakes happen. I always made a habit of just being straightforward about my forecast even if they weren't going to like it. I found it better to be truthful about the challenges I would face in the upcoming period that would affect my sales. It was a less-severe "beating" than overpromising and underdelivering.

Proverbs 22:22-25

> [22] Do not exploit the poor because they are poor and do not crush the needy in court, [23] for the LORD will take up their case and will plunder those who plunder them. [24] Do not make friends with a hot-tempered man, do not associate with one easily angered, [25] or you may learn his ways and get yourself ensnared.

We could use examples of world leaders or dictators to teach the lessons found in Proverbs 22:22-23, but let's not do that. Instead, let's make this more personal by addressing the attitude and discipline we need to work in challenging times and uncertain environments. We are living in a time where there has been major, negative financial upheaval. Many people have been laid off, and jobs are scarce. That can bring out the best in people. However, it often brings out the absolute worst in people because they become frantic about the possibility of losing their job.

First, when we dwell upon losing a job, we're probably attracting those very elements that will lead us to job loss. Instead, our energy needs to be focused on improving our performance and being more productive for the companies we work for or looking for a company that is a better fit. And the side effect is that we become better and more productive to those around us. There are plenty of toxic, intolerant, closed-minded, negative people in the world. We can make a real impact by being a positive influence.

Unfortunately, everyone we encounter doesn't have that enlightened approach, and ultimately they are going to experience adverse situations as a result. In the case of bad economic times, we have seen people targeted personally and laid off, and not every situation seems fair at the time. It's also possible that we could be laid off even though our performance is good. Downsizing head count in a company can be a subjective process, and it doesn't always make sense. Then, of course, God sometimes has other plans for us and the layoff can be the catalyst.

Layoffs are painful in many ways, and job security can be uncertain during even the best economic conditions. We have to make plans for the inevitable, prepare ourselves financially, and make sure that we are constantly updating our skills so we are attractive to other employers.

Hopefully, you aren't in a workplace where the managers attempt to motivate by fear and you hear things such as, "I'm going to fire you," "The company is going to lay everyone off," "We're going to close down if you don't meet your sales goals," "You need more sales or you're going to get fired." In a toxic environment like that, sentences no longer have periods. They are punctuated with hostile comments such as "Heads will roll" and "Joe and Dave are going to be fired if they don't shape up." That's not productive, and it creates an environment where people stop thinking "out of the box" to find new ways to make things better. Instead, they just play it safe. Even the best performance never thrives in that environment. It becomes counterproductive.

Proverbs 22:22-23 promises that there is justice somewhere down the line even though we may or may not see it. It isn't our responsibility to provide it. We have to trust God to take care of it in His time. It may not appear to us that it happens fast enough for many of the people involved, but for some reason, events have a way of rectifying themselves over time.

Proverbs 22:24-25 speaks to exercising caution in who we spend time with. Have you heard the phrase: "Show me the six people you spend the most time with, and I will show you who you are and who you are going to be"? That probably rings true because we tend to be like the people we spend time with. If we spend time with negative, toxic people who are engaged in appalling, immoral, unethical, criminal behavior, guess what? That's probably how we'll become. Unless you have been tasked to show them better life skills and they are buying into it, you're probably not doing yourself a service. Spending social time with toxic people usually causes us to be affected by them rather than the other way around.

Be cautious how you spend your time. There is nothing wrong with trying to help people and put them on the right path. However, if you're going along to get along with people who are heading in the wrong direction, you too will end up lost.

Proverbs 22:28

[28] Do not move an ancient boundary stone set up by your forefathers.

There is a good example of this in Joshua chapters 13 through 21 where Joshua is taking back the land for the Israelites. He is dividing it up amongst his tribes in a very specific fashion while adhering to Moses' direction. It is a long read but interesting in its approach and reasoning. The example provides a broader concept that applies to everyday life.

Moses had warned the people that when they reached the promised land, they should not cheat their neighbors by moving boundary markers and dividing lines so that they could have more land. In our life today, the message is that we should accept what has been biblically promised to us. We should be fair in how we go about living with our neighbors — or love your neighbor as you would love yourself, and do unto others as you would have them do unto you. You can find more information on this subject in Deuteronomy 19 and again in Deuteronomy 27.

Let's end here by looking to treat others fairly and treating them as we would like to be treated. One way to do this is by controlling our emotions — in particular, our anger. Anger is contagious, so limit your exposure within reason to situations that generate an angry response. Also, learn to recognize the behavior when it begins, and notice what generates it in you.

If you are serious about changing the habit of inappropriate anger, then you need to start hanging out with other people who know how to manage their anger. That's one of the benefits of a church or true spiritual environment. By being involved in my church, I've absorbed positive values, habits, and behavior. And if you are a parent, don't forget your children are watching you closely.

Action Steps on the Life Path

God approves of foresight, restraint, and intelligence when utilizing credit. The average American family has close to $10,000 in debt. Write down your credit cards and their balances. How does your total compare with your income?

_____

_____

_____

_____

_____

_____

_____

_____

_____

_____

_____

_____

_____

_____

_____

_____

_____

_____

_____

List your other expenses such as utilities, transportation, and day care. What are some ways you can trim those expenses to put more toward paying off your credit card debt?

_____

_____

_____

_____

_____

_____

_____

_____

_____

_____

_____

_____

_____

_____

_____

_____

_____

_____

_____

_____

_____

_____

Evaluate your rent or mortgage. If you currently rent and aspire to purchase a home, are you in a place that will allow you to save for a home? If you have a mortgage already, does is make sense to stay with the current payment or refinance your mortgage? Does it make sense to make extra payments toward the principal on the loan?

_____

_____

_____

_____

_____

_____

You'll find many articles on financial management on my website at www.theodorehenderson.com. Some of them concern paying down mortgages and paying off large credit card debts.

In addition, www.thewisdomcompass.com will contain articles on the topics covered in the book as well as other general life matters with spiritual guidance.

Too Much Food Plus Too Much Wine Equal Too Much Trouble

"Apply your heart to instruction and your ears to words of knowledge."

Proverbs 23:12

Today's lesson centers on Proverbs 23 of the Proverbs of Solomon. Even though you may not think so at first, this text spends a lot of time discussing proper behavior before a ruler. What really emerges from these verses is the behavior expected from a professional person when in the company of other professionals — especially if they are in superior business positions to you or you are attempting to consummate a business relationship.

The use of food and wine is quite ingenious in that wine in too large a quantity allows you to drop your guard to the point you may not use good judgment. Lack of caution in such situations provides a false sense of security allowing you to be open to bad decision making, improper actions, and unnecessary business losses.

The key is discipline, and this is continually presented as the answer to maintaining the proper attitude and behavior.

Proverbs 23:1-3

[1] When you sit to dine with a ruler, note well what [a] is before you, [2] and put a knife to your throat if you are given to gluttony. [3] Do not crave his delicacies, for that food is deceptive.

The whole point of certain portions of this proverb is one of professional caution. When you dine with influential or important people, be cautious because they may be trying to influence or even bribe you. The meal may have less to do with the food and more to do with seizing the opportunity to gather and impose one's will on another.

If you read the headlines that frequently appear about business corruption, you will notice the stories of scandal usually center around influence, buying trips, dinners, and special privileges. That moral compass at work is especially important in tough times. In addition to using the wisdom in your decision making, be very careful when taking gifts from important and powerful people — even if that gift is just dinner or entertainment. For example, look at the following headline from the Department of Justice from Thursday, September 4, 2008:

> WWW.USDOJ.GOV "WASHINGTON - Former lobbyist Jack A. Abramoff was sentenced today to forty-eight months in prison and ordered to pay $23,134,695 in restitution to victims based on his guilty plea to conspiracy, honest services fraud, and tax evasion charges, Acting Assistant Attorney General Matthew Friedrich of the Criminal Division and Nathan J. Hochman, Assistant Attorney General for the Tax Division announced."

One last point on this topic, lobbyists (solo or part of a firm) are perfectly legal as long as they adhere to the federal guidelines that define their behavior. Abramoff went way over the line and eventually was caught.

Proverbs 23:4-5

[4] Do not wear yourself out to get rich; have the wisdom to show restraint. [5] Cast but a glance at riches, and they are gone, for they will surely sprout wings and fly off to the sky like an eagle.

These verses speak to the issue of being rich or possessing wealth and pursuing treasure. We all hear or read stories about lottery winners. They

Too Much Food Plus Too Much Wine Equal Too Much Trouble

win millions of dollars, and then, a number of years later, they're broke. We should note that no amount of money used incorrectly or without wise stewardship — also known as good management — can last forever.

For clarity, I would like to define *stewardship*[5] as defined by *Merriam-Webster's Collegiate® Dictionary, 11th Edition*. This word captures the responsibility of managing money or any other part our life.

> 1: the office, duties, and obligations of a steward

> 2: the conducting, supervising, or managing of something; especially: the careful and responsible management of something entrusted to one's care <stewardship of our natural resources>

During an economic downturn, scandals emerge where billions of dollars have been squandered in scams and schemes. The scammer or the schemer isn't the only one at fault although he or she will face years in jail, destroyed reputations, and damaged family relations. Part of the problem in these cases is poor stewardship of one's wealth.

If you have figured out how to earn your money, the chances are good you have some idea about how to keep it. Financial stewardship requires continual education and reading — again successful people are generally readers and communicators. A windfall for someone who has never had a large sum of money to manage can present many challenges. For instance, take someone who makes a modest income such as a person who works on an assembly line or as a server in a restaurant who wins the lottery. All of the sudden, she goes from making a small amount of money per week to having a huge amount of money overnight. Even though it is a blessing, it arrives with some unexpected burdens of caring for the wealth.

The first burden is that the winner discovers she has "friends" who now need loans, and she's going to feel obligated and compelled to give them money. However, this starts to change the dynamic of the friendship because now they are indebted to her — even if she is not expecting it back. And chances are good they will show up again because they don't know how to manage wealth or money someone has given to them.

I read a very sad story about a billionaire who had invested all of his money with Bernie Madoff, the scammer who turned his wealth management

[5] By permission. From *Merriam-Webster's Collegiate® Dictionary, 11th Edition* ©2010 by Merriam-Webster, Incorporated (www.Merriam-Webster.com).

business into a massive Ponzi scheme. By the time the totals from client accounts and the fabricated gains were totaled, it amounted to almost $65 billion. The court-appointed trustee estimated the actual losses to investors to be $18 billion. The billionaire lost everything in the Madoff scandal and did the unfathomable — he committed suicide.

It's hard to know exactly why the billionaire committed suicide. Perhaps it was the thought of not being a billionaire or having to make the money again. Maybe he couldn't stand losing the lifestyle his wealth afforded. Perhaps he looked in the mirror and feared he wasn't quite as smart as he once was. Whatever the reason, it was a tragic loss for him, his family, and his friends.

Wise stewardship of your wealth helps you safeguard your resources. Managing large sums of money involves diversifying the investment wisely. When we don't build our knowledge of financial stewardship, it becomes tough to make wise decisions. In the case of Bernie Madoff (and others like him), he became ethically challenged along the way, lost his moral compass, and became a criminal.

This is why we need to be on guard about receiving windfall money — large amounts that come from winnings, inheritances, and short-term investments. We need to learn how to manage it and our expectations because there are so many people who are looking to take the money and take advantage of us.

Proverbs 23:6-8

> [6] Do not eat the food of a stingy man, do not crave his delicacies;
> [7] for he is the kind of man who is always thinking about the cost.
> [b] "Eat and drink," he says to you, but his heart is not with you.
> [8] You will vomit up the little you have eaten and will have wasted your compliments.

The verses warn us not to be envious of people who have wealthy lifestyles or, more importantly, who have become rich by being stingy, mean-spirited, and miserly — like Ebenezer Scrooge from Charles Dickens' *A Christmas Carol*. People who become wealthy by hoarding their money really don't get much back in return. They are miserly in their wealth despite the fact they may be very smart. They may pay their people well, but their charitable giving amounts to a few dollars to the local symphony or their alma mater's football team. While these are good causes, there are greater needs in the world.

Put your wealth — whether it's the small amount of wealth that most people have or it's a great amount of wealth that multimillionaires and billionaires have — to work aiding or solving the world's problems such as hunger, illiteracy, and a lack of proper health care. Use your wealth to shore up the spiritual base of your faith through mission work. You may be fond of pets, animal causes, and environmental issues and choose to give to those in addition to faith-based charities and initiatives.

Be free in your giving and use your money to help make the world a better place. Besides, the miserly existence is a lonely, miserable one. Mean-spirited, stingy people don't have any friends unless they buy them. Those aren't the kind of "friends" you want anyway.

Proverbs 23:10-12

> [10] Do not move an ancient boundary stone or encroach on the fields of the fatherless, [11] for their Defender is strong; he will take up their case against you. [12] Apply your heart to instruction and your ears to words of knowledge.

God is a redeemer; however, a redeemer was also someone during this time period — maybe a family member or friend — who bought someone back out of slavery. When people fell onto hard times, they may have indentured themselves or sold themselves into slavery to pay that debt off in biblical times. So a redeemer can be a person, or it can be God.

There's also an additional meaning — a redeemer was someone who had an obligation to marry a widow of a family member. While that tradition is not done now, it was quite common during that period of time — particularly in the Hebrew or Jewish culture. Chapter 4 in the book of Ruth is one such story.

Proverbs 23:12 refers to a redeemer as someone who is able to learn, listen, gather knowledge, and use it wisely. We all know smart people who don't listen. Even though they get to a certain point in life and even seem successful, they never reach their full potential because they know everything already and won't listen to anyone. No matter how intelligent or successful we are, we can often find less-successful people who have valuable knowledge.

Carefully observe the people around you to learn from the them. You don't go to a bricklayer to learn how to do the foxtrot. You go to a dance teacher. You go to a mason to learn how to lay the bricks. Likewise, take your advice from the people who are experts in subjects you want to learn or understand. Don't worry about whether they are financially successful or equal to you. Choose people who have the knowledge you need to propel yourself to achieve whatever goal you're pursuing.

These scriptures tell us not to become so fixed in our ways of living or approach to life that we prevent ourselves from gaining knowledge from people who are eager or willing to help us grow. Accordingly, be eager to listen, continue to learn, and make learning and growth something that happens regularly in your life.

Proverbs 23:13-14

> [13] Do not withhold discipline from a child; if you punish him with the rod, he will not die. [14] Punish him with the rod and save his soul from death.

In this use, "punish" is meant as discipline but doesn't necessarily mean a spanking or hitting. Parents are sometimes reluctant to discipline their children; instead, they are interested in being their best buddy. Unfortunately, that is not God's will for the parent's role. Parents should raise their children to understand the world around them and to act wisely in making decisions both during their youth and when they leave the nest and go out on their own.

Parents often make the mistake of indulging and not disciplining. They stifle and corrode their children's development because they're not giving them the necessary feedback. If children don't receive proper discipline at home, they will find the world will deliver dramatically harsher discipline once they are an adult.

The ultimate corrosive effect happens when parents keep their children home as adults. Adults who continue to live in the protective environment of their parents will still receive feedback from the world just like adults who left home. However, being sheltered will make them less successful and less of a valuable contributor to the environment around them. Eventually a fully functioning bird leaves the parent's nest.

Discipline is very important for young people as well as important for adults. As a student in a Catholic school in the sixties and seventies, I did not always enjoy that correction, but I am a more disciplined person to this day (despite any past failures) because of it. I understand proper conduct and how to properly go about pursuing my objectives. Without the discipline of my youth, I doubt I would have been able to write this book.

If you are a parent, evaluate how well you do in the area of discipline. Be honest with yourself, and make note of those areas where you are having trouble in your relationship with your children — especially those who are getting older. Teenagers can be particularly difficult. No matter how angry or sad they are making you at any given moment, ask yourself if you are helping them the best way possible or are you being an overindulgent, overprotective parent?

Proverbs 23:17-18

> [17] Do not let your heart envy sinners, but always be zealous for the fear of the LORD. [18] There is surely a future hope for you, and your hope will not be cut off.

It is almost human nature to envy those who seem to be doing well (or better than we're doing). Christians should want to see people doing well, but sometimes we fall into the jealousy trap. I want to do well also, but I don't always live up to what I should. Then I notice how easy things look for other people, and I find myself in the jealousy trap. As I grow in my personal development and my faith, I'm more able to quickly recognize my negative outlook and move to correct myself.

Envy and jealousy sidetracks us. It starts to put negative energy to work and when that happens, we begin to make compromises and become ethically challenged. It causes us to initiate all types of things that we normally wouldn't do if we were focused on staying positive and utilizing these biblical principles to gain and utilize wisdom.

It's dangerous to fall into the trap of envying people — especially those who are not "hampered" by trying to adhere to God's laws. It doesn't necessarily make them bad people; however, it does not necessarily mean they are prospering in the way that someone of faith looks to prosper. Instead of being envious about what other people are doing, learn from their example and stay focused on what you are trying to accomplish.

God promises a wonderful life to those who adhere to His Word. However, that wonderful life isn't necessarily in this life nor is it trouble-free. So if you believe that, you know you are living according to biblical principles, and you are following the Word, then you will achieve the life that God has ordained for you.

Proverbs 23:30-35

[30] Those who linger over wine, who go to sample bowls of mixed wine. [31] Do not gaze at wine when it is red, when it sparkles in the cup, when it goes down smoothly! [32] In the end it bites like a snake and poisons like a viper. [33] Your eyes will see strange sights and your mind imagine confusing things. [34] You will be like one sleeping on the high seas, lying on top of the rigging. [35] "They hit me," you will say, "but I'm not hurt! They beat me, but I don't feel it! When will I wake up so I can find another drink?"

Alcohol can be very comforting. Unfortunately, it is only temporary. The only real relief that we get from the trials and tribulations of life is from dealing with the cause of our problems and turning to God for peace.

Alcohol is just another drug when abused. People who struggle with alcohol use need to avoid losing themselves in booze and instead pursue finding themselves in the Lord. These verses provide a warning for those who have issues with drinking too much or who must interact with people who abuse alcohol or even drugs.

I'm not suggesting you assume the role of counselor. However, sharing these verses can open up the dialogue around the issues that someone may be going through. People abuse alcohol and drugs to escape the trials of life but really find no escape at all. If you find yourself involved in this activity either as an abuser or a loved one of an abuser, seek professional counseling for all parties involved.

There is a lot to this chapter that bears re-reading, but the most important lessons are about discipline and receptiveness to instruction. Discipline will allow you to conduct yourself appropriately in both professional and personal settings. Secondly, listening and being open to good advice will help you learn from others' mistakes. Imagine all the "hard-knock" lessons you will not have to experience.

Action Steps on the Life Path

Get into the habit of identifying people who can aid your effort in pursuit of your goals. Think of five people you know who have a skill or knowledge about a topic that you need to learn more about. Write their name and that skill or area of knowledge below. You will want to contact them after you have formed a coherent plan for what you are pursuing.

_____

_____

_____

_____

_____

_____

_____

_____

_____

_____

What areas of your professional behavior or professional social conduct could use improvement? Be honest with yourself.

_____

_____

_____

_____

_____

_____

_____

Too Much Food Plus Too Much Wine Equal Too Much Trouble

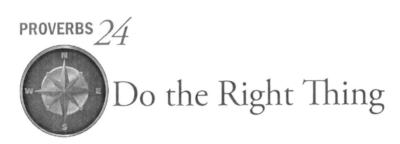

PROVERBS *24*

Do the Right Thing

"By wisdom a house is built, and through understanding it is established; through knowledge its rooms are filled with rare and beautiful treasures."

Proverbs 24:3-4

The opening verses capture the spirit of this chapter. The house is your home, and in your home is your family. Nowhere is wisdom, understanding, wise thinking, and integrity more important than in your home, so don't defile it. If you do, you are defiling your spouse and your children. One of the greatest gifts you can provide is to be a true model and a blessing to your children, other children, and the next generation.

Proverbs 24:5

⁵ A wise man has great power, and a man of knowledge increases strength.

Basketball, football, or any sport that requires teamwork has multiple operations that go onto the field of battle together to coordinate their efforts as one unit. Many times, you will see a team on paper who isn't as big, strong, or fast beat the team that has the greater individual talent. They do it through teamwork and smarts. I remember watching the battles between the old Boston Celtics with Larry Bird and the Lakers with Magic Johnson. When they initially met in the championship rounds of the 1984, 1985, and

1987 seasons, the Celtics weren't quite as fast, tall, or athletic. But when they beat the Lakers, they won by executing better.

The Lakers were so athletic that they depended on that athleticism to a great degree. When they got older, they had to learn to execute better than the younger, more athletically gifted teams. It is really the wisdom, preparation, and the strategy execution that creates a winning team's advantage. If a basketball player spends more time taking foul shots in practice, his foul shooting is generally better during the game. His individual skills will improve by focusing on executing basics such as taking jump shots, dribbling, and passing.

Besides working on individual skills, champions practice their coordination with their teammates. That requires an extra level of dedication because it's not all about the individual accomplishment anymore. The wisdom lies in understanding that we have to sacrifice some of our personal and individual goals for the team's overall goals. Individuals win when they help another teammate be better because everyone can benefit and win.

In the end, it's not just strength, speed, or athletic gifts. It's actually the wisdom to understand how best to use them and meld together that creates a winning team.

Another sports example that illustrates this point is John Wooden and his book, *Pyramid of Success*. Even though he has passed away, his legacy lives on in the men he coached and influenced. Each of his success principles are anchored in Christian principles. He was a strong person of faith who lived it by example — the way I strive to but haven't been consistently successful at yet. He conducted himself personally and professionally as what I would consider a true person of faith. He walked the Scripture instead of just speaking it and hammering others with it.

What made his teachings so powerful is when his former players and employees speak of him, they speak of him using the principles to describe how he was and how he encouraged others to be the best they could be and to be part of the team.

Proverbs 24:6

> [6] For waging war you need guidance, and for victory many advisers.

Do the Right Thing

The verse uses war for the example, but this message applies to any major decision that you need to make in life. When making a major decision, seek out people who are more experienced or knowledgeable about the subject matter than you are. That often means seeking people who are older and wiser. However, just being old does not make them wise, and being wise doesn't mean they're old.

Choose advisors carefully. They may not be in your current network of contacts. Ask people you know to connect you to people who can advise you on certain subjects. Watch for people in your life who function in a manner you would like to operate in or have some gift that you'd like to understand better. Reach out to them and find out how you can spend some time together. Consider forming a mentoring relationship with them where you meet on a regular basis.

Who you choose as advisors depends on your current phase of life. If you are raising children, you likely have older relatives — parents, grandparents, aunts — who can provide trusted advice. You don't want the advice of someone who has never had a child. You want the advice of someone who can provide specific examples of how best to bring your toddler along or to keep your sanity if you have a young infant crying continuously because of colic. As your children grow into their teen years, you may need to seek the advice of people such as counselors and parents of grown children.

If you are considering going to college, choose a school that is well-known in the field you want to study and reach out to other people who have also gone to college. They can advise you on many things from setting up your degree plan to locating financial aid to managing your time to accommodate your class work. You may seek the opinions of many people, but choose your close advisors carefully based on their wisdom, experience, and a proven track record.

Proverbs 24:8-10

> [8] He who plots evil will be known as a schemer. [9] The schemes of folly are sin, and men detest a mocker. [10] If you falter in times of trouble, how small is your strength!

God wants a pure heart — one that is not engaged in thinking about or committing sin. Just thinking of sin continuously and purposefully is as bad as committing the act. Engaging in fantasies of doing evil will eventually lead to action.

Instead, dwell on doing the right thing and feeling the right way. We need to police our thoughts. Evil can start when a married person starts fantasizing about someone he works with or sees on a regular basis. If he focuses on her strongly enough, he'll initiate an inappropriate conversation that could turn into an inappropriate act. If the other person is weak or willing, the fantasy can become reality. The act of adultery involves secrecy and escalates to more irresponsible acts that destroy relationships and maybe even marriages.

If you find yourself falling into evil thoughts of any kind, you can interrupt those thoughts actively and purposefully. I use some very specific Bible verses as well as some quotes, sayings, and affirmations that aren't necessarily biblical. They help interrupt thoughts that could lead me down a path of evil. I use these "interrupts" to stop myself from dwelling on the wrong things.

One example is the use of interrupts to reorient yourself toward more positive thoughts when you're angry at someone and find yourself focusing on it. I was such a grudge holder that I couldn't break the behavior at first. Finally, I said to myself, "I'm carrying that person with me whether they know I'm angry at them or not." Sometimes people don't even realize how we feel about them or a situation they are involved in.

I found that when I've got an "anger monkey" on my back, if I stop and interrupt it, the monkey leaves and lightens my load. My thoughts are free to turn to ways to spend time more positively such as better quality time with my spouse, family, or friends. I can concentrate on positive pursuits such as determining ways to spend more quality time developing myself, planning leisure activities such as going to see a movie, or simply planning dinner. Any of those are a better use of time than dwelling on revenge, hatred, and vile, twisted thoughts. Believe me, dwelling on sick thoughts will eventually make you sick. Kick the monkey to the curb and feel a little freedom.

When I was younger, I used to enjoy professional wrestling. There was something about these guys in robes and tights who jumped around the ring and made all those athletic-looking moves. Obviously, they were not really fighting — it was ballet, theatre, and stuntmanship at its best. They always used to cut promo interviews with the wrestlers to advertise upcoming matches. I'll never forget this one guy called Double A. He used to say, "Adversity introduces a man to himself," and he would apply it to the context of whatever story line the wrestlers were running. I thought it was an interesting phrase and, for whatever reason, it stuck with me. Adversity, if used correctly, can be a benefit because is reveals the real you before you know it.

You'll encounter the trials of life occasionally, and you'll come to a wall that you'll have to climb over. Clearly there are some situations so negative in your life that it seems like you'll never see a benefit from them; however, the benefit can manifest itself. You just have to keep the faith until you reach the other (positive) side.

When we encounter trials and problems, we need to do whatever it takes to get to the other side of trouble. If it's a job loss, you need to become re-employed, whether it's in the same field, a different field, or in business for yourself. If you're getting divorced, you have to work through the hard feelings so you can heal and prepare for a healthy relationship. We can be in denial of the situation and feel sorry for ourselves, but that's not going to help us work through it.

I met someone at a seminar at church who was divorced, unhappy, and unemployed. He was a sad case because he never made any progress. I saw him about a year or so later and nothing had changed. Clearly, he was not willing to take action.

Sometimes people are not willing to take action because the pain, sickness, affliction, and "victimhood" become their comfort zone and friend. It's easy to use victimization to gather the attention people are looking for from others.

Facing adversity in a positive manner can make you stronger. Think about situations in your life where you had trouble. When you came out on the other side of it, were things dramatically better for you? What did you learn about life and about yourself?

I have come through every job loss with a better opportunity than the one I had before. I think it had a lot to do with how I handled adversity. Never think that adversity means something's wrong. Adversity is actually fine-tuning you for whatever future and blessing that lies ahead.

Proverbs 24:17-18

> [17] Do not gloat when your enemy falls; when he stumbles, do not let your heart rejoice, [18] or the LORD will see and disapprove and turn his wrath away from him.

We've all had people do mean things to us and have probably felt good about seeing them "get what they had coming to them." Even though it might seem quite unnatural, it's beneficial for you to: A) forgive someone for what they have done to you that's wrong; and B) not gloat when they get some form of punishment for their actions.

Sometimes people hurt others because they are in pain. If that's the case, you really don't want to enjoy whatever is going to be happening to them. They need us to say a prayer for them instead. It's not always easy because sometimes our anger gets the best of us. But when we come back with a cool head, we realize we ought to think about blessing everyone. That would make the world a much better place. At times, we need to bless people who have been our enemies instead of fueling the fire.

Proverbs 24:29

> [29] Do not say, "I'll do to him as he has done to me; I'll pay that man back for what he did."

This chapter has given us several opportunities to explore the negative side effects of thinking evil thoughts, focusing on bad things, being sinful in attitude, and engaging in toxic behavior. You can be toxic to yourself as well as to others. Worrying about revenge is counterproductive. When you are focused on revenge, it becomes difficult to take action in your life.

This verse is not talking about proper punishment enforced by our local, state, or federal government. This verse addresses the individual who is seeking revenge. It is evil to take the role of vigilante like Charles Bronson in *Death Wish* or Clint Eastwood as *The Enforcer*. Those are interesting movies and good actors, but the characters are not real and should not be emulated in the real world.

If you catch yourself plotting revenge, think about the thoughts and attitudes that you are having. Are you being toxic? Are you participating in the noxious state of affairs? If someone has wronged you, use the legislative ability of our government. Use the freedom to be able to pursue certain forms of retribution for the sake of law and for public safety. When you take matters into your own hands, you're not doing yourself any good. You are also not acting in concert with justice and a safe society.

Wisdom is the only road map to a prosperous, balanced life — and a truly happy and engaging life. Is it wise to continually rebel against legitimate authority? No. If someone lies or spreads falsehoods about you, is it wise to do the same to them? No. Some might say honesty is the best policy. If that is the case, is that a good reason to be honest in all your interactions with others? No. Do it because it is God's will AND the right thing to do.

Action Steps on the Life Path

Think of two or three situations when you deliberately lied and did the wrong thing strictly for your own personal benefit. Why did you do it? Who did you hurt? Why did you feel the need to do it? Do you still think it was right? Would you do it again or would you tell the truth?

_____

_____

_____

_____

_____

_____

_____

_____

_____

_____

_____

_____

_____

_____

_____

_____

_____

_____

PROVERBS 25

The Wisdom of Leadership

"If you argue your case with a neighbor, do not betray another man's confidence, or he who hears it may shame you and you will never lose your bad reputation."

Proverbs 25:9-10

Proverbs 25 through 31 focus on wisdom specifically for leaders. These proverbs were collected by the advisors to King Hezekiah, a biblical king. The first section was written by Solomon and the next two sections were written by others. While we can all learn from these proverbs, many were originally directed toward the king or those who actually dealt with or advised the king. As a result, they are particularly helpful for those who are currently leading or aspire to become leaders.

This section of the book of Proverbs ends with the description of a truly good wife — one of my favorites. I like to call it the "Proverbs 31 Wife" or "Proverbs 31 Woman." In many areas of the Bible, a woman is used as an example — some cases are in a flattering sense and other cases are not so flattering. They just happen to use a female reference given the time it was written. But the characteristics, both good and evil, are not gender-bound and apply to both men and women. However, I particularly like the fact that Proverbs ends with the highest example of godly wisdom embodied in the female.

Proverbs 25:2

> ² It is the glory of God to conceal a matter; to search out a matter is the glory of kings.

To best understand Hezekiah, read II Kings 18-20 and II Chronicles 29-32. There are also comments on Hezekiah in II Chronicles 36-39. Interestingly enough, he was one of the few kings of Judah who honored the Lord. Once you start studying the Old Testament and the biblical principles that the kings practiced or did not practice, you will understand that God's relationship with many of the kings was complex (to be kind). In many cases, the kings seemed (based on their behavior) to be directly at odds with God's teachings as given by the judges and prophets.

Hezekiah restored the temple which had been destroyed by his father, Ahas. It is interesting to find that a very wise king who honored the Lord was at odds with his father. However, it earned him the respect of surrounding nations of the time. Many of them recognized the Israelites or Judea's God as something very special and brought gifts to honor Him in whatever the custom of the time was. Ultimately, Hezekiah had the proverbs collected, copied, and read. The quote says, "In all that he did in the service of the temple of God and in his efforts to follow God's laws and commands."

Hezekiah embodies Proverbs 25:2 because he diligently searched for God's guidance. He was an extremely successful king because he sought God's wisdom and followed the wisdom and the laws of God and of the time. If we repeat that behavior and model the activities of a successful person who operates morally, the chances are good we will achieve some level of success. Your success may not necessarily be the same level as the person that you are modeling. It could be less, or it could be more.

Proverbs 25:3-6

> ³ As the heavens are high and the earth is deep, so the hearts of kings are unsearchable. ⁴ Remove the dross from the silver, and out comes material for [a] the silversmith; ⁵ remove the wicked from the king's presence, and his throne will be established through righteousness. ⁶ Do not exalt yourself in the king's presence, and do not claim a place among great men.

These verses are speaking to the King, but let's personalize it. Proverbs 25:2-6 continues to reinforce the importance of discovering truth and wisdom. This is followed by a warning on the value of keeping your own counsel and making up your own mind. The first key is to avoid talking too much and spreading your ideas around — it's never clear who could be lurking in the shadows to undermine you. Secondly, make sure you fully develop your ideas into goals, desires, and objectives that you will pursue wholeheartedly. By the time anyone sees them who might try to undermine them, you will be secure in your decision, and they cannot succeed in sidetracking you. Their attempts will fail, and you will continue to focus forward.

Even though you should seek advice and counsel from others, carefully evaluate where that advice or counsel is coming from. Make sure your advisors are consistently honest and supportive of you and your goals even though they may not necessarily always agree with you. When your ideas are not quite fully formed and they are still driven by the passion within you, you will face a particularly steep climb toward difficult obstacles and objectives. It is easy to become derailed. Don't be afraid to change advisors if your current one no longer works for you.

Lastly, these verses speak to being a good steward of the king's time and managing your own time properly. You have demands from your professional life that you must balance with your family life, friends, and individual pursuits such as hobbies. Carefully discern and balance the justifiable demands on your time versus unjustifiable ones.

Say you need to do homework because you're pursuing an advanced degree, studying for some particular purpose, preparing for a big meeting the next day, or have an important speech you have to make. If someone is actively trying to distract you with something frivolous like a party or some other activity that would undermine your effort to perform, you need to draw a line in the sand. Make sure that person understands that you have different priorities. I'm not saying you should never have any fun. On the contrary, actively schedule in fun time. However, the timing you choose should not interfere with the goals you are pursuing.

Proverbs 25:7 says, "It's better to wait for an invitation to the head table than to be sent away in public disgrace." In Luke 14:7-11, there was a parable that Jesus spoke that also illustrates this point quite clearly. Jesus is always referred to in the gospels as "Teacher." People also referred to him as "Rabbi" which means *teacher*. He was a teacher, and many of the lessons and parables he used instructed people to conduct themselves properly in their everyday life as well as their spiritual life.

The lesson in these verses suggests that we should not look to seek honor for ourselves before the time is right. Many times, it is better to quietly, diligently, and faithfully complete the work we've been given to do. In some cases, the work may be divinely inspired.

Additionally, when you do God's work, you have the opportunity to lead by example. Forcing people to do what you want them to do is not leading. If people are willing to follow your example, you are leading. Whether the people are age ninety or nine, they pay a lot less attention to what you say than what you do. The act and the words must line up.

Proverbs 25:13-14

> ¹³ Like the coolness of snow at harvest time is a trustworthy messenger to those who send him; he refreshes the spirit of his masters. ¹⁴ Like clouds and wind without rain is a man who boasts of gifts he does not give.

Many times, it is difficult to find someone we can trust. That is why so many of us have few real friends. Even though we may associate with many people, they may not necessarily be real friends.

Trust is especially important with employees. If you're a business owner, you want to be trustworthy and dependable and have trustworthy, dependable, faithful employees. You want the same thing if you are a manager in a company. You want to be trustworthy, dependable, and have like-minded employees working for you. To get and keep the kind of employees you want, you have to lead by example. You must be an example of a good employee — punctual, responsible, honest, and hardworking — and operate in an ethical and above-board manner. When you do that, you will attract like-minded people who are invaluable assets to your company.

Creating an environment where everyone has the opportunity to give honest feedback will also be invaluable to the company whether you own it or you're an employee of it. Fostering honest feedback will enable the company to prosper. The decisions that need to be made will come from the right mind-set, and the company will be a great place to work. Open and honest feedback will open doors that lead to the next opportunity because team members feel their ideas are valued and are more willing to contribute.

The business environment may be very challenging, and we may work with difficult people or in a difficult office. However, we must strive do the best we can as employees, managers, and owners to understand what is needed to make the job easier for all concerned. Ultimately, our goal should be to provide the best products and services for our clients.

Proverbs 25:14 says when you make a pledge or promise, keep your word. Sometimes we have to go back on our word because we made a commitment before a difficult situation caused us to alter our plans. For example, you might have promised to give a charity $100 but you only have $90. Even though you can't give the full amount, give what you have. If you have promised to volunteer time that you suddenly realize you don't have, help them find a replacement who can volunteer instead. Not only will this reinforce that you are someone who keeps your word, but the people who made plans based on your promise will not be impacted as if you did not fulfill any of your promise.

Non-profit organizations such as churches, synagogues, temples, missions, civic clubs, and service organizations depend on gifts of time and money from people to keep their doors open and serve their clients. When those commitments aren't honored, it makes it impossible for them to fulfill their mission. Biblical principle is very clear here: if you make a pledge, keep your word.

Sometimes we feel pressured to make a commitment we know we can't keep. Be honest with yourself and with the organization and only pledge what you know you can honor. Not being honest to those who depend on you will set you up for disaster in addition to hurting the efforts of others.

Proverbs 25:18

[18] Like a club or a sword or a sharp arrow is the man who gives false testimony against his neighbor.

The point in this verse is don't lie! Lying is considered an act as vicious as a physical attack because its effects can be as serious as any type of inflicted wound. It creates scars and hard feelings amongst people. Who knows what damage a single lie can cause?

One of the great examples in the Old Testament is the lie told by Joseph's brothers. They sold Joseph into slavery, but they lied to their father and told him he was dead. Later in captivity, Joseph was serving in the house of an Egyptian ruler, Potiphar. The Egyptian ruler's wife lied and said that Joseph had tried to rape her. Such an attempt against a powerful individual or a ruler was severely punished, so Joseph was thrown into prison. If you've read the story, you know that Joseph overcame the lies and went on to become empowered in Egypt and even helped his family and the Jews during a time of great famine and hardship.

I recently watched a movie released in 1987 directed by John Sayles called *Matewan*. It is about the coal miners in West Virginia in 1920 and their efforts to form a union. The economic exploitation was to the advantage of the state authorities, which is why the company was allowed set up and maintain an abusive situation. Part of the story had to do with the miners trying bring in a union and fight back against the exploitation of the company.

One of the townspeople, C.E. Lively, was a spy for the company and also had an informal leadership position with the townspeople. He tried to set up the union organizer (Joe Kenehan) who had come to town to help them start the union. He initiated a smear campaign against him by trying to convince a woman named Bridey Mae Tolliver — who had a romantic interest in Joe — to turn against him because she felt bad due to his lack of interest in her. He was very pleasant to this young lady but had no romantic interest in her. His passion was the union. He was going to be moving on, so he conducted himself as a gentleman at all times in the movie. However, the traitor convinced the woman — and for some reason she agreed — to tell a lie that he had actually raped her and that the men ought to do something about it.

Luckily, the scheme was discovered before it was too late, and C. E. went running off into the night. He basically snuck out with his tail between his legs. They did get their union; but there is another point to the story. Here is someone who was a traitor, who manipulated a young lady to tell lies, and who almost destroyed an entire town's access to a better livelihood.

A lie is not something innocent that we need to look the other way from or quickly forgive. Many people have told damaging lies even though they thought no one would be hurt. We need to be genuinely sorry if we fall into that trap and apologize to those that we may have hurt if possible. We also need to forgive those who have lied to us if they are truly sorry and even sometimes when they are not. Yes, someone's lie might be damaging and hurtful and some form of restitution in the form of at least an apology is warranted. However, forgiveness — regardless of the other party's reaction — allows us to move on instead of letting bad feelings spoil the rest of our life.

Where has lying hurt you? Is there someone you need to forgive and apologize to?

Proverbs 25: 21-22

[21] If your enemy is hungry, give him food to eat; if he is thirsty, give him water to drink. [22] In doing this, you will heap burning coals on his head, and the LORD will reward you.

God makes life a little difficult for us sometimes because our egos are in the way. In fact, Paul quotes this proverb in Romans 12:19-21 and in Matthew 5. Jesus, of course, encourages us to pray for and forgive those who have hurt us. Remember, His words on the cross were: "Father, forgive them, for they know not what they do."

By returning good for evil, we are acknowledging God as the entity that will make it all right. I cannot think of any situation — personal or on a larger, global scale — where a continual, never-ending, eye-for-an-eye, retaliatory posture produces good. At some point, cooler heads need to prevail, and someone needs to stand down. Those involved must start talking and stop fighting. More importantly, they need to forgive. If we don't, we carry the burden with us everywhere we go. If you have two like-minded people or entities that understand we need to forgive, move on, and negotiate a better place, it can only lead to a better, safer, more secure life for everyone involved.

Think about your life. Are you spending time retaliating and holding grudges when you would be better off forgiving, making peace, and moving on using your energy in a much more beneficial manner?

²⁶ Like a muddied spring or a polluted well is a righteous man who gives way to the wicked. ²⁷ It is not good to eat too much honey, nor is it honorable to seek one's own honor. ²⁸ Like a city whose walls are broken down is a man who lacks self-control.

If we make compromises with evil or wrong doing, we are setting aside the ethical standards of right and wrong. To do so is acting unwisely and helping no one. The lesson is not saying we should not enjoy honors. We should enjoy the honors that we receive, and we should be grateful to the people who honor us. However, dwelling on the honors that we "deserve" can only be harmful. Yes, sometimes we may deserve something and we are not acknowledged, but so what? Even though we know we did a good job or did the right, wise, or ethical thing, we may not be acknowledged for it.

Have you ever been upset that you weren't given credit for something at work? We're human and not perfect so sometimes we can be upset when that happens. Even when we don't receive recognition we deserve, we still receive a paycheck — a form of appreciation. People don't always acknowledge when we do something good or right. Regardless of their own motivations, move forward because you have created a strong spiritual base. It will prevent you from being derailed when someone doesn't give you the proper acknowledgement. By not moving on, we end up bitter, angry, discouraged, negative, mean-spirited, or small-minded. When we move on, we can be successful, balanced, and happy.

Lastly, city boundaries can be walls, fences, rivers, or roads. The boundaries restrict the inhabitants of the city and their movements. Particularly in ancient times, the boundaries were necessary to protect the occupants and the city they lived in, so people were happy to have them. The walls, like discipline, offer protection which is what self-control provides us. Once a city was conquered, the first thing any smart ruler or general did was to have the occupants tear down the walls so they could not defend themselves again. This allowed the occupier to retake the city or take some form of action against the inhabitants.

So let's end here by thinking of self-control as the city walls meant to defend and protect you from evil. They also provide boundaries that allow you to conduct yourself in a wise manner. Other lessons in this chapter discuss the danger of lies and the lack of integrity. We saw situations from the story of

Matewan and the story of Joseph where someone lied because their ego was bruised. There were far-reaching consequences beyond the one or two individuals immediately involved. Finally, as a leader, we should create an environment where the people we lead are encouraged to be honest.

Action Steps on the Life Path

What are some areas of your life that require change? There may be two or more.

_____

_____

_____

_____

_____

_____

_____

What are some situations where you needed to exercise more self-discipline and more self-control?

_____

_____

_____

_____

_____

_____

Do you have any out-of-control behavior that you need to overcome? If so, what is it?

_____

_____

_____

_____

The Wisdom of Leadership

Do you have an area of your life where you are having trouble and it is preventing you from living and pursuing a more balanced, useful existence? What would remedy the situation? If you need more room, consider writing your answer in a journal.

_____

_____

_____

_____

_____

_____

_____

_____

Ultimately, an out-of-control life is open to all sorts of attacks and distractions. List some of those below.

_____

_____

_____

_____

_____

If you exercise discipline and self-control, what benefits might you receive if you are not subject to this limiting behavior?

_____

_____

_____

_____

_____

PROVERBS *26*

Such a Fool

"As a dog returns to its vomit, so a fool repeats his folly."

Proverbs 26:11

Sometimes, we are subjected to an environment where there are plans, plots, schemes, vendettas, etc. We have already covered this to a great degree in the previous lessons. We know that evil begets evil. However, we also understand there are times we are not in a position to directly fight people who are cursing us, gossiping about us, or plotting against us. Sometimes we have to "walk it out." We need to be steadfast in our faith — faith in the Word, faith in God, faith in the plan that we have put together, and faith in ourselves.

Faith is necessary even when we truly believe we're doing the right, ethical, moral, and wise thing. We need to be steadfast in our belief and stand tall through the inevitable setbacks. Sometimes, bad things happen to good people. Many times, the positive outcome arrives right after the storm has finished. Getting through the challenging experiences is one of the many ways that we fight the seemingly undeserved curses that the enemy places in our way to distract us from God's plan for our life.

Proverbs 26:4-5

> [4] Do not answer a fool according to his folly, or you will be like him yourself. [5] Answer a fool according to his folly, or he will be wise in his own eyes.

These verses point out that there is a contradiction between intelligence, wisdom, sound reasoning, foolishness, or folly. A fool remains a fool whether or not you respond to him. However, a wise person whose mind is open to knowledge and learning has a choice to respond based on what he sees as the greatest need of the fool.

Some fools don't deserve an answer because they are clearly not interested in anything that will change or expand their mind. They instead put themselves in a position where they can continue being a fool. As Proverbs 26:2 says, "Like a fluttering sparrow or a darting swallow, an undeserved curse does not come to rest." Therefore, in the process of trying to engage them in an intelligent exchange, you end up dropping yourself down to their level. It is futile trying to interact with them as if they are looking for wisdom.

You may sometimes find yourself in situations where you need to answer someone so that you can expose their imprudent ideas. Many times, you are exposing their foolishness to those around them to prevent them from hurting someone. That's a choice that you need to consider carefully.

Proverbs 26:6-7

> [6] Like cutting off one's feet or drinking violence is the sending of a message by the hand of a fool. [7] Like a lame man's legs that hang limp is a proverb in the mouth of a fool.

Proverbs 26:6 reminds me of *The Field* (1990), a movie based on the fictionalized 1930 murder of a farmer in Ireland. The central character , Bull McCabe, was played by Richard Harris, and that name started to have more meaning as the movie went on.

Bull McCabe was a very strong man. He was part of that last generation that drove the British out of Ireland to create the free part of Ireland. The plot centered around Bull's desire to buy a field the landlord (who actually happens to be English) was going to sell because she felt isolated and terrorized at the time. She wanted to move on.

The story involved his son, Tadgh, and a person he employed who was the town idiot and drunk, Bird O'Donnellv. Bird was like a court jester and was good at stirring up trouble and delivering messages to Bull that ultimately led Bull down the wrong path. Bull became enraged about the circumstances that were going on around his attempt to acquire the land he rented. His son subsequently was killed. His death was inadvertently caused by Bull's actions, and some other things happened that were equally disastrous. In the end, his life came apart.

Bird went off on his merry way continuing to do what fools do — observing and giving information that leads people down the wrong path and making fun of others along the way. Even though Bull understood this, he was blind to it because the fool fed the ego in him that had developed. It overshadowed his good characteristics — common sense included. Many times in the movie, Bull used the fool to convey a false message, not understanding that the fool also conveyed a false message back to him.

There is a danger in being surrounded by people who can be manipulated by others. Even though they may be fools, their actions can boomerang back on the manipulator. Fools can often be skilled manipulators themselves.

In Proverbs 26:7, remember that Proverbs is not a formula. Instead, it is an approach that allows us to take advantage of our faith, wisdom, and knowledge. Some people aren't going to take advantage of it and won't learn the lesson because their minds are dull. Maybe they are dull from too much of the wrong type of experience or from self-medicating. Maybe they are dull for a different reason. Mindlessly quoting Proverbs is of no value to the fool. It is like a paralyzed body part that just keeps twitching. Only those who want to actually do better, be better, make wise decisions, open their mind up to knowledge, and possess a receptive attitude will get the most out of the words and approach of Proverbs.

Use these principles to open your mind, deepen your faith in God, and activate the best parts of yourself. You'll find that you also gain salvation — part of the communion of a spiritual relationship. When we earnestly seek to learn from God, he will respond and pour out His heart to us.

Proverbs 26:8-9

> [8] Like tying a stone in a sling is the giving of honor to a fool. [9] Like a thornbush in a drunkard's hand is a proverb in the mouth of a fool.

It is foolish to tie a stone to a slingshot and expect to hit something. It is just as foolish to praise or reward someone who doesn't deserve it. Perhaps you've seen it happen in your workplace when a problem team member has issues or is causing dissension. Sometimes the team's leader will try to make that person better, more loyal, or more productive because he thinks he can do something that will turn the problem team member around. The team leader will even try giving him more authority or responsibility. I've never seen that work.

As a manager, I tried it with a young salesperson who reported to me a number of years back. He was not a skilled, high-level salesperson. We were trying to sell to very large companies and financial houses, and this individual lacked the experience for the environment we were in.

This young man should never have been hired for the position because he wasn't qualified. We needed a senior-level salesperson experienced in selling complex information technology solutions to complex and large environments. The rudimentary skills that he did have — making phone calls and appointments — would have been better suited for a different sales environment such as an inside sales roles or at least something dramatically less complex.

This salesman and I reported to the same manager when he joined the company. Besides being under-qualified, he undermined his boss. I initially thought the issue was due to a personal conflict between the two. However, when I was promoted and became his supervisor, I realized he was just a negative, scheming, subversive individual. He was able to instigate unrest among other newer team members who were equally negative and banded together to undermine whoever was in charge. Their personal life was equally miserable and unhappy. They seemed to enjoy dwelling in their victimhood. Even though they didn't know each other before they arrived, their personalities drew them together. Like attracts like.

If you are on the Proverbs road to wisdom, you will find yourself repelled by these people. I have found myself drawn to people who want to be successful. Since then, my life has gone dramatically better both personally and professionally.

All the support and faith thrown at negative people is not going to transform them into positive leaders without the right attitude and foundation. People should earn the right to get additional responsibility and privileges in order to move ahead with ethical and morally sound behavior.

Proverbs 26:9 highlights another way to view this. Fools are not going to understand how to apply the wisdom and lessons of Proverbs. Instead they are going to view the adversity that comes their way through the same lens they always have. They will see themselves as a victim — it's the church's fault, it's their boss' fault, it's the company's fault, it's their spouse's fault, it's their neighbor's fault. It's everyone else's fault but their own. They rationalize, "If this or that were different, I would be okay because they're all against me," or "No one knows how to do anything other than me. That's why I have to do everything myself."

When you hear phrases like this on a consistent basis from someone, it is a sure sign that he is negative, subversive, and unsuccessful even though he may appear to be financially and professionally successful. When you look at the totality of his life, you realize he is so miserable and toxic that no one would want to live like that. Instead, take the high road and go for the balance offered in the Proverbs way of life.

Proverbs 26:13-16

> [13] The sluggard says, "There is a lion in the road, a fierce lion roaming the streets!" [14] As a door turns on its hinges, so a sluggard turns on his bed. [15] The sluggard buries his hand in the dish; he is too lazy to bring it back to his mouth. [16] The sluggard is wiser in his own eyes than seven men who answer discreetly.

These verses set the tone for a lot of failure in life. From personal experience, I have been lazy about some things at various times in my life, and it's no surprise that I didn't achieve success when that was a factor. In contrast, I have rarely been disappointed when I have worked diligently at something I was capable of — even if I didn't achieve the very thing that I was going after. I found that my hard work opened up doors and helped me to achieve other goals.

For example, I played a lot of basketball when I was a teenager growing up in New York City. I learned that most people aren't blessed with some kind of unseen hand that just whips the talent on them. Whether people dream of being a professional basketball player or just want to improve so they have bragging rights on the playground, they need to go out and practice.

Particularly in the summer when I wasn't in school, I would practice a couple hundred jump shots taken from different angles on the court each morning. At night, I practiced dribbling with my left hand so I could dribble as well with it as I could with my right hand. I lived in a small house with a little basement. You could always find me down there or out in our little backyard dribbling with my left hand. I started practicing layups and other moves with the left hand so I would have additional weapons in the arsenal.

I never made it to any great level in the world of basketball, but the diligence and the self-discipline paid off in many other ways down the road. It taught me to motivate myself to pursue certain goals. That translated into achieving various educational goals which helped further my career. I needed that tenacity when I set out to earn my MBA by attending classes at night and on the weekends. I started on it in my late twenties when we didn't have online courses and every school didn't have an MBA program. At that time, you needed to fight pretty hard to get into a decent school if you didn't make the Ivy League versions.

I was accepted into a school and started the four-year journey of attending school nights and weekends to earn my degree. I enjoyed learning which was important since I spent two-and-a-half hours in class two nights a week. I learned to stop focusing on the end and start concentrating on looking forward to the next class. Inevitably, I started concerning myself only with what I needed to prepare for the next class or whatever project was coming up for that class during the semester. Subsequently, I finished in three years and I earned what is considered a B-plus or A-minus average if you put a letter grade to it.

I majored in finance and information systems and even though I did not go on to a career in finance, having that on my résumé has always been a plus. As things have progressed, the additional educational degree has become much more of a requirement, even for sales and sales management positions or situations that normally didn't require it. The reason is simple: employers want employees who are self-motivated, self-directed, and self-organizing.

In my case most of the time, I was going two nights a week (including the summer) and then all day on Saturday. I gave up a lot of partying and fun and ended up leaving some people behind. But I also met some new people along the way. As my career advanced, my circles expanded to include like-minded people who were interested in furthering their career and their position in life. I found myself in a world I wouldn't have been exposed to without dedication and commitment. I also found myself needing to ignore the people who urged me to take a different, less successful course in life.

All this simply means is that if I were lazy, I wouldn't have taken two hundred jump shots in the morning nor would I have gone to school two nights a week and all day Saturday while working full time and studying when I could have been doing something else. Because I was focused on advancing my education and career, I was able to do so with sacrifice and planning.

People who want to overcome laziness should take a good look at themselves. If they spend their evenings after work on the couch frequently but daydream about moving ahead in life, they will only move ahead if the couch slides across the floor. What people do after five o'clock is more important than what they do before five o'clock in terms of what the future may hold — particularly if they are looking to transition into running their own business, have an additional business, or go back to school. It all starts with a few small steps toward that change such as setting some concrete, realistic goals and just stepping toward them gently. Most people find a self-organizational tool such as a day planner helpful. Whatever you decide, set goals, take some steps, and stick to your plan.

Proverbs 26:17

> [7] Like one who seizes a dog by the ears is a passer-by who meddles in a quarrel not his own.

No matter how docile dogs are, if you yank their ears, you will get their attention — and most of the time in the form of teeth.

Conflict in a marriage or relationship between two people is best handled by the two people in the relationship. No matter how close you are to one or both parties, resist the urge to get involved. If someone is being physically harmed by another person (whether they are in a relationship or you just happen to pass a couple arguing on the street), that's the time to call the authorities. They are trained to insert themselves as legal professionals to handle the conflict. You especially do not want to get in the middle of someone's marriage conflict. Take care of your own business. Chances are you have enough problems running your own life that you don't have the energy left to really have any intelligent, positive effect on anyone else's relationship.

If family members or friends are having problems, recommend that they get professional counseling or faith-based counseling. It will be resolved much faster with someone who is trained to deal with relationship issues. In relationship conflicts, it's hard to get both sides of the story, and you may only get bits and pieces. It is one thing to lend a sympathetic ear. It is totally another to give advice and interject your opinions. You'll find yourself giving advice that may not address all the issues and then wind up confused because they aren't taking it anyway. You don't want to be the one who helped drive them apart — even if it is the best thing for both parties. Part of the growth of a relationship is learning to resolve conflict together.

Stay out of the conflict and keep your opinion to yourself. You'll be much more help if you recommend counseling, wish the best for them, and pray for them. Unless there is something illegal going on or some kind of dangerous situation that may be life-threatening such as physical abuse, mind your business. Until you walk in their shoes, you have no idea what they are going through, and it's best to urge them to seek professional help.

Proverbs 26:20

[20] Without wood a fire goes out; without gossip a quarrel dies down.

Gossip is just as harmful as taking drugs, drinking too much, or smoking. Constantly dwelling on every little bit of trouble or irritation only keeps the fire of conflict and emotional unrest burning and injects unnecessary drama into a situation. Avoiding that negative behavior is like taking the wood from the fire — it eventually goes out.

Letting go of the past is key to stopping the drama. We need to forgive and move on. When we continue to dwell on past issues, the other person doesn't suffer but we continue to experience the mental anguish. When we forgive, we get the most out of it. We forgive for ourselves and not for the other people involved. If someone has wronged you, not forgiving that person is like carrying them around with you. No matter how badly you were treated and how wrong the infraction was, you will benefit greatly through forgiveness.

Letting it go can be difficult. It needs to be an active, intentional gesture. You could verbally say you are letting it go and forgiving them. You could also write it on a piece of paper and then throw it away. Be creative. By doing that, you release yourself and the associated pent-up emotion so you can move on. Have you ever found that you are holding a grudge against someone who doesn't even know you're holding a grudge and doesn't care? Maybe that person doesn't even know you. Hanging on to the grudge doesn't do anyone any good. Let it go and do something useful with that energy. Plow it back into acquiring wisdom and leveraging knowledge to better your life.

As we have seen from reading this chapter, being a fool can take many forms, and we should do our best to recognize and avoid this behavior. One way is by gossip. Mean-spirited gossip may damage the person you are speaking about, but it can also boomerang back to you in a negative way.

Another foolish method is false flattery — otherwise known as lying — to ingratiate yourself with someone. If you are doing it to make friends, you will have to keep it up to maintain the friendship. If you are going to expend that type of energy, put it into something positive instead.

Lastly, don't be foolish and continue to fuel your anger. Be honest with yourself about who you are and start to work through it scripturally or in another way. Remember it will eat away at you causing the most damage to the one who continues to harbor the poison of angry grudge holding.

Action Steps on the Life Path

Write down two instances when you resisted listening to good advice because you either didn't want to hear it or take it. Were you acting foolish? If so, why? How will you correct this moving forward for your own good?

_____

_____

_____

_____

_____

Have you ever found yourself behaving like Bird O'Donnelly or Bull McCabe? If so, when and under what circumstances? What were the results for you and the others involved? Is this ethical behavior? Why or why not?

_____

_____

_____

_____

_____

List your three to five best talents. Are you properly exploiting them? If not, why and how will you do better in the future? How will you apply discipline to yourself and your time to make your talents work to your best advantage?

_____

_____

_____

_____

_____

_____

PROVERBS *27*

Still Foolish?

> *"Be sure you know the condition of your flocks, give careful*
> *attention to your herds; for riches do not endure forever,*
> *and a crown is not secure for all generations."*
>
> *Proverbs 27:23-24*

Today's lesson comes from Proverbs 27 — one of the Proverbs of Solomon that was part of the collection written by King Hezekiah's advisors. I entitled this chapter "Still Foolish" because we clearly defined foolish behavior in Chapter 26, and we explore ways to both avoid and prevent foolish behavior in this chapter.

For example, boasting about what you will do before executing or putting together a plan to get it done is foolish. It is smart to follow the advice of a true friend rather than someone who says what you want to hear or reinforces the easy way out. Seeking honest counsel as opposed to following bad advice can prevent you from making a fool of yourself. Lastly, pay careful attention to your personal and business affairs. Don't assume it will all just work itself out.

Proverbs 27:1

> [1] Do not boast about tomorrow for you do not know what a day may bring forth;

You may brag about what you are going to accomplish somewhere down the road; however, stay firmly grounded. Think about what you are doing right now and the effect it has not only on you but on those around you. Don't go too far down the road living out the successes of the future until you have started laying the groundwork for those successes. This scripture advises everyone to keep a level head and stay reasonable.

It doesn't mean that you shouldn't see yourself in success scenarios out in the future. Instead, it indicates that we shouldn't live out there without doing what is necessary to become successful. A simple example is spending your bonus money before you've received it. You may dream about being a multimillionaire. You may dream about having a successful relationship with your spouse. You may dream about being successful at work. You may dream about being a championship swimmer. However, someone who spends the majority of her time on the couch with cheese doodles watching mind-numbing programming probably is not going to achieve those goals. So lay the groundwork, and do the homework. Only then will future take care of itself.

Proverbs 27:6

> 6 Wounds from a friend can be trusted, but an enemy multiplies kisses;

Consider the sources of advice or interaction you have. A friend who has your best interests at heart sometimes will have to tell you the truth — even though it may hurt. Being sincere about having the kind of friends who will listen to you and be honest means being willing to listen to their feedback and advice. Good friends can be a reliable source of advice that is honest, sincere, ethical, and wise even when you don't want to hear it. However, the advice can force you to evaluate your own behavior and compel you to then consider next steps.

Take, for example, someone who is one hundred pounds overweight and doing nothing about the issue. That person is focused on concentrating exclusively on the symptoms caused by being overweight such as adult-onset diabetes and high blood pressure. They should instead address the root cause and not use medication as the only answer but rather part of a broader solution that involves lifestyle change. The answer can be as simple as eating the right foods and getting a moderate amount of exercise.

Therefore, in addition to any medication used to control the symptoms, that individual should see a nutritionist and health expert to put together a personalized program of lifestyle change.

It may not be easy at first, but the payoff is worth it. A healthy lifestyle can lengthen a person's life, give them a better quality of life, and allow them to be a better parent, spouse, and employee. Not taking positive steps such as these can leave someone sick and moody and cause them to struggle to work and interact with others.

This is an important issue for me not only because I have lost friends and family members prematurely but also because I see the negative results of bad lifestyle choices daily. Health concerns will probably require some tough choices to reverse the problems related to a lifetime of behavior such as overeating or smoking. The end result will be good, but it will take determination initially. He may have to reduce or eliminate some foods he has enjoyed eating for a lifetime. He will probably have to start exercising even though he doesn't enjoy exercise. He may have to fight the urge to hit the snooze alarm when it goes off at five o'clock in the morning so he can do a run or a fast walk before work. He may initially feel left out by not joining the other smokers outside the office on a break. However, the positive health benefits far outweigh any transitory discomfort.

A caring friend would probably suggest that his overweight buddy change some things in his life. That advice might include eliminating processed and fatty foods. He might suggest some exercises his friend could try to get him started on the right path. A caring friend would be there to encourage him along the way.

Not all friends are encouraging. Someone who doesn't have your best interests at heart may reinforce the self-destructive behavior of eating an improper diet, skipping exercise, continuing to smoke, and drinking too much. We all have to reassess our relationships occasionally. If a friend drags us down, it might be important to cut him loose. Start considering the source of the advice you receive from friends. Do your friends truly care about your success and have a positive effect on your life? Or are they toxic and unempowering?

Proverbs 27:15-16

> [15] A quarrelsome wife is like a constant dripping on a rainy day;
> [16] Restraining her is like restraining the wind or grasping oil with the hand;

Nagging — a continual, steady stream of "advice" — is a slow, torturous experience. We characterize women as the naggers, but men nag too. Generally, naggers are well-meaning people who think they are not getting through to the other person. Unfortunately, this behavior is forcing the recipient to shut down tight. When that happens, naggers cannot accomplish their objective. When nagging turns into torture, it becomes destructive and ruins the relationship leaving the other party feeling trapped. Nagging can become a habit.

Are you a nagger? If you are, take an honest look in the mirror. If the nagging is not getting through, you may want to try a different approach. First, ask yourself about your own motivation for engaging in the behavior. Is it about being right and getting your way? Is it about winning or showing the other person they're wrong? If you are truly concerned about the other person, nagging isn't going to work. You need to find a more effective way to get through to them. I suggest counseling for married couples where this is a factor. For Christian couples, strive to find a faith-based counselor.

Counseling helps shed light on issues for both parties. Ultimately, it is up to the individuals to determine whether or not they will take the advice and implement a new behavior. But it can provide great alternatives to nagging. It can help the individuals develop more effective ways of communicating which is a foundation for a great relationship.

Proverbs 27:18

> [18] He who tends a fig tree, will eat its fruit, and he who looks after his master will be honored;

When we're in a leadership position, we are called to lead. Just because someone has been given a management title and meets the company's standards in the job description doesn't mean he is equipped to lead a team. A business owner may be good at planning and organizing. However, leadership skills are necessary for leading a team that is empowered, effective, and productive.

Assess your leadership technique. Do you allow people to share their concerns with you and give honest feedback? Is it give and take both ways even though clearly the buck stops with you in terms of making a decision? Are you recognizing the people who deserve your attention because they are reliable team members or are you overlooking them? Are you taking the time to recognize them for their hard work? Do you address issues when they arise or is your attention diverted elsewhere? Do you help them resolve issues or unfairly blame others to make them look like your problems are everyone else's problem?

People want to follow a strong leader. They want to receive recognition, honest feedback, and encouragement. They notice poor leadership. They notice when someone consistently responds in a negative way. I call them "yes, but" people. They say things like, "*Yes,* this was good, *but* something else had happened before, so it's not as good as it could be."

Regardless of what type of leadership role you occupy, acknowledge and support the people who earnestly try to be the most reliable and helpful they can. And when it's time to address problems, make sure you are engaged in the solution and address poor behavior and performance in your team members.

Proverbs 27:21

[21] The crucible for silver and the furnace for gold, but man is tested by the praise he receives;

In these lessons, we have recognized adversity as a teacher; but praise is a teacher as well. How we handle it reveals how we are made much like high temperatures test a precious metal. So how do praise and accolades affect you? Are you motivated by them? Do you work more diligently after you receive them? Your attitude toward praise says a lot about you just like your attitude toward adversity reveals your character. Anyone with a high degree of integrity is not swayed by praise or the lack of it. This verse says we should temper our reaction to praise. Focusing on the pursuit of praise can cause you to lose your way. It can be used as a weapon to manipulate you when someone puts you in a position that makes you feel that you can do no wrong and make no mistakes.

Do what you sincerely believe is right given the situation and the people that you are dealing with rather than what you will be praised for. It is more important to do what is right, wise, ethical, and moral.

Proverbs 27:23-27

> [23] Be sure you know the conditions of your flocks, give careful attention to your herds; [24] For riches do not endure forever, and a crown is not secure for all generations; [25] When the hay is removed and new growth appears, and the grass from the hills is gathered in; [26] The lambs will provide you with clothing, and the goats with the price of a field; [27] You will have plenty of goat's milk to feed you, and your family and to nourish your servant girls;

As I write this book, we are enduring a time of intense recession. We have come out of a period of plenty for some but not for others. It is time to reflect and ask if we are doing all we can to make it through this phase. Some prepared for it while others did not.

Regardless, now that it is upon us, we should do all we can to make it through this period of lack so we can take advantage of the opportunities that follow a recession. Economic conditions are cyclical. We can't depend upon the president of the United States to make the changes that we need in our individual life. The president's job is to lead the nation and his section of the government and interact with Congress and the judicial branch. But ultimately, the citizens have to act responsibly and set the standard for our leaders of what we expect from them and what we will and will not tolerate.

If you have not saved appropriately for this recessionary period, you are probably feeling the pain now. You may have been let go from your job, and you may not have put away enough money to make it through a year's worth of unemployment or hard times. If you are in this situation, it doesn't make you a bad person, but you most likely want to prepare for the next recession.

So be diligent and prepare for the future even though we are moving through a very challenging era. Try to gain as much foresight as possible and give responsible attention to things that matter such as your family, home, and career. Be a good, responsible steward of the resources you have at your disposal so they can shield you better during the next recessionary period. Think ahead intelligently and plan. It's not an option to "play it by ear." That doesn't work very well. You may get away with it once or twice,

Still Foolish?

but life requires a plan for the future. Those who plan and execute on their plans tend to come out better than those who don't.

Take a look at the various areas of your personal and professional life. How are you going to move ahead? It may involve getting additional education, attaining additional resources of some type, or studying something on your own that will help propel things forward. Evaluate everything and make note of the areas of your life that need attention so you can design the plan necessary to make that happen.

This chapter began with verses that warn us to pay attention to our business, and I would like to summarize it in the same way. As surely as following foolish advice will adversely affect you and your family in a negative way, so will undue reliance on the false shield of money. The good thing about a recession or depression is that after you come out of it, you should have learned the hard lesson that no amount of money can protect you from bad investments or "taking your eye off the ball." Just when you think you are safe, poor planning and lack of focus will put you in the position of losing everything.

Action Steps on the Life Path

What is the best way to change your behavior and become a more effective communicator?

_____

_____

_____

Fights, quarrels, and nagging are sometimes symptomatic of other things that aren't being said. Other times, we are fight "ghosts" from previous relationships where we are acting out unresolved issues that we had somewhere else along the line. Is there someone in your life that you find yourself nagging or quarreling with? If so, what is the real reason? What are your motivations when you're engaged in self-destructive behavior of this type?

_____

_____

_____

_____

_____

What are the three things you are going to do over the next thirty days, six months, and twelve months to make a dramatic change in some area your life? Be specific and put a date of completion next to the action.

_____

_____

_____

_____

_____

_____

_____

Wise Living Is Learning from Your Mistakes

"He who conceals his sins does not prosper, but whoever
confesses and renounces them finds mercy."

Proverbs 28:13

This chapter addresses our relationship with money, wealth, family, friends, and the poor. At first glance, Proverbs 28:13 would seem to be out of place. But upon closer inspection, it is very appropriate. The wrong relationship with money and wealth leads us down a sinful path. If we sin, then how do we right the wrong and heal the wounds?

Confession and acknowledgement are the cure. People strongly resist doing this which is why we are fascinated with, admire, and are willing to forgive those who do. Always being "right" is not only wrong-headed but impossible. The quest to make more and keep all of what we make or possess will force us to make the wrong decisions. It will also lead us to possibly hurt people and multiply poor decisions unless we are able to take the first step toward being forgiven — to admit we did something wrong in the first place. Even though we have addressed this previously, Proverbs 28 will shed more light on the topic.

² When a country is rebellious, it has many rulers, but a man of understanding and knowledge maintains order.

This verse is particularly relevant in the period of recession (or any time of turmoil) that we live in now. The excesses of the early part of the new millennium have revealed themselves through too much deregulation, practices to weaken financial industry oversight, and the acts of some greedy, irresponsible people who have acted illegally. During this era, those who operate and police our financial and governmental institutions have brought it to near collapse. Now we have leaders who are putting forth a plan that will hopefully bring us out of it. Time will tell if that is the case.

Our country has had many recessions during its history. We shouldn't point fingers during a time of recession. Rather, we should focus on the solution and prevent future events from occurring in the exact same way. Economic downturns highlight how irresponsible leadership can put us into this position, but we need wise, intelligent, thoughtful, and accountable direction to bring us out of it.

We are called to study how society reacts when it reaches a crisis point. We also must review the tone or the style of management that brought us into the crisis. Even though they may not have caused it, they were on duty when it hit. By and large, when the government changes hands during a crisis, it goes in a completely opposite direction in terms of style and approach because people believe — and many times rightly so — that we need a new way of doing, approaching, and looking at things.

Most believe that to get out of the crisis, they need someone who is knowledgeable, intelligent, and trustworthy. Those are traits that we should always look for, but we seem to become much more focused in our search for them after a crisis hits.

The same thing can occur in a workplace. For example, many employees steal from their employers. You might say, "No, not me." But theft happens is subtle ways. It's not just taking home paperclips or an extra pen. Workplace theft happens when we don't give our employers one hundred percent in effort and attitude. Slacking, particularly during a crisis period, is stealing from the company. Being distracted in such a way that productivity is lowered is stealing from the company as well.

Look in the mirror and ask yourself, "Am I stealing from my employer? If the answer is "yes," then adjust your attitude. People who show up for work — no matter where that work is — with a negative, small-minded, or mean-spirited attitude are probably not giving all they can give. And people who do that aren't just stealing from their employer — they are robbing themselves too.

A positive attitude and one-hundred-percent effort are really what we should give. Those traits will get us through many more tough situations than we believe. It is better to have that in many cases than to be well-skilled but lazy and ineffective with a poor attitude.

Now let's relate that to a marriage or romantic relationship between two people because the dynamic is so powerful. If someone is not giving the relationship one hundred percent or has a negative attitude, the relationship will suffer or even disintegrate. Giving a one-hundred-percent effort and positive attitude expands and strengthens your personal relationship and makes it something you can depend on when the rest of the world becomes a hostile place. It can provide a haven to retreat to when you need to recharge your battery so you can go out and fight again.

Proverbs 28:5

> 5 Evil men do not understand justice, but those who seek the Lord understand it fully;

Being a person of faith can be a challenge, but justice and love are what God is about. We aren't called to be a doormat to be run over and abused. And there is nothing wrong with being a fierce competitor or an uncompromising business person as long as you are moral, ethical, and just.

In business, all parties need to reach an amicable agreement in negotiations. If one party feels that he entered into an agreement where he is not getting full value, it will adversely affect the relationship. Even if the slight was unintentional, as Christians, we are called to handle it justly and resolve the issue.

Ignoring human suffering is bad for all. We are called to help our fellow man in a way that makes sense for each individual. I choose to do it through my support of charitable activities and through my church. For someone else, it might mean helping an elderly neighbor or a young family member who is having a tough time. Pay attention to the needs around you and around the world, and ask yourself how you can help to be an active part of correcting injustice and human suffering. Don't wait to be asked.

Proverbs 28:9-11

> [9] If anyone turns a deaf ear to the law, even his prayers are detestable; [10] He who leads the upright along an evil path, will fall into his own trap; But the blameless, will receive a good inheritance; [11] A rich man may be wise in his own eyes, but a poor man who has discernment sees through him;

These scriptures tell us that God doesn't answer your prayers when you engage in negative behavior. He understands your intention as well as hears your words.

Let's apply this at a personal level. Say someone's goal is to improve her health, and she prayed for God to help her lose weight as one of the steps. All the prayer in the world isn't going to help her if she doesn't want to change her diet and get some exercise. She has to be sincere and give up the cupcakes, cheese doodles, fatty foods, soda, processed flour, and the excess sugar. Jumping on the fad-diet bandwagon doesn't build the discipline to create the lifestyle change needed to keep the weight off. When we engage in behavior that is at odds with the outcome we are praying for, God can't help us.

Losing weight and then keeping it off requires new habits. The benefit is improved health and vitality. In many cases, it can improve adult-onset diabetes and hypertension. Subtle but diligent changes in your behavior can make a big difference. It might be difficult to work in that morning walk, but you could walk to lunch or to the appointment that is ten minutes away instead of taking a taxi or driving.

These scriptures advise us to be consistent in our words and our actions. If we say we love our children or spouse but our actions don't reflect love, they don't believe us. Some of us are only acting the way we saw our parents act, but we have to break that cycle of negativity. It can be as easy are starting with a simple compliment to your spouse. If your spouse spends a lot of time at work, tell him or her that you'd love to spend more time together even if it means giving up some luxuries. Thank them for what they are doing for your family. Compliment them on the meal.

Praising the behavior you want to see more of can be much more powerful than nagging someone about the behavior you want changed.

How are you applying this to your career? Are you praying for a career change or advancement? Are you doing the things you need to do to support that desire? Are you updating your education or your skills? Are you networking? Are you involved in professional organizations. All of these things will help you reach your goal of being successful, employed in the type of role you desire, and being more prosperous.

The alternative to making those positive changes is engaging in the group pity party by the water cooler complaining: "The job's not paying me enough," "My commute is too long," and "This job isn't getting me anywhere." That behavior is not making you a dime or helping your future. If those are indeed real issues, it's time to take a look in the mirror and ask why those conditions exist and what you can do about them. What can you do to increase your skills so you can advance. Is your long commute worth it? What companies are closer to home? What kind of jobs are you qualified for that offer the advancement opportunities you desire. If you don't qualify, determine what you need to do to change that.

We may not love our current job, but it's not a volunteer role. We get paid to be there and our employer deserves our earnest efforts as long as we are engaged in that relationship. If, for some reason, that does not fit with the overall balance of our life and it skews things in a painful manner, it's time to find another way to make a living. But standing around complaining about it to other coworkers when we should be doing something productive is foolish.

Proverbs 28:11 touches on a different concern that I call in some cases: "The rising-tide-lifts-all-boats syndrome." Just making money does not make you wonderful. At various times, we go through these national or global economic bubble periods where people make money easily. We might be fortunate enough to work for a company with stock options that increased quickly in value. Perhaps someone came up with an idea that sold really well and allowed people to make an incredible amount of extra income because the conditions were right. It seems as if when everything is going our way, the good times are never going to end.

However, we know from history that the economy is cyclical. Having so much helps us develop a dangerous habit of spending too much. It's not unlikely that someone could end up with a fourth mortgage on his home to resolve his consumer debt issues and then immediately invest in more consumer items to run that debt up again. Even during the transition to an economic downturn, he can still feel pretty confident and forget that money does not make us smarter or more wonderful. At some point, the piper has to be paid.

We need balance in good times and bad. We need diligence to keep the amount in our checkbook from steering us away from the things that are important. We need to continue to develop the moral grounding, faith, meditation, and prayer and continue to invest in ourselves spiritually throughout the process.

Conversely, don't think badly of yourself if you are poor. The same process and the richness of a spirit developed by a prosperous spiritual life will help you through a tough period and help you overcome and improve your circumstances.

No matter what your condition — rich or poor — think about where you are, the benefits of that situation, where you are going, and the end goal.

Proverbs 28:13

> [13] He who conceals his sins does not prosper, but whoever confesses and renounces them finds mercy;

Let's not dwell on sin right now. Let's address mistakes because ultimately committing a sin is making a mistake. Consider something simple like taking a test. Say you're a good student, and you take a test and only miss one or two questions. Do you ever notice how you never again forget the correct answers to those questions? The reason you missed the questions is clear and you can't hide from the red marks on your test. You admit it, learn from it, and strive to not make the same mistake again.

So why do we treat sin differently? Why should we hide it and not learn from it? Not admitting our mistakes only hurts us. It is easy to rationalize that if no one notices our mistakes, we don't need to confess them. The learning begins when we confess our mistakes.

Think about the people you know who try to hide wrong behavior. Can you imagine reporting to someone who can never admit he is wrong? Everyone else is always wrong — the people who report to him, his boss, the company, and the rest of the world. To him, it is always someone else who

Wise Living Is Learning from Your Mistakes

made the mistake. People who can't admit they are wrong don't grow or learn, and they become increasingly difficult to deal with.

We have all dealt with people who will not admit to mistakes. They tend to build a wall around themselves and see others as enemies. I've caught myself in the same trap, but once I moved past the struggle to admit that I am wrong, it was liberating. There is a freedom to be able to say, "You know what? I was wrong about that and I need to do it a different way," or apologize to someone by saying, "You know what? My apologies on that one." People get caught off guard because they are not used to hearing others admit they are wrong. Too many try to make a case for why their view is right instead of just admitting the mistake. It's a pleasant surprise to hear someone say, "No, my apologies, I didn't jot it down correctly. I'll do better next time." I find when I commit to do better next time, I inevitably do — maybe because I know someone will hold me accountable to that commitment.

On the other side of the coin, you want to create an environment where people can feel safe to admit and learn from their mistakes. When we vilify and demonize people because they make a mistake, we stop getting information. You want people to feel that they can make mistakes for the sake of learning. Now there is a difference between an honest mistake and lazy sloppiness on a continual basis (intellectually or physically); but even when people are giving one hundred percent, the effort does not always guarantee perfection. No one is perfect. But when people strive to learn from mistakes, inevitably they improve.

We don't always have to be right to feel good about ourselves. Even when we make an error, we can feel good about what we learned and how we overcame it. Life is not a test in school. It is a continuous-improvement process with failure as the ultimate teacher, and we have to treat it that way.

Remember, the most important step toward forgiveness — including forgiving yourself — is to confess. It is a courageous act to say, "I did something wrong, it's not going to happen again, and it was an honest mistake." You don't always have to be right to feel good about yourself. In fact, you will increase and reinforce a strong self-image in the process. I wasn't always like that, and I've found new freedom and peace of mind in being able to learn and grow from my mistakes and help others to grow through theirs. Even if you work around people who can't admit to mistakes, don't do as those individuals do. Take the high road, and do what you know is right.

Proverbs 28:17-18

> [17] A man tormented by the guilt of murder, will be a fugitive till death, let no one support him; [18] He whose walk is blameless is kept safe, but he whose ways are perverse will suddenly fall;

In this scripture, the author has used murder to symbolize the transgressions that we commit against other people or they commit against us. In addition to wisdom, part of the theme in Proverbs is the need to forgive others and forgive ourselves. However, we haven't covered how important it is to hold the person we are forgiving accountable for their actions. Whether or not the person who wronged you is aware of or acknowledges his guilt, it is important that we strive to forgive him. If we don't, we begin to experience all of the emotional and psychological turmoil that a grudge entails. Forgiveness, while difficult to do, will free you.

Forgiving someone doesn't mean that you can't hold that person accountable. You are not under any obligation to make them feel better about what they have done if they are not sincerely acknowledging their guilt. Depending on the infraction, the individual should feel remorse whether he committed wrong accidentally or intentionally. That person needs to voluntarily come forward to apologize sincerely and try to make restitution. If he does that, forgive him and acknowledge his apology. He should understand the full weight of what he did.

This process of acknowledging the wrongdoing, apologizing, and offering restitution helps clean the slate so that you both can move forward. Particularly in the instance where you have to continue to either work or live with this person, it allows the sin to be cleansed away so that some measure of trust can be regained and the relationship can mend.

We don't want to interfere with the natural process of someone acknowledging their guilt, understanding to consequences of their actions, and letting their conscience reveal their mistake. My dear mother was from the South and she used to say, "Ohhh yeah, their conscience is probably whipping them. That's why I haven't heard from them!" I used to chuckle at her and didn't quite know what she was saying when I was younger. Now that I am older and understand the importance of forgiveness and acknowledgement of guilt, I get it. When I have done something wrong and had to acknowledge my guilt, apologize, and make restitution, in some way, my conscience was "whipping" me. It was a natural consequence of maturity to come to the realization that I was not always right and that — whether in the case of an honest mistake or trying to get away with something I knew was wrong — I was accountable for acknowledging it and apologizing for it.

You don't have to believe in God to understand the power of forgiveness and move away from retribution. But through sincere forgiveness for genuine acknowledgement comes the power of absolution and the ability to free yourself from the emotional baggage. Are there situations in your life that you are still hanging on to where you can apply this concept?

Proverbs 28:19

> [19] He who works his land will have abundant food, but the one who chases fantasies will have his fill of poverty.

I will put aside my "spiritual" hat for a second and address this one in a slightly different way. If you have dreams of working for yourself and having a dramatically shorter work week (less than forty hours), forget it; that falls squarely under the heading of fantasy. Unless you are working part-time to supplement retirement benefits, the great likelihood is that to make your business profitable, you will work harder than you ever have.

Most of us work for companies — even if we have part-time businesses — and we should use the "work-your-land-slowly" approach. Take for example our relationship with credit. Buying now and paying later without planning can land you in bankruptcy or foreclosure. However, careful tilling of your land allows you to avoid these two disasters. Here are some things to know about successfully using credit.

- Manage debt and credit. Debt and instant credit are part of our everyday life. This use of instant credit, however, has taken its toll. Many use credit cards to spend more than their means, and a few actually build themselves a prison that buries them alive. Wise management is the only way to intelligently use credit.

- Sparingly use installment debt. Use a mortgage to buy a home and pay cash for everything else.

- Avoid revolving credit. Avoid these cards and instead use a charge card that must be paid in full monthly. The interest rates are so high, they virtually make you an indentured servant if you fall behind.
- Use credit wisely. Use credit intelligently. Examine the terms of the cards you are currently using. Keep track of your cards, their rates, and your current balances as this will help you to be aware of how you use credit cards.
- Eliminate credit card debt. Based on your current spending practices, create a realistic budget to pay off your credit card debt in the shortest time possible while not adding any more debt to it.
- Limit the role of debt. Buy a home and eliminate consumer debt.

Taking this type of action on just the debt in your life will eliminate an incredible burden from your financial life which will help you improve many other aspects of your life.

Proverbs 28:26

> [26] Those who trust their own insight are foolish, but anyone who walks in wisdom is safe;

Picture for a second an old Western movie or a modern version such as Clint Eastwood's *Dirty Harry*. This rugged individual rides into town alone, and for the next two hours, he cleans up the place and roots out the bad guys. He never seeks advice but periodically gives advice as he dispenses justice at the end of a six-shooter.

That's a great image for Hollywood, and it makes for neat storytelling. There is something so romantic and alluring about that whole Clint Eastwood or John Wayne type of image. On the big screen, they are bold, they take action, and they don't suffer fools easily. However, that is the movie screen, and it doesn't work in reality. Anyone who operates like that in real life may achieve a certain amount of success but will eventually be doomed to failure.

We all see images in the news of dictators and political "strong men." History is filled with people who were able to steamroll their way up to a certain point before complete collapse and implosion. We can look back and easily find a dictator, businessperson, or public figure who has failed because of their fearless, strong-armed approach. You see it happen with celebrities who surround themselves with enough "yes" people that they no longer have insight from real people with real advice. They become insulated and start to make mistakes because they don't interact with the greater world so that they can listen to and take cues from it.

Take the wisdom-based or spiritual path — God's way — and admit, acknowledge, and operate this way. No one can predict the future. We can't predict the consequences of our life with any certainty. You can take certain actions and attempt to create a certain outcome, but that is all you can do. We're not totally self-reliant or totally dependent. The wisdom we need to exercise comes from being interdependent with others.

Interdependence allows us to take advice, learn from situations, and understand the benefit of collaborating with intelligent, like-minded, wise people. Like-minded people may not necessarily think the same way you do on a particular topic, and they may indeed even disagree. However, they are wise in and of themselves, and their viewpoint is valuable.

If our work is blessed with success, we should enjoy it in a humble manner — not because we aren't proud of our accomplishments but instead to show respect to divine guidance and those around us who helped us along the way. Wealth is a deceptive defense and weapon because it is only a tool that affords us certain opportunities. Rather, it is the wisdom employed to attain wealth and the judicious use of it that transforms money into a formidable weapon. In actual fact, the wrong attitude toward money and wealth can completely wreck relationships both inside and outside your home. Use wise thinking for balanced connections with money and healthy relationships with people.

Action Steps on the Life Path

Examine your behavior for a moment. Write down two or three types of behavior that are critical to your life right now. Do you have any behavior that is at odds with your success?

_____

_____

_____

_____

Make note of areas where you are unwilling to admit mistakes. Do you want to change this approach? How will you accomplish that?

_____

_____

_____

_____

_____

Give careful thought to Proverbs 28:28: "When the wicked rise to power, people go into hiding; but when the wicked perish the righteous thrive." Take three to five minutes and write down your reaction to this verse. How does this verse apply to our world today? If you need more space, consider writing your thoughts in a journal.

_____

_____

_____

_____

_____

_____

What you think about helping the poor? How can you personally make your community and your world a better place?

_____

_____

_____

_____

_____

_____

_____

Many of these verses cover being unfaithful, being stingy, and stealing. What did you think when you read those passages? Did you think about some things you do or see other people doing differently?

_____

_____

_____

_____

_____

_____

_____

Wise Living Is Learning from Your Mistakes

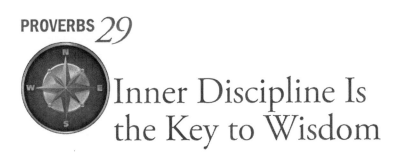

PROVERBS *29*

Inner Discipline Is the Key to Wisdom

"A fool gives full vent to his anger, but a wise man keeps himself under control."

Proverbs 29:11

This chapter covers several themes which resonate with me because of their emphasis on discipline — not the discipline of physical violence or corporal punishment but rather the discipline of correcting character flaws that feed poor decision making. Discipline is something we must exercise personally; otherwise, we can't teach it to others such as our children or employees. People are more likely to learn from us when we model the correct behavior. Of course, you can force someone to do what you tell them or act in a certain way when you can see them, but this doesn't require inner wisdom. Instead, it just requires fear. We are better people and a more productive society when we do the right thing because it is the right thing to do. Discipline ensures that we will do the right thing when no one is looking.

Remember one of the definitions of *discipline*[6] as given to us by *Merriam-Webster's Collegiate® Dictionary, 11th Edition* is *training that corrects, molds, or*

---

[6] By permission. From *Merriam-Webster's Collegiate® Dictionary, 11th Edition* ©2010 by Merriam-Webster, Incorporated (www.Merriam-Webster.com).

perfects the mental faculties or moral character. In other words, discipline is the companion of wisdom.

Proverbs 29:1

> [1] A man who remains stiff-necked after many rebukes will suddenly be destroyed — without remedy.

We should be willing to listen to input from people who are wise in their area of expertise and can help us navigate our personal, business, and spiritual paths. When we accept wise counsel, the likelihood of making a mistake we can't recover from is reduced significantly.

Unfortunately, some individuals are so stubborn that they discard wise counsel and take dangerous chances. We never know when we are getting our last chance. In the case of someone involved in gang life, drug dealing, or criminal activity, it ends in jail or death. If that individual is lucky, it may end in a short sentence and allow him to recover his life. Most likely though, that person who kept taking risky chances and making foolish decisions ends up serving a life sentence or on death row which dramatically limits any second chances.

This verse also advises us to recognize the fact that we need to immediately change negative behavior that is counterproductive to how we should conduct our life. One of my favorite life coaches — entrepreneur, author, and peak performance strategist Tony Robbins — says "We need to take massive action," — whatever that massive action might be. It could be a dramatic new health regime under the guidance of your doctor, some kind of radical educational approach, something new you are going to be doing at work, or some kind of massive action to improve or save your marriage or relationship. Whatever the change agent is, it needs to be life-altering and must be conducted with a sense of urgency.

Understand the urgency of the situation — even if it seemingly isn't urgent for you. It might end up being the last straw. For a smoker, for instance, chest pains or some other physical signal might provide that wake-up call that things need to change and it's time to stop smoking. A good friend of mine who was a smoker hurt himself, and he couldn't get to the store on his own. His immediate family didn't respond to his request for cigarettes.

It was a wake-up call that he needed to break his smoking habit, and he saw this as an opportunity to do it. He understood smoking was going to negatively affect his health, and he took this opportunity to free himself of it. God bless him because his friends and family will have him around longer. He had to choose to take the massive action of breaking his addiction to cigarettes.

Cigarettes are a good example because of their ubiquitous presence, their emotional triggers in our society, the addictive nature, and the massive health costs they generate. My mother smoked for many years. She started smoking before she was pregnant with me, stopped while she was pregnant, and then started again shortly after I was born. Throughout her life, she smoked and drank some. She also developed diabetes and even though she took medication, she did not eat properly. In her early sixties, she got sick.

One day, she passed out. Luckily, some neighbors were able to find her in time. After a short stay in the hospital, she was able to bounce back. Obeying her doctor's orders, she stopped smoking and drinking. When I previously begged her to do the same thing all those years, she accused me of nagging her. She would say, "Well you have to die of something." Fortunately, when it came to that point, she wasn't ready to die yet. She decided that cigarettes were not going to be it, and she went on to live another couple of decades. I had her around for a lot longer, and I am a better person for it. It was time for her to take massive action, and she took it. She was able to stop immediately because the motivation to quit abusing her body and keep on living was greater than her addictions.

Proverbs 29:13

> [13] The poor man and the oppressor have this in common: The LORD gives sight to the eyes of both.

This verse could refer to a president, dictator, king, or maybe some type of ruling group who is responsible for leading a nation. It is good to look out for oppressive situations and do what we can to alleviate suffering associated with oppression.

In this case, let's not look at the greater world. Let's look at individual situations where everyday interactions between people create oppression and negatively influence their life because of some temporary authority that exists in the relationship.

For example, I once participated in a sales-planning exercise for the group of salespeople and sales management who reported to a vice president in the company. To be honest, after seeing the pre-work we were supposed to complete prior to the exercise, I tried to get out of it. I did have a legitimate reason but, to no avail, I had to attend.

The format called for each person to get up and present what they were working on and what they were going to do for the balance of the year. This was in the first quarter so we were supposed to project out the business we were looking to bring in for the next nine months.

As a professional salesperson and manager for most of my adult life, I recognize the benefit of a well-planned group planning session. However, this one wasn't well-planned. She had asked that everyone sit together all day to do it. This took all of us away from our normal revenue-producing activities for what amounted to no good reason. Next, she spent the entire session making negative comments, taking calls from her daughter, and planning her flight back home. She basically ignored the people she had called together for the day.

For some of us, it took two days to put our presentations together and in the end, it was a waste of time. This is just one example of an ordinary way people abuse their authority and kill off the creativity in those around them or who report to them.

Proverbs 29:15 and 29:17

> [15] The rod of correction imparts wisdom, but a child left to himself disgraces his mother.
>
> [17] Discipline your son, and he will give you peace; he will bring delight to your soul.

This is a verse for all children (sons AND daughters) as well as instruction for parents. As parents, we just get tired of disciplining, scolding, and investing all of the energy that goes with raising children. Periodically, we get tired so we throw our hands up and just say, "Whatever!"

We have to discipline ourselves not to do that because we don't have an infinite number of chances to positively affect a child's life. We must remember that even when your young daughter is telling a convoluted story about why she didn't do something simple — a task that would have

Inner Discipline Is the Key to Wisdom

taken less time than weaving this long-winded story to cover it up. Just stick to your guns and say, "Enough already. Please go do it and get it over with." Sometimes that isn't the easy thing to do because you are tired, you don't want to lose your temper and say the wrong thing, and she is nine years old.

We have to discipline them properly. That doesn't necessarily mean spanking. It may be something as simple as explaining to a child that he is making no sense and that he needs to do what you asked him to do. Even when you want to throw your hands up and ignore the behavior, continue to find the strength to mete out discipline without nagging, hurting his feelings, and losing your temper. You owe it to your children to make sure that you discipline yourself to discipline them. You brought them into the world, and it is your responsibility to raise them and give them life's lessons along the way. It is not always easy, and no one promised it would be — particularly when they become teenagers. If you stick to it and have done your job well, you will have given them a foundation that will, in most cases, create decent adults on the other side of "teenagehood."

Bear in mind that loving, consistent correction — not harsh, negative, mean-spirited, or small-minded correction — will help them learn. It will make them wise, and they will be more receptive to learning. People are interesting characters. Even when they are tiny and they haven't grown to adulthood, they respond well to positive correction in most cases. Positively motivating people creates a better atmosphere and a better world than correcting negatively.

Proverbs 29:18

> [18] Where there is no revelation, the people cast off restraint; but blessed is he who keeps the law.

In some translations, the word *revelation* is replaced by *divine guidance* and simply refers to *the word of God that is received by the prophets or judges* (in the biblical sense). Where there is ignorance or rejection of God or biblical principle, there is no moral compass, so crime, sin, and different types of transgressions result. The absence of a moral compass leads individuals as well as society into chaos. I dread the thought of any society where man does not recognize that there is something greater than himself. We are free to believe what we want, but how can people feel life is an accident — that they are here by chance? A spiritual component can be such a powerful "glue" that binds society in a positive way.

I visited Hawaii several times and became fascinated by Hawaiian culture. On one tour, I heard the story of Queen Ka'ahumanu (1768-1832). The queen decided that she wanted to do away with *kapu* — the whole system of sacred laws governing every aspect of Hawaiian life under the guidance of the rulers with ascent of their gods. Breaking a kapu resulted in severe punishment — usually immediate death.

Because of her influence, they did away with the kapu system in 1819. She also championed rights for native Hawaiian women that allowed her to be a ruler after her husband's death alongside their son, Liholiho (also known as Kamehameha II). She also broke kapus regarding certain restrictions on the way a woman could interact with men.

In the post-kapu system, Ka'ahumanu found that the Hawaiians had lost their moral compass. Society started to drift into chaos because there was no longer a spiritual governing mechanism. When the limitations on wrong or hurtful behavior are removed, it begins to diminish the authority of the leaders.

Ka'ahumanu reached out to Christianity in 1824 and was baptized in 1825. She recognized that Christianity would not limit her from exercising control as queen and that it gave her something around which to build a moral compass for Hawaiian society. Also in 1824, she presented Hawaii with a new set of codified laws based on Christian ethics and the Ten Commandments. This groundwork gave moral authority to the missionaries at the time. It eventually led to the dissolution of Hawaii as a kingdom, the destruction of their culture, a ban of the language, the wholesale selling off of Hawaiian land to become large, foreign-owned plantations, and decades of exploitation of the native population. Hawaii joined the United States in 1959.

No matter where you go, society demands some form of greater spiritual and moral bonding — a moral compass to act as the glue for society. It's an acknowledgment that there is something so much greater than ourselves that we need to conduct our life in a particular way — whether you look at a society which legislates against God such as the old Soviet Union or some Communist republics and dictatorships. There is always a breakdown in the moral fiber of the people involved when the society is not guided by a moral compass.

Inner Discipline Is the Key to Wisdom

That is not to say that you won't have the same issues in societies where religion is allowed or encouraged. However, in a society guided by a moral compass, there is something that you can point to that firmly identifies right and wrong. A society can only exist without it for so long. Of course, having God's word and instruction means nothing unless we are actually obeying it.

Proverbs 29:25

> [25] Fear of man will prove to be a snare, but whoever trusts in the LORD is kept safe.

If someone was holding a gun on you, you would probably have good reason to be afraid. For whatever amount of time that person had that gun trained on you, they would have control over how many more breaths you are going to take in this life.

However, let's apply this verse to a real-life work scenario. Say, for instance, you are in a difficult work situation and are continually threatened with being fired. Or, you feel because the company is downsizing, you are going to be caught in a layoff, and you live paycheck-to-paycheck without any savings. You are very insecure and frightened of what the future could hold for you. Perhaps it is another scenario that could shake up your whole world as you know it. Maybe it's gangs in the neighborhood or someone you fear because of the physical or psychological action they may take against you.

Perhaps your fear is a phobia. Is something preventing you from carrying on your life in an orderly and enjoyable way? Maybe you fear water, flying, heights, or being in closed places like elevators. Phobias like these can prevent you from living in a place that you might otherwise want to live or enjoying vacations such as cruises or boating. Perhaps you fear reptiles or other types of animals. Phobias don't have to be based in logic to produce some form of psychological limitation. Regardless, fear can ensnare and prevent us from moving forward in our life.

Faith in God can liberate you. Having a spiritual relationship with God makes you dramatically more capable of dealing with the fear associated with living or working in a toxic or hostile environment. It can provide significant relief in an atmosphere where you might like your job but the management structure or individuals make it extremely difficult for you to perform in your occupation and enjoy it. You might have the right skill for the right role, but you're just in the wrong place. By having that spiritual relationship — that spiritual grounding, that moral compass — you are able to negotiate the trials and tribulations that come along much better than someone without this preparation.

I watch people around me at work and reflect on previous work settings I have been in. I notice the people without this basic knowledge always look as if they have more trouble than anyone else. They don't seem to be able to handle the trouble and the difficulty because their god is the company, the job, the boss, or their boss' boss. To overcome a difficult situation, you have to enter the workplace and remind yourself that the environment is not in control of your life. Difficult people in your workplace may have some immediate transitory control, but they don't have ultimate control in how we allow that challenging state of affairs to affect us. Developing the spiritual basis, the moral compass, and a relationship with the Creator allows us to get through those troubled times.

Give some thought to those situations in your life where developing a broader spiritual relationship, a belief in God, or a greater relationship with God through prayer and meditation will be to your benefit.

In summary, a life of discipline should not be lonely and isolated. Take the correct action in your life. Choosing the ethical and morally correct action should be reinforced, not discouraged. Therefore choose the environments you will spend time in carefully. As a person of faith, be especially careful in your choice of friends. Friendships based on money or other artificial measurements will be disappointing as will those with bad character traits such as temper tantrums. The quality of your environment will have a direct relationship to your ability to operate consistently with wisdom.

Action Steps on the Life Path

We talked a lot about the effect on us when someone abuses power and influence. There are no excuses for abusing other people. Take a look at your own life now. Is there someone whose life you have some control over — your child or employee or many some young people you coach on a team? Is your conduct appropriate? Are you abusing your authority? If so, what undisciplined behavior would you most like to change in yourself?

_____

_____

_____

_____

_____

_____

_____

What character trait in yourself do you want to correct immediately? Pick one that will have the most impact on your life. What actions will you take to begin the correction?

_____

_____

_____

_____

_____

_____

_____

_____

_____

Inner Discipline Is the Key to Wisdom

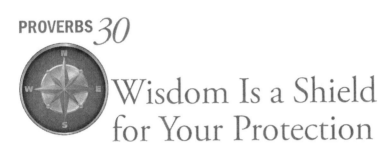

PROVERBS *30*

Wisdom Is a Shield for Your Protection

"Every word of God is flawless; he is a shield to those who take refuge in him."

Proverbs 30:5

As a Christian, I believe the Scriptures contain the word of God. I depend upon the divinely inspired writings and their teachings to be a guide for my life. If you are using divine wisdom as your compass, in my opinion you have the best chance there is to arrive at the destination you should. Think of the consequences of not following this type of instruction. The potential for an unfulfilling personal life rises dramatically. You are sabotaging your spiritual life and the list goes on from here.

The issues that confront the average person haven't changed over the millennia. Technology has changed, but human nature hasn't. If you feed yourself with the wisdom of Scripture, you will not go hungry for instruction.

Today's lesson will center around Proverbs 30, also known as the Sayings of Agur. Proverbs 30 is part of the collection of the Proverbs of Solomon; but these are the extra Proverbs of Solomon that were collected by the advisors of King Hezekiah. Agur ben Jakeh is credited with compiling Proverbs 30.

There is little known about Agur except that he was a wise teacher who was part of Lemuel's kingdom.

Proverbs 30:2-4

> [2] "I am the most ignorant of men; I do not have a man's understanding. [3] I have not learned wisdom, nor have I knowledge of the Holy One. [4] Who has gone up to heaven and come down? Who has gathered up the wind in the hollow of his hands? Who has wrapped up the waters in his cloak? Who has established all the ends of the earth? What is his name, and the name of his son? Tell me if you know!

The author begins by crying out. He is weary, and he is seeking something greater than himself that he knows exists. He is humbling himself to the Creator. When we humble ourselves, we open our hearts and minds to the infinite knowledge of the Creator. We don't know everything. We become frustrated with not knowing everything, not having all of the answers, and running into roadblocks.

The verses simply reinforce that we have to be humble about the fact there is more than us — an intelligence infinitely greater and smarter beyond us. We should accept it and learn from this infinite wisdom and the gift that has been given to us. Go easy on yourself and understand that you don't know everything; but you can pray to the Creator to help you understand those things greater than you.

Proverbs 30:7-9

> [7] "Two things I ask of you, O LORD; do not refuse me before I die: [8] Keep falsehood and lies far from me; give me neither poverty nor riches, but give me only my daily bread. [9] Otherwise, I may have too much and disown you and say, 'Who is the LORD?' Or I may become poor and steal, and so dishonor the name of my God.

Having too much money at once and being too focused on it is very dangerous. It can corrupt you and stimulate moral decay. It can throw your moral compass off stride so that you stop making ethical decisions. In the end, it makes decisions difficult when the most-important objective is to hold on to your money or make more. It doesn't mean that being rich is bad. Being rich is good because it places you in a position to leverage your financial resources to help as many people as possible while still providing safety and comfort for your family and the greater community.

However, being poor is no blessing! Somehow people get lost in misguided thinking when reviewing Christian text that somehow being poor is a blessing. Anyone who has ever been in a position where they could not to pay bills or put food on the table for their family knows that poverty isn't a blessing. And being poor can be hazardous to your spiritual health as well as your physical health because your condition can fill you with doubt. Over a prolonged period, doubt can produce massive stress-related diseases such as hypertension. You may end up being blessed by the experience of working your way out of it. By maintaining the right attitude toward life, you can plow ahead and blessings may hit you along the way, but being poor or living in poverty is not answer.

The very condition of poverty is not a blessing, and we should not wish people into that position. We should leverage our individual efforts through organizations to aid the larger community and provide a helping hand so those who need and want a helping hand can do better on their own.

Being rich is not the answer either. Being balanced is the answer! Pursuing your career in an intelligent manner can safeguard your ability to provide for your family. That means being ready for the changes that come in the economy. Look at how the world around you has changed. The opportunities and benefits that existed for your grandparents and your parents no longer exist for you. There is a world of new opportunity for you in this age of information, but it requires operating according to different rules.

In addition to being focused on and evolving your career and being ready for advancement, focus on how you can best interact in your community. And that community can be a small town, a big city, or even the greater global society. How can you leverage your resources for the best possible use so that all people can benefit by your ability to generate wealth for yourself? Through wise stewardship of what God provides for you, you may be able to generate comfort, education, and safety for other people.

A lot of my charitable activities center around helping children born to disadvantage in third-world countries as well as those in the United States. In many third-world countries, a child may be an orphan simply because a man does not live in the home. Living in a country that is not technologically advanced can be a sentence of poverty for the mother as well as the child. In an unstable political area, people may not have access to the nutritional needs, educational needs, or safety. I like to participate in organizations that support people with these types of needs. I mention this not to pat myself on the back but to give you ideas about how best to work in your immediate community and the greater society.

Proverbs 30:11-14

> [11] "There are those who curse their fathers and do not bless their mothers; [12] those who are pure in their own eyes and yet are not cleansed of their filth; [13] those whose eyes are ever so haughty, whose glances are so disdainful; [14] those whose teeth are swords and whose jaws are set with knives to devour the poor from the earth, the needy from among mankind.

This is a powerful series of verses specifically focusing on arrogant behavior. Not many things will bring us to a fall quicker than arrogance.

As we travel through life, we'll find times when we need to make peace with the past and forgive people. They may not necessarily want forgiveness or know we are forgiving them, but it will allow us to make peace with things that have happened so we can move on. Even if that entails getting counseling, do it. When someone starts out in life and creates a legacy of cursing his father and mother, that becomes a powerful burden to carry around. Cursing the very people that bore, raised, and cared for him along the way will make it difficult — if not impossible — to move forward in a meaningful way. Finding peace with our past wrongs as well as the wrongs of others allows us to move forward to lead a productive and satisfying life.

Even though you find peace in a situation so that you can move on doesn't mean necessarily that the other person is going to. Someone's abusive parents are not magically going to make up whatever they've done to their child, but she can move on if she can find peace in those circumstances. When people cannot find peace, it creates issues for them. They end up with corrupted attitudes toward the world around them and the people they may live and work with. One way we can see the result is in people who are always blaming others.

It's tough to work with someone who knows everything. It is especially challenging when that type of person has a lot of influence on your life. He may lie because he is unwilling to accept responsibility when something goes wrong or he makes a mistake. It becomes everyone else's fault. However, you can find him quite easily when something good happens. These people also tend to speak about themselves as victims of one thing or another. Perhaps their health is poor or somebody crossed them or their mother or father didn't quite live up to their expectations of what a parent is.

You need to be extremely careful if you start to recognize yourself as this type of individual. You could be the boss that never has a good way to say anything — the glass is always half empty. Even though you're working on a tough project that is going well, you can't bring yourself to say, "Good job, I know it's going to come through; I know we can do it." People in this blaming, victimized mentality are always operating from a negative, poisonous position and say things like, "If you don't do it, I'm going to get you!" "I'm going to put you on report." "I'm going to deduct money from your salary."

They are unhappy people, and no one ever knows why they are unhappy. If you work with them, you need to recognize that you can only control *your* reaction to their behavior. Make sure you are not mimicking or exhibiting that behavior as well. Operating in the same manner is arrogant, and it will prevent you from making wise, ethical, morally correct choices. You want to strive to be better than that and make wise choices.

Proverbs 30:24-28

> [24] "Four things on earth are small, yet they are extremely wise: [25] Ants are creatures of little strength, yet they store up their food in the summer; [26] coneys [d] are creatures of little power, yet they make their home in the crags; [27] locusts have no king, yet they advance together in ranks; [28] a lizard can be caught with the hand, yet it is found in kings' palaces.

These small creatures operate with such wisdom. They cooperate — either by instinct or some unseen intelligence we can't quite fathom — to accomplish the mission they are called to serve. We spray, chase, bat away, and do whatever we can to interrupt their mission. Eventually, they go away after they have accomplished their goal, and they reappear somewhere else in their natural cycle. We need to approach our world in this way.

We need to stay focused on the good things across our personal, business, and spiritual life. We're going to have distractions along with way.

Sometimes those distractions are mild, and sometimes they really get our attention because they hit us so negatively. Maybe we lose our job, experience some other disaster, or encounter the death of a friend or family member, and it upends us. Despite the interruption, we need to continue moving forward and recognize how blessed we are. In the good times and bad, it's up to us to operate wisely, morally, and ethically with that moral compass I've mentioned before.

Understand that giving is a way to expand your wealth because, by helping others, you ultimately help yourself. By hoarding and only focusing on what you have and holding on to it, you inevitably put yourself in a position to lose it. Plus, you're not enriching the world around you.

So ask yourself, "What are two or three things that I'm focused on and care about?" Then, start to contact some local organizations that you may want to investigate further about how you can immediately get involved.

Action Steps on the Life Path

Jot down some causes that interest you. Maybe it's children's health, assisting the elderly, helping people who are subject to a particular disease, education, or faith-based initiatives.

_____

_____

_____

_____

What are two or three charitable activities that relate to those causes that interest you? Contact local organizations to investigate further and ask how you can immediately get involved.

_____

_____

_____

_____

Think through some of these verses highlighted in this chapter again. How are they relevant to your personal situation?

_____

_____

_____

_____

_____

_____

_____

Wisdom Is a Shield for Your Protection

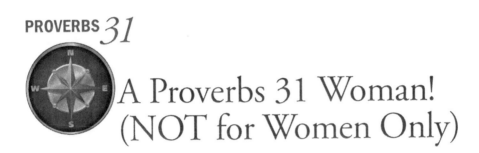

PROVERBS *31*

A Proverbs 31 Woman! (NOT for Women Only)

"A wife of noble character who can find? She is worth far more than rubies. Her husband has full confidence in her and lacks nothing of value."

Proverbs 31:10-11

Even though Proverbs 31 is the last lesson, it is not the end of the learning. I expect that you have received the blessing of experiencing improvement in yourself and learned much from the thirty lessons of transformation so far. Continue to refer back to the Bible because, like any good book, it is a reference that you can continue to use as you go through life. The Proverbs series is so practical and has so many great ideas. It is an excellent guide for navigating the personal, business and spiritual areas of your life.

Proverbs 31 and Proverbs 1 are my favorites. Remember in Proverbs 1, the purpose of Proverbs was clearly laid out. It was written to teach people wisdom and discipline. Through the lessons and direction, it was meant to help people understand the insights from the wise people around them as well as from wise people of the past. The intended outcome was to develop the wise people of the future who will leave more lessons behind.

Proverbs 31 uses the example of a wife as the ultimate model of someone who embodies all of the wisdom and discipline of Proverbs. It is pleasing to see them use a woman in this regard because in many other instances, the Bible uses a woman to illustrate points of failure, decline, or defeat. It is very fitting that they use a female to embody the ultimate success we should aspire to reach — especially considering the time in which it was written. But even though the illustration here is a woman, the lessons, conduct, wisdom, and discipline she embodies is suitable for all. Gender doesn't matter at this point.

Proverbs 31, known as the Sayings of King Lemuel, is the last selection of the collection that King Hezekiah's advisors assembled from the Proverbs of Solomon. Not a lot is known about King Lemuel except that he was a king who received wise teachings, apparently from his mother. His name means *devoted to God*. Some believe that Lemuel and Agur (who I mentioned before as one of the advisors and authors) were both from the Kingdom of Massa in Northern Arabia.

Proverbs 31:4-7

> [4] "It is not for kings, O Lemuel not for kings to drink wine, not for rulers to crave beer, [5] lest they drink and forget what the law decrees, and deprive all the oppressed of their rights. [6] Give beer to those who are perishing, wine to those who are in anguish; [7] let them drink and forget their poverty and remember their misery no more.

These verses center around personal behavior as it relates to drinking. The verse is actually talking about drinking too much, not the fact that they are having wine. The verse isn't saying that you can't have wine with your meal. It is talking about using moderation, discipline, and limitation as opposed to overdoing it because drinking too much makes people act foolish. People who drink excessively hurt themselves and damage their health, relationships, and careers.

Certainly in biblical times, wine was one of the safer beverages to drink because they did not have the high sanitation standards or the technology to provide safe drinking water in many cases. And, of course, it gave you a certain amount of pleasure. You could really consider their wine organic because they did not use the preservatives and sulphites that we put into wine today. As a result, drinking it didn't have that same immediate effect as drinking some of today's chemical-filled wines.

The lesson here is not to be a drunkard, not to drink too much, and not to crave alcohol. It will only skew your judgment when you have guzzled it and had too much.

The admonishment in these verses is also directed toward national leaders. We expect a lot from them. It doesn't mean that they cannot have some wine or an occasional alcoholic drink, but clearly a national leader who is drunk and disorderly is not someone we can trust to make rational decisions. When they drink too much, they are under the influence of a drug that impairs judgment and the ability to make decisions of national interest. It changes their mental state as they drink more and more of it, especially if they consume so much that they pass out.

Although the lesson here is aimed at national leaders, we can apply it on a personal level. We are all leaders in some areas of our life, and bad decision making affects us and those we lead.

I'm not talking about a just glass of wine with dinner. If someone is prone to excessive drink and drunkenness, can he really do the best for his family? Can someone make wise decisions if she has had so much to drink that her judgment is impaired? Can they interact with their family members and coworkers properly? Are they doing the right thing for their health? Leaders are called to use self-discipline so they can make decisions when action is called for.

Taking in too much alcohol is addressed in these verses, but it also extends to our medicine cabinet. Some take prescription drugs for some particular ailment — real or imagined — that impair their judgment in the professional, personal, or spiritual areas of their life. Think of those in public life who have died either immediately or from cumulative abuse of prescription drugs.

There is an added lesson here even if it starts out with drinking too much wine: we should ensure justice for those who cannot defend themselves — justice for the poor and for those who are hurting and in distress. This directive is intended for the king as he need not do anything that prevents him from doing his job of ruling wisely over the kingdom. If you are a leader or advisor to the king or administrator, you have the same responsibility. Also, the verses address social justice and advise us to speak up for the poor and helpless.

Proverbs 31:10-13

> [10] A wife of noble character who can find? She is worth far more than rubies. [11] Her husband has full confidence in her and lacks nothing of value. [12] She brings him good, not harm, all the days of her life. [13] She selects wool and flax and works with eager hands.

These verses highlight a woman of exceptionally strong character and tremendous wisdom who has various skills and is incredibly compassionate. This describes someone you want to spend time with. Male or female, we would be blessed to find someone with these characteristics to marry and build a family with.

The person in the mirror can become this person too. Even if you don't think you fit this picture of perfection, you can continue to work toward this goal as you apply the key points you've learned through this Proverbs study. Becoming this person is a journey, and you shouldn't beat yourself up if you aren't already there.

Notice how the woman described in these scriptures is different from the stereotype or the mistaken idea of a woman's role in Middle Eastern society at this point in time. This woman is not stooped over, barefoot, pregnant, illiterate, and terrorized by a menacing husband at home. The Proverbs 31 woman is a businesswoman. Her business is taking care of her children, husband, and household although she could also be engaged in an income-generating activity as well. She is a woman of strong character who has the compassion to operate with different types of people in different situations. She has the skills to make her home better while improving the life of those people around her. It is definitely a role model that women and men alike should strive to emulate.

Proverbs 14-29

> [14] She is like the merchant ships, bringing her food from afar. [15] She gets up while it is still dark; she provides food for her family and portions for her servant girls. [16] She considers a field and buys it; out of her earnings she plants a vineyard. [17] She sets about her work vigorously; her arms are strong for her tasks. [18] She sees that her trading is profitable, and her lamp does not go out at night. [19] In her hand she holds the distaff and grasps the spindle with her fingers.

A Proverbs 31 Woman! (NOT for Women Only)

²⁰ She opens her arms to the poor and extends her hands to the needy. ²¹ When it snows, she has no fear for her household; for all of them are clothed in scarlet. ²² She makes coverings for her bed; she is clothed in fine linen and purple. ²³ Her husband is respected at the city gate, where he takes his seat among the elders of the land. ²⁴ She makes linen garments and sells them, and supplies the merchants with sashes. ²⁵ She is clothed with strength and dignity; she can laugh at the days to come. ²⁶ She speaks with wisdom, and faithful instruction is on her tongue. ²⁷ She watches over the affairs of her household and does not eat the bread of idleness. ²⁸ Her children arise and call her blessed; her husband also, and he praises her: ²⁹ "Many women do noble things, but you surpass them all."

Proverbs 31:14-29 paint a detailed picture of this woman. She is an excellent wife and mother. Any parent knows that it takes work to do good parenting. You can't outsource that job. She is not only a wife and mother, she is a skilled businessperson. She is a seamstress and a merchant involved in real estate. She understands farming, management, importing, and manufacturing.

A Proverbs 31 woman is someone who is using her skills and developing new ones. Look at your own life regardless of whether you are a woman or a man. Are you using the skills and talents God gave you? Are you developing new ones?

Notice that her strength and power doesn't come from her incredible achievements. They are a result of her reverence for God. Her spiritual life is an anchor for these personal and professional achievements. That is why we must go through Bible studies in this way, engage in prayer and meditation, and continue to build our understanding of biblical principle and God's will for our life. It isn't really about spending more time in a church. It is about engaging in practices that anchor you spiritually and allow you to utilize and improve your skills.

Even though the scriptures don't say this woman is beautiful, isn't it easy to assume she is? She seems to be the kind of person you are immediately drawn to. Her attractiveness comes entirely from her strength of character and the ability to utilize her gifts and talents in everyday life. Her apparent beauty isn't necessarily physical beauty, but it is deep and long-lasting because of her ability to positively affect the lives of others. Amazing, isn't it? Beauty is only skin deep, but it is important to our interaction with someone.

The woman described in these verses is probably a composite of many of the best traits of women in their role as wife, mother, and businessperson, but they could also be a composite of a man. The real issue at hand is not about achieving perfection. Instead the issue is about becoming someone who is seen as a model of inspiration to those around us. We are not inspiring simply because of great oratory. We can inspire others when we utilize wisdom and discipline and conduct ourselves with attention to integrity. That is how we become an attractive, model companion who inspires others. People love to spend time with and seek advice from that type of person.

Proverbs 31:30-31

> [30] Charm is deceptive, and beauty is fleeting; but a woman who fears the LORD is to be praised. [31] Give her the reward she has earned, and let her works bring her praise at the city gate.

The book of Proverbs begins with the command to fear the Lord. It ends with the picture of a woman — a wife, mother, and businessperson who fulfills this command. She finds success in her fear and reverence of the Lord. He is her spiritual anchor. She works hard, respects and cares for her spouse and children, and provides proper discipline in a compassionate way that is not mean-spirited or hateful. She possesses good foresight, encourages others, shows compassion and caring for others, expresses concern for those who are less fortunate, utilizes wisdom, and handles family finances wisely. These are qualities we all should aspire to possess.

Even though none of us are perfect, we want to make sure we are using our talents for the best purpose possible with these biblical lessons and spiritual anchors. Take these lessons that we have learned throughout the thirty-one chapters of the Book of Proverbs to go forth, be successful, and enjoy your life. If you receive honors along the way, which I am sure you will, enjoy those honors and elevate your self-worth by enjoying the fruits of your labor. Never forget the real lesson which makes the Book of Proverbs special for us: it is our road map and shows us how to become much wiser so we make good decisions and live according to a greater ideal.

As you move forward and do the things according to the Book of Proverbs, please share your experiences at our website www.thewisdomcompass.com. We are very interested in your experiences, and we look forward to giving

A Proverbs 31 Woman! (NOT for Women Only)

practical feedback and following up with our readers. Please do not be shy about going online and keeping us informed of your progress and asking questions. Thank you for traveling on this journey with me. Go forth and enjoy. I look forward to interacting with you.

Action Steps on the Life Path

Spend five minutes writing down the passages we discussed in this chapter that were meaningful to you. What made them meaningful?

_____

_____

_____

_____

_____

_____

_____

_____

_____

_____

_____

_____

_____

_____

_____

_____

_____

_____

_____

_____

_____

_____

_____

_____

_____

A Proverbs 31 Woman! (NOT for Women Only)

What are some examples in your life that they highlight?

_____

_____

_____

_____

_____

_____

Being spiritually anchored is the key to living a balanced life and being someone who is utilizing their skills for the purpose for which they were made. Are you anchored spiritually? If not, why do you think it would it help you?

_____

_____

_____

_____

_____

_____

How you are going to become more spiritually anchored?

_____

_____

_____

_____

_____

_____

Spend two to three minutes making a list of your skills. What action can you take immediately to implement those skills that are the most important to your life?

_____

_____

_____

_____

_____

_____

_____

_____

_____

_____

_____

_____

_____

_____

_____

_____

_____

_____

_____

_____

_____

_____

A Proverbs 31 Woman! (NOT for Women Only)

# Final Thought

In 2 Timothy 4:7-8, it says, "I have fought the good fight, I have finished the race, I have kept the faith. Now there is in store for me the crown of righteousness, which the Lord, the righteous Judge, will award to me on that day ..."

Your reward for staying the course with this program is a greater insight into your life and faith. You are now better equipped to use wisdom to benefit everyone around you. Most importantly, as a person of faith, I hope you have made the connection between the spiritual and the practical for a richer life.

For more information and inspiration, visit www.thewisdomcompass.com.

Theodore Henderson

During a career that spans more than twenty years, Theodore Henderson has excelled as an articulate, organized, and successful business manager, consultant, seminar leader, and public speaker. He has demonstrated a proven ability to build and maintain profitable, long-term relationships with a sophisticated client base.

In 2003, he launched a New York City-based firm providing both non-profit and for-profit consulting in entrepreneurship, education, and self-development. The firm specialized in facilitating a thorough business-planning process that delivers a coherent, easy-to-read business plan appropriate for new business owners as well as for prospective lenders and investors. He spent three years doing this as an after-school program aimed at young people as well as coaching adults under the banner of his church before returning to corporate life.

Theodore now works with individuals who want to use biblical principles and Christian faith as a guide to success in all the key areas of life: spiritual, social, personal, family, and business. He is also still involved in youth leadership training.

He is passionate about speech, communication, and the application of biblical principals to business and personal success. Whether in his keynote speeches, his published articles, or in his seminars on faith-based approaches to personal financial issues and self-development, that passion is clearly demonstrated. Specific topics on which he speaks and writes include faith, God, and financial empowerment; communication and financial success; and dynamic communication.

Theodore holds a Master's degree in Business Administration with a concentration in Finance and Information Systems. He is active in Toastmasters International and has achieved the level of Distinguished Toastmaster (DTM) — the highest educational level currently offered by the organization — in recognition of his superior leadership and communication skills. He is also active in the New York City chapter of the National Speakers Association as well as other charitable activities.

Theodore is a lifelong New Yorker and is passionate about his native city. As a real estate investor, he purchased and completely renovated properties. Theodore is very involved in his neighborhood and church, periodically volunteering for other charitable activities. He has taken a special interest in mentoring and tutoring urban youth and the disadvantaged. He has guided youth in the completion of business plans and coached them to win business plan competitions.

Despite such a hectic schedule, he still finds time for his family as well as biking, skiing, Latin dancing, and playing with his chihuahuas and cats.

For more information on Theodore's work, visit www.thewisdomcompass.com.

Order More Copies

Online To pay by credit card, place your order online
at www.thewisdomcompass.com

Postal Mail To pay by check, send your completed order form to:
Theodore Henderson
THJ and Associates
459 Columbus Avenue, Suite 182
New York, NY 10024 USA
Attention: The Wisdom Compass
(888) 994-3343

Order Form for Mailing

The Wisdom Compass: A 31-Day Journey to   _____ x $24.95 = _____
Wisdom-Filled Living
292 pages

Please add 8.875% sales tax for orders shipped to New York addresses.

Shipping and Handling

USA: Add $5 for the first book and $1 for each additional book.
International: $9 for the first book; $5 for each additional book.

Your Information

Name _____

Address _____

City_____ State _____ Zip_____

Telephone _____

E-mail Address_____

Breinigsville, PA USA
28 October 2010
248187BV00005B/2/P